BEYOND FICTION

BEYOND FICTION

The Recovery of the Feminine
in the Novels of Cervantes

RUTH EL SAFFAR

UNIVERSITY OF CALIFORNIA PRESS
Berkeley   Los Angeles   London

193907

University of California Press
Berkeley and Los Angeles, California
University of California Press, Ltd.
London, England
©1984 by
The Regents of the University of California

Library of Congress Cataloging in Publication Data
El Saffar, Ruth, 1941–
Beyond Fiction.
Includes bibliographical references.
1. Cervantes Saavedra, Miguel de, 1547–1616—
Characters—Women. 2. Women in literature. I. Title.
PQ6357.A3W636 1983   863′.3   83-1067
ISBN 0-522-04866-0

1 2 3 4 5 6 7 8 9

*For Cambof Petapel
and his author,
beyond fiction*

"The real world is beyond time, but can be reached only by a process that goes on in time."

Northrop Frye, *The Great Code*

"Now learn this lesson from the fig tree: As soon as its twigs get tender and its leaves come out, you know that summer is near."

Matthew 24:32

Contents

Preface

"Is there a text in this class?"* has become, overnight, *the* classic poststructuralist question, subject like Descartes' "I think, therefore I am" to infinite variation and parody. "Is there a woman in this text?" has already surfaced as one alternate version, and another, equally appropriate, "Is there a text in this woman?" could easily follow. Both variants, along with the original query, have often teased away at me over the years during which I labored on this book.

I have come, finally, to see all three as interlinked. When, other than in the present century, have women in such relatively great numbers been able to discover a text within themselves? The venture is still, to be sure, a precarious one, for texts have generally been products made by men. Is something in the very nature of woman disturbed when she enters the realm of the text? Throughout the process of writing this book I have reminded myself of this question.

I did so because I came to feel, somewhere along the line, that there is really no such thing as "object" and "observer"— something Heisenberg already told us early in this century. Instead, I felt, as I was writing this book, that I was involved in a process in which my own integrity as a being was on the line in everything I saw, read, analyzed, and expressed. The woman I found in the text, in other words, made possible and was made possible by the text in this woman. It is now clear to me that I could not have written this book fifteen years ago, not only because I had less literary experience then, but because I was

*The reference is to Stanley Fish's *Is There a Text in This Class? The Authority of Interpretive Communication* (Harvard University Press, 1982).

less conscious of my beingness, less aware of my life sources. My text is conditioned by a whole range of experiences that make it uniquely mine.

The deepening of the sense of selfhood, which I consider as important for the process of interpretation as the conventional procedures of researching and analyzing, is not, however, to be confused with ego- or even eccentricity. The woman I have found emerging in Cervantes' text is unmistakably there, as the pages that follow will show. When the lost woman is recovered, as she regularly is in Cervantes' last works, from *La Gitanilla,* to *La ilustre fregona,* to *La española inglesa,* to the *Persiles,* she brings back into the society from which she had been stolen or ejected health, prosperity, harmony, and wholeness. The woman is most assuredly in the text, but she needs, in order to be brought out of the shadow, to be read *from* a "text" in which the feminine has been activated. Once the light has been cast on her and her role, she becomes visible to anyone. Like any lost object, once she is found, she is found for all to see.

The woman—or better, the *feminine*—in Cervantes' text functions exactly as the stone the builder cast aside. The old prison-houses of fiction, all of which Cervantes systematically tested and demolished, were constructed without her. For the greater part of this century we have treasured most those fabrications of Cervantes that have written into them their own instability. We have delighted in making fun of or sympathizing with (it really doesn't matter which) the eccentricities of his alienated heroes, from Don Quixote to the mad Licenciate to the jealous Extremaduran, ignoring, until very recently, the stories that trace another pattern. In those other stories, most of them written late in Cervantes' life, the male heroes experience a breakdown of received values as they make contact with a socially devalued female through whom, while redeeming her, they are redeemed. This is the structure of Cervantes' late romances, a structure built on the recovery of a *fourth* term, one that resolves the triangle of unfulfilled love and makes a resolution beyond madness or death possible.

I hope that through this study a new text can be introduced into the class. It is my feeling that the time is right, that the new cornerstone is already about to be set in place. Writers as apparently different as Northrop Frye, Walter Ong, and Jacques Derrida have all signalled a change taking place in Western culture—a movement that will finally lead us past the spectral certainties of logocentrism to a surer ground. What is needed in the sometimes terrifying process—so often represented by Cervantes as a shipwreck in stormy seas—is the realization that the "deconstruction" is as much a beginning as an end. When we find the text again, it will be because we have recovered the class as well.

In the process of completing this study I have been forced to make a habit of expecting miracles. It often seemed to me that this book could not possibly be done. As I worked along pulling time out of nowhere, I finally began to realize with what regularity what I needed became available to me. The people who were witting or unwitting instruments in this book's unfolding are too numerous to name, and many, were I to mention them, would be puzzled to find themselves here. I will confine myself to the overt suppliers of support in what follows.

I have first to acknowledge in gratitude the money and time that have been made available to me from foundations and institutions for completing this work. The University of Illinois at Chicago has been wonderfully generous with both, supplying small grants for typing and publication cost and providing me with several quarters of research time. In 1978, when I thought this book was near completion, the American Council of Learned Societies gave me a grant-in-aid that pushed my project forward over one summer. Finally, in 1982, with the book at publication stage, the Consul General of Spain in Chicago and the Association of Hispanists of the Midwest gave generous donations to the University of California Press to help bring down the final cost per copy of this book.

Through the several drafts of this study I was blessed with a typist, Kristina Lykos, whose phenomenal speed in turning out completed typescripts was equalled only by her uncanny ability to find her way through the morass of cross-outs and write-overs that constituted my handwritten version. At the last minute when everything seemed to be hopelessly scattered in pieces, expert and unexpected help came from MaryAlice Kobler, who typed all the Spanish quotations into the final copy, gratis, and from Diana Wilson, whose sympathetic and expert reading saved me from many an error, stylistic as well as orthographic.

Other friends along the way read and discussed with me all

or parts of the manuscript. I had very helpful commentary from Lucille Braun, Douglas Carey, Andrew McKenna, Mary Beth Rose, and Cesáreo Bandera, and to all of them I am deeply grateful. I am also grateful to more distant mentors—Elias Rivers and Bruce Wardropper—for general encouragement when progress seemed slow. Finally, I must thank, once again, Mario Valdés, without whose generosity to me when he was chairman of my department at the University of Illinois at Chicago I would never even have begun work on this book.

The full story, as I have said, is too long to tell. Suffice it to say that every star was in place along the way and that I am grateful for it all.

Chicago, August 12, 1982

Note on Texts

All quotations from Cervantes' works appear first in English, with the original Spanish version immediately following in parentheses. The sources and page references for all quoted material are as follows:

Translations from *La Galatea* are my own. The Spanish citations come from Juan Bautista Avalle-Arce's two-volume edition (Madrid: Clásicos Castellanos, 1961) and are identified by book and page (e.g., III, 210).

The translations to both parts of *Don Quixote* come from J. M. Cohen's *The Adventures of Don Quixote* (New York: Penguin Books, 1950) and are cited by part, chapter, and page (e.g., I, 15, 175). I have taken the Spanish from Avalle-Arce's two-volume edition (Madrid: Editorial Alhambra, 1979) also citing the reference by part, chapter, and page.

Like *La Galatea*, the *Persiles* has no acceptable modern version in English. The translations that appear here, therefore, are once again my own. The citations in Spanish come from Avalle-Arce's edition (Madrid: Clásicos Castalia, 1969) and are referred to by book, chapter, and page.

CHAPTER ONE

Introduction

CAUTIONARY NOTES

Today's writer or critic feels perhaps more acutely than his or her counterpart of former times the limitations of words, of codes, of systems. Some have dedicated whole careers to showing the utter futility of building interpretive systems, of making affirmations of value, of expressing truth. We find ourselves drawn nonetheless to the very frail networks of letters and sounds that constitute our various languages and often divert our disappointments about their inadequacy into meticulous studies of the way these networks form and transform themselves. The semiotician Umberto Eco has expressed as a simple rule the essence of all such networks and of all the codes by which we exchange information: *"Thus semiotics is in principle the discipline studying everything which can be used in order to lie. . . .* I think that the definition of a 'theory of the lie' should be taken as a pretty comprehensive program for a general semiotics" (emphasis his).[1]

Yet we are discomfited by the radical assault upon meaning that reduces the literary text—in exegeses that become larger as the task of finding meaning becomes more hopeless—to an arena of infinite free play in which sand castles are endlessly built and torn down in seeming mockery of all preconceived notions of truth. There is no doubt that language, and by extension literature, inhabits a realm of opposites. In that realm, every affirmation comes conjoined to that which would deny it. Derrida and those who have followed him have provided an excellent service by sensitizing us to the limitations of the written text and of all systems designed by the intellect to capture truth. Edward Said, whose discussion of the novel requires him to distinguish it

1

carefully from absolute truth, has noted that "any absolute truth cannot be expressed in words, for only diminished, flawed versions of the truth are available in language. This is as much as to say that *fiction alone speaks or is written*—for truth has no need of words—*and that all voices are assumed ones"* (emphasis his).[2]

Moving closer to the topic of the present study, Cesáreo Bandera has discussed in *Mimesis conflictiva* how Cervantes came to discover the "fiction of fiction" through writing *Don Quixote*.[3] Recognizing the "fiction of fiction" represents a gigantic step toward discovering the nature of truth, a step that is bound to affect all that the author who makes that discovery writes afterwards. The discovery is an extremely dangerous one, however, leading as easily to chaos as to illumination. For when the house—the illusion that there is *a* system that properly nullifies all others, a nameable *right* against which all else is judged as wrong—falls, one can easily fall with it into despair. To avoid recognizing the illusion for what it is, one is tempted to keep spinning out endless constructs, mocking each one yet not daring to abandon the enterprise for fear of the emptiness that looms beneath it. This avoidance is very clearly expressed by J. Hillis Miller, who, though speaking of criticism, could easily have been speaking of fiction: "Criticism is the production of more thread to embroider the texture or textile already there. This thread is like a filament of ink which flows from the pen of the writer, keeping him in the web but suspending him also over the chasm, the blank page that the thin line hides."[4] But what if one allows oneself to fall into the "chasm" of a wordless universe only to find that the very chasm itself was an illusion?

Paolo Pasolini's film *The Passion According to St. Matthew* contains the wonderful scene where Jesus instructs a lame man to throw down his crutches and walk. The sequence captures the doubt, the literal fear of falling that bound the man to his crutches those many years, the fear that was itself the root of his lameness. It required faith to throw the crutches away, faith without which the healing could not have taken place.

It also requires faith, in this late day, when the whole critical enterprise appears to be covered with uncertainty, to undertake a study such as this one. No critic seems able to determine what Cervantes was all about; moreover, no critic seems certain that his or her continuing efforts can do anything but perpetuate the lie. To write another book of criticism, to try once more to represent Cervantes accurately, requires a faith that "passes all understanding." I cannot prove that what I see in Cervantes is anything more than an accurate reflection of my own private construct of him. I will assert the presence of a pattern in his works that makes sense of all their differences, and I will sometimes tread in the forbidden forest of symbol, archetype, and dream in my analysis of particular works. I will claim that through a close analysis of the role of the narrator, the relation of primary to secondary characters, and the integration of plot and episode one can follow the subtle shifts that mark Cervantes' movement from "fiction" (to use Bandera's term once again) to Truth. I offer all that follows believing that it is clearly so. I have found a pattern underlying the four long pieces of fiction that define Cervantes' career; the pattern works from many different perspectives, each of which seems to confirm the others, and the conclusions I have reached here fit with all that we know of Cervantes and the dates of composition of his works.

ILLUSION AND REALITY

My thesis is most easily captured, on the level of the plot, by the often-disputed deathbed scene at the end of *Don Quixote* Part II. The scene is repeated in many of the shorter works as well—in Anselmo's belated forgiveness of Camila and Lotario in "The Tale of Foolish Curiosity," in Carrizales' ultimate acceptance of responsibility for what has befallen him in *El celoso extremeño*—and depicts a final laying to rest of illusion. In Don Quixote's case, the shedding of the illusion, which like the armor he wore exposed him to the very batterings from which it was designed to protect him, resulted from an illumination that came to him in sleep. The book makes it clear that it was not the importunings of his housemaid and niece, nor the schemes of Sansón Carrasco, nor even the painful realization that Dulcinea could not be found that freed Alonso Quijano from the iron grip of Don Quixote's illusion, but divine grace. "Blessed be Almighty God, who has vouchsafed me this great blessing! Indeed his mercies are boundless, nor can the sins of men limit or hinder them" (II, 74, 935) (¡Bendito sea el poderoso Dios, que tanto bien me ha hecho! En fin, sus misericordias no tienen límite, ni las abrevian ni impiden los pecados de los hombres [II, 74, 603]) was his exclamation upon awakening.

The deathbed scene, then, is nothing less than a scene of conversion: "Congratulate me, good sirs, for I am Don Quixote de la Mancha no longer, but Alonso Quixano, called for my way of life the Good" (II, 74, 936) (Dadme albricias, buenos señores, de que ya yo no soy don Quijote de la Mancha, sino Alonso Quijano a quien mis costumbres me dieron renombre de *Bueno* [II, 74, 604]). Of such conversions and their reflection on the author, René Girard has written eloquently in the last chapter of his *Deceit, Desire, and the Novel*. To understand the mechanisms of the conversion one must see that the character's failure as a fictional entity and his final awakening to Truth are aspects of one another. That is, again staying within the context of the plot, the objections of housekeeper and niece and the endless cruelties of Don Quixote's many adversaries play an essential role in preparing Don Quixote for his release. Were Don Quixote to meet with unqualified success, the piercing of the illusion would be impossible. Success would blur the fact that the assumptions on which he was working were illusory.

The hero's success or failure, then, tells us something about the author and how he sees the world. The fact that Cervantes allows for a relentless assault on his hero throughout Part II suggests that he is not trapped in the world view of his character and that, furthermore, he knows that the character's limited view does not suspend him over a void. The progressive battering to which Don Quixote is subjected in Part II is part of a process designed not to undermine but to restore the dignity of the character, Alonso Quijano, hidden beneath his disguise as knight-errant and creature of fiction. In the chapter on *Don Quixote* Part II, I will show how carefully ordered is Don Quixote's undoing and how neatly structured—when compared to the *Don Quixote* published in 1605—is the 1615 novel.

Don Quixote's conversion presupposes the author's previous conversion. Cervantes, who made his mark on Western letters by challenging the literature of illusion on which Don Quixote modeled himself, did not begin his writing career free of the encumbrances of that literature, however. Cesáreo Bandera has clearly shown that Cervantes' very attack on Don Quixote, and through him on the romances of chivalry, was made from the position of one still caught in the structures he set out to ridicule. What I am proposing in this study is to trace the stages by which Cervantes moves from participation in, to resistance against, to freedom from the entanglements of desire that are the essence of fiction.

TRIANGULAR DESIRE AND FICTION

When I speak of "desire" I introduce, intentionally, the terminology of René Girard, who has established the relation between fiction and metaphysical desire. The desire of which Girard speaks has a triangular configuration that systematically prevents union with the desiring subject's ostensible goal. The typical novelistic expression of metaphysical desire is the love triangle, and in Cervantes' work as well as in most works of the pastoral and chivalric genres love triangles are everywhere: Cardenio and Fernando love Luscinda; Anselmo and Lotario love Camila; Eugenio and Anselmo love Leandra, and on and on. Because of its self-destructive character, the desire each participant in the triangle experiences breeds conflict and usually results in madness, death, or chaos.

To fully appreciate the implications of Girard's analysis, the important point is to see that the love triangle is an emblem of a misplaced desire for God. Lacking an Absolute Other on which to attach itself, the desire is displaced onto a secondary other who then acquires the attributes of God, and in seeming absolute renders the desiring self ancillary and trivial by comparison. The third term, in such an imbalanced relationship, automatically emerges as a rival to guarantee the infrangibility of the separation of the subject from the object of desire, thus preventing discovery of the object's mundane reality.

In most of Cervantes' expressions of the situation, the main male character views the rival as a being like the loved one, superior to him and therefore more worthy of the love to which he so vainly aspires—think, for example, of Silerio's Timbrio in *La Galatea*, or Cardenio's Fernando and Anselmo's Lotario in *Don Quixote* Part I. As a superior being, the rival becomes someone to be venerated and emulated; as inhibitor of the lover's aspirations, the rival is also the object of the lover's fear and hatred. Caught between two mutually contradictory valuations of the "third term"—the same-sex rival—the lover plunges into an ever-deepening cycle of despair that leads inevitably to his destruction.

It is no wonder that the story of unfulfilled desire is the very substance of fiction. Fulfilled desire leaves nothing to say, nothing to hope for, no shining tomorrow (or yesterday) against which to lament the insufficiencies of today. Language rushes in to fill the void that is created when the self perceives itself as isolated and essentially different from the other. But language only perpetuates the split it is designed to conceal, and the search within it for the way to Truth is bound to be abortive. Like the Lady and the Rival, the Word, when granted a power it cannot possibly possess, leads the deluded into all manner of confusion.

In the author's case, the union to which he aspires is that between the written word and "reality." Mediating that desire and arising as a spectral "third term" are the dominant literary forms of his day, all those pastoral and chivalric romances that were so popular and yet so false. The analysis I have made here of Cervantes and his work asserts a homology between the effort on Cervantes' part to achieve expression of his own experience without the intervention of other literary forms and the effort of his characters to free themselves from the inhibiting power of the rival. When the characters are shown convincingly working from courtship to marriage in the story, they will find themselves within a literary structure that is coherent, no longer grounded in irony, and capable of true closure.

When the other is recognized in all his or her imperfection, in other words, as an *expression* of God but not God himself, a signal is given within the story that the author outside it has assumed a like attitude toward the literary artifact, which becomes in its turn an *instrument* of the expression of Truth and not itself its bearer. The shift in attitude is a fundamental one, and one that can explain Cervantes' movement away from the novel in his last work toward a highly literate appropriation of what Alban Forcione has called the "Christian Romance."[5]

Evidence that Cervantes struggled with the problem of desire and literature is present in his earliest published work, *La Galatea*. The problem manifests itself in the many ways Cervantes attempts to draw his characters out of the love triangle that is the essence of the courtly love mystique and in his covert resistance to the structure of the pastoral novel whose framework he nonetheless borrowed. In *La Galatea* we find rivals unconscious of their rivalry (Elicio and Erastro); rivals who resolve their conflictive mutual desire for the same woman when one agrees to marry the loved one's sister (Timbrio and Silerio); lovers who have made a profession out of their lover's plight, becoming philosophers and poets of love (Damon and Tirsi); lovers who commit suicide or try to (Lenio and Galercio); a lover who becomes a murderer (Lisandro); and a lover who renounces the loved one (Lauso). What stands out in this panoply of responses to the problem of romantic love is the fact of such love's inevitable failure. The only truly resolved love story, that of Timbrio and Silerio, takes the form of a mini-Byzantine novel that sprawls over four of the work's six books and still seems contrived at the end.

Just as Cervantes can be seen to struggle fitfully for a solution to the problem of the love triangle in *La Galatea,* he resists falling into the established patterns for the pastoral. He brings in far too much of the "real" world to fit comfortably into the tradition made popular in Spain by Montemayor, and he insists on a touch of rusticity entirely out of keeping with the world of literary shepherds and shepherdesses. He also refuses facile solutions and therefore winds up without a real ending for the characters who are supposed to be the hero and heroine of the piece.

From the very beginning, Cervantes appears to have had his doubts about Arcadia and the set of assumptions on which it rested. By *Don Quixote* Part I his objections seem to have sharpened, and he demonstrates more openly his determination to undercut the artificial social and literary hierarchies that caused him trouble in his life as well as in his work. In the Prologue to Part I he challenges the lettered establishment, the tradition of laudatory poems by noblemen and recognized poets, and the very necessity of writing a prologue. *Don Quixote* itself carries the attack to the chivalric and pastoral romances and to those characters who build their lives around literature.

THE PROBLEM OF STRUCTURE IN THE FOUR LONG WORKS

Don Quixote Part I, like *La Galatea,* is studded with tales of unfulfilled love and failed expectations, most of which are poorly woven into the fabric of the plot. The secondary stories are hardly extraneous, however, as critics have now almost unanimously come to agree. For the most part, the interpolated material reflects the unresolved and unresolvable conflicts with which the main characters are dealing. Some minor characters, however—Silerio and Timbrio in *La Galatea;* Dorotea and the Captive in *Don Quixote* Part I—give hints that Cervantes was looking for a way out of the labyrinth in which almost everyone else is caught.

In the study of Cervantes' long works of fiction offered here I will closely examine the interpolated tales, seeing them as indices of the stage of development of the primary characters and as efforts to reach beyond the confines—literary and metaphysical—in which those characters are trapped. The interpolated tales also reveal the author's stage of development. His first two works fail to truly integrate the various levels of the text and fail at the same time to arrive at a conclusion. Only in *Don Quixote* Part II does one find a stabilized narrator and a clearly organized plot structure. There, for the first time, Cervantes uses literature to suit his own aims, rather than being confined by literary structures whose insufficiencies are nonetheless obvious to him. In Part II Cervantes, and through him Cide Hamete, demonstrates a control over his material not nearly so evident in his two previous works. There we are no longer witnessing a struggle between Don Quixote's chivalric and the narrator's "realistic" versions of the main character's adventures. Cervantes is fully in charge, controlling the material carefully from beginning to end and integrating far more successfully than in Part I the secondary characters and their stories.

What must also be noted and accounted for in Part II is the female characters' final escape from their exclusive role as objects of the erotic fantasies of their desiring lovers. The love triangle as the only structure for representing characters in fiction has been not so much resolved as abandoned. The woman defined solely as the object of desire is replaced in Part II by a whole collection of women—single and married, young and old—who exist independent of the erotic conflict. The female characters' escape from the confinement of externally imposed roles is duplicated by the male characters, many of whom show skill in slipping out of the conventions that held them fast in Part I. A good example is Basilio, who wins Quiteria from his more powerful rival Camacho by *playing at,* but not identifying with, the role of distraught lover. Other minor and not-so-minor characters—Master Peter and Sancho—also demonstrate the ability to assert control that Cervantes has achieved over his literary universe. The conclusion is inescapable that the freeing up of the love triangle is intimately connected with the liberation of the author. Cervantes in his last works exhibits a freedom to use the literary material, words, and narrative structures of others without having constantly to remind the reader of their limitations.

In Cervantes' final work, the *Persiles,* irony and the scoffing narrative voice that we have taken as the hallmarks of Cervantes' fiction are almost completely absent. Also absent is the solitary hero, dreaming about an impossible lady while doggedly working toward his own destruction. In his place is a hero whose adventures figure not as isolated events of interest in themselves but as steps along a clearly marked journey that leads from the northern countries to Rome and, correspondingly, from confusion to certainty. The new hero travels with a lady, who must perforce lose the sheen of perfection and inaccessibility that characterized the ladies of the chivalric and pastoral romances.

The journey on which the hero and heroine embark in the *Persiles,* furthermore, is one instigated not by the traditional source of authority, the male ruler (for he is off at war), but by the figure most severely neglected in Golden Age letters, the mother. It is Queen Eustoquia who urges her younger son Persiles to take matters into his own hands and to go with his beloved Sigismunda on a pilgrimage to Rome. The pilgrimage, like Basilio's deception in *Don Quixote* Part II, removes Persiles from the horns of the dilemma confronting him, giving him an alternative to the yielding to or fighting with the rival that characterizes the triangular relationship of desire. Sigismunda remains just a hair's breadth away from being a classic object of rivalry among men, however, for Persiles' older brother Magsimino has declared his intention to marry her when he returns from war. The work itself is threatened by the possibility of becoming yet another escapist romance, which may be why Cervantes, while obviously proud of the *Persiles,* expressed doubts about it. The only indication that the work and the love it describes are grounded in Truth and not in desire can be found in their continual orientation toward Rome and the faith that the Heavenly City represents.

The substance of the *Persiles* concerns the obstacles and delays that inhibit the couple's marriage and their concommitant embracing of Truth, but the work is constructed so that for once the hero and heroine enact the possibility of fulfillment and not the inevitability of failure. The changes that such an approach implies for the structure of the work will be the subject of Chapter 5 of this study. What must be noted here is that the form of the Byzantine novel that first appeared in the extended secondary tale of Timbrio and Silerio in *La Galatea* takes over the *Persiles* entirely, becoming, as a form that carries the allegory of the pilgrim, the literary vehicle through which Cervantes can express the "fiction of fiction."

TRIANGULAR DESIRE AND THE HIDDEN FOURTH TERM

From the very earliest of Cervantes' works, the triangular structure, which condemns desire to failure, can be seen competing with another, quadrangular structure that suggests another conception of desire. That alternate structure introduces an element alien to literature and eventually leads the author out of its confines. In demonstrating the presence of the nonliterary order in Cervantes' works, I will refer to what I call the "fourth term." Four is traditionally associated with the natural world in which terms in opposition—summer/winter, spring/fall; fire/water, earth/air—while remaining distinct, belong to a totality that gives order and meaning to their differences. Viewed from within, the terms appear to be in irreconcilable conflict. From without, however, they form a whole that requires the proper functioning of each for the well-being of the system. Four, then, offers the *potential* for harmony that the pointed, forward-moving configuration of the triangle cannot. The former is associated with the natural world; the latter, with fiction.

In all of Cervantes' stories of love fulfilled in marriage, the resolution comes about through the introduction of a fourth figure who had formerly been neglected by the characters who saw themselves locked into the endless frustration of the triangle. Thus Blanca emerges in *La Galatea*, as if from nowhere, to allow Timbrio and Silerio to free themselves from the bondage of their rivalry, and Dorotea in *Don Quixote* Part I appears miraculously from the burning triangle of Cardenio's despair to lead him out of his madness and into marriage with Luscinda. The fourth figure in Cervantes' earliest works, however, exists primarily in a virtual state. She is there as Florisa, the intimate, though nearly faceless friend of Galatea, and appears as a balancing figure throughout Cervantes' works whenever the attracting female character is too highly valued by her lover. Whenever she is recognized and brought out of her anonymity, this fourth, scarcely noticeable figure brings with her the secret to resolution that eludes the other three protagonists. The specific situations in which the fourth figure emerges will be analyzed in detail in the chapters to follow.

It is no accident, as the reader might have already noticed, that the shadowy fourth figure in Cervantes' stories is always the undesired, undesirable female. She is literally rejected—sent underground—when the lover deifies the lady of his desires. Since that lady is in reality just another good/bad, beautiful/ugly being like the lover himself, to idealize her is to chase from consciousness all of her aspects that do not conform to the image he has projected on her. The banished negative attributes, as the Marcela/Maritornes opposition in *Don Quixote* Part I reveals clearly, then accumulate to produce grotesque creatures who are not only repulsive but also destructive.

To redeem the undesired and undesirable female is no easy task. The more lofty her attractive counterpart, the more unattractive, frightful, and aggressive she will seem. Don Quixote meets only foul-smelling inn prostitutes because his goal is Dulcinea. His steadfast determination, right through 72 chapters of *Don Quixote* Part II, to have the lady *his* way conjures up, in compensation, increasingly violent demonstrations of the reality of the carnal world, first depicted by inn prostitutes and peasant girls and then degenerating into female tormentors and herds of trampling bulls and pigs. In the face of such insistent demonstrations of his error, it is no wonder that Don Quixote was reluctant to give up his illusions. Being the cause of his problems, the illusion of the Lady appears finally to be his sole protection against the ever more powerful insistence from the banished fourth term that it be recognized. Given the gravity of the situation, only divine grace could save Don Quixote from the horrors that arose in the wake of his illusion.

Other characters in Cervantes' works, however, being less severely trapped in the triangle of metaphysical desire, have an easier task of it. But it is hard enough for the carefree young nobleman Fernando of *Don Quixote* Part I to accept the farmer's daughter Dorotea for his wife. Fernando's reluctant acquiescence has rightly been seen as another sign of divine grace at work.[6] The "conversion" for Fernando could not be other than miraculous, for nothing in his experience truly prepared him for it.

The cases of Tomás de Avendaño in *La ilustre fregona* and Juan de Cárcamo in *La Gitanilla* are much better described by Cervantes, who seems, by the time he wrote those works, to have had a clearer grasp of the transformation process. Those two gentlemen have an easier time, since they actually desire the (socially) undesirable woman. Even so, to redeem her (i.e., marry her and discover her true "nobility"), they must undergo a process of undoing not unlike Don Quixote's in Part II. They must divest themselves of all that belongs to their given place in society, shedding name, costume, and status to win her. The only difference between Don Quixote and the heroes of *La Gitanilla* and *La ilustre fregona* is that the latter submit voluntarily to the dismantling of their given set of assumptions about themselves, while Don Quixote resists.

ILLUSION BREAKING AND THE STRUCTURE OF THE BYZANTINE NOVEL

Even in the earliest works, the hero who succeeds in marrying the loved one must undergo severe trials that break down his sense of superiority and self-containment. Timbrio in *La Galatea,* like the Captive in *Don Quixote* Part I and Ricardo in *El amante liberal,* must fall victim to storms at sea, shipwreck, and captivity at the hands of the enemy. Such a process becomes central to the entire structure of the *Persiles,* and in all cases the male character in question later marries the woman, who participates with him in many of his travails.

What one sees, when considering Cervantes' works as a whole, is a struggle between a whole host of terms in opposition—the temporal and the eternal, the literary and the natural, the individual and the social, fiction and Truth—that were best resolved for Cervantes by appropriating the structure of the Byzantine novel. The struggle in all the works is expressed in the plot through the efforts of loved ones to get married and of heroes to reach their goals. It is expressed structurally in the effort to assimilate the secondary and primary narratives, to make effective use of the formal subdivisions—chapters and books—within the text, to establish a stable narrative perspective, and to come to a satisfactory conclusion.

Signs that Cervantes was not content with a strictly temporal, literary, individualistic fictional approach to the world are evident from his earliest work. The discontent, however, was one felt from within the parameters of the temporal and literary. The Timbrio/Silerio story in *La Galatea* and the Captive's tale in *Don Quixote* Part II reveal that to break out of those limited boundaries would require, for Cervantes, an assault upon all the comfortable assumptions of the sedentary, lettered life.[7] The two stories also show that when the hero can achieve such a breakthrough, the lady, apparently miraculously, becomes not a distant dream but a reality, and the rival simply drops out of the picture.

The absence of the rival as a significant figure changes the focus of the hero's struggle. The change is apparent in *Don Quixote* Part II when Don Quixote observes to Sancho that the giants and the enchanters—once very real figures in the knight's imagination—are actually emblems of sloth, envy, and lust that must be overcome in himself.[8] Don Quixote is in fact much less aggressive toward his supposed adversaries in Part II than in Part I, as almost everyone has noticed. In the *Persiles* the hero never attacks his rivals directly. He focuses his attention solely on overcoming the obstacles that hinder his journey to Rome. The struggle with the "other" has been internalized, and the travails figure as symbols of limitations the hero must break through.

Before the journey to the loved one and to Truth can become the major theme of a long work by Cervantes, he must see the lie of escapist literature, with its emphasis on the Rival and the Impossible Lady. When Cervantes tears Don Quixote down, as he does in Part II, he is at the same time clearing the way for a fruitful assimilation of all the terms in opposition that battled for supremacy in his earlier works. The temporal in the last work can now be seen as an aspect of the eternal, the literary as an expression of the natural, the individual as an essential component of the social, and fiction as a cover for an underlying truth. The Byzantine novel, adopted in earlier works as a subgenre, finally emerges in the *Persiles* as the dominant vehicle through which to express not only the "fiction of fiction" but the path beyond leading to Truth.

FINAL REFLECTIONS

The problems Cervantes was working with were not confined to literature. Essential to the process being described here

is the realization that "fiction" reaches far beyond the borders
of the written text. Fiction reigns whenever the elements of the
natural world are stacked into hierarchies so that some things
are raised up beyond their worth and, as an inevitable corollary,
others are brought down.[9] I have highlighted the position of
the undesirable woman because she represents the neglected
element that guarantees the continuation of fiction in all its instability and violence. She stands quite literally for the unconscious
—that element systematically excluded from awareness—in the
Spanish Golden Age. Only the briefest glance at Golden Age
literature would reveal to what extent she represents a taboo.
She rarely appears at all, and when she does, it is to be either
chastized or redeemed, but never to be herself an instrument of
transformation. When Cervantes struggles with the literary
problem posed by courtly love, he is also struggling with the
dominant consciousness of his day. And when he finally reaches
a point in his fiction when the "undesirable" or off-limits woman
becomes the object of the hero's desire, he will impose on that
hero travails that will undercut every assumption he holds
dear.

I have made considerable use of C. G. Jung in working out
this analysis because he is particularly concerned with the problem of the feminine as it relates to the larger problem of
establishing harmony between the self and the other in a period
that has been characterized by an overvaluation of the masculine. The triangle of desire afflicts women as well as men, but
Cervantes represents this desire primarily as it is experienced
by male characters.[10] For them, as for Cervantes and his age, the
task is to throw off the limitations of their personal view and to
see women as they actually are. I emphasize this because the
fourth figure that emerges in the resolution of the triangle is
bound to be a nonideal female figure.

Jung's description of the structure of the psyche has also
been particularly helpful here because it maps the journey from
and the return to the unconscious. In this context, the unconscious is synonymous with the natural order, which the neglected
feminine represents.[11] The pattern Jung describes in his many
discussions on the assimilation of the anima is simply the pattern
of conversion mentioned at the beginning of this introduction.

I have also adapted aspects of Jung's scheme to my reading
of Cervantes because of startling homologies between Cervantes'

works and Jung's theories. The stages of self-discovery he discusses, from development of the ego to assimilation of the
shadow, to development of a relationship to the anima, seem to
be clearly revealed in a sequential reading of Cervantes' works.
Most persuasive, however, are the recurrences in Cervantes'
work of symbols to be found also in Jung, as will be discussed
in detail in the chapters to follow.

On a theoretical level, little else will explain the growing
importance, in Cervantes' later works, of the independent female
character. Her emergence at the same time as the male characters
are undergoing conversion suggests that the two phenomena
are linked. In recognition of this coincidence of events I have
used Jung's theories and applied to Cervantes' long works my
intuition, developed through a study of the *Novelas ejemplares* in
Novel to Romance,[12] that Cervantes underwent a change in orientation over the course of his writing life now clearly detectable
in his works.

CHAPTER TWO

La Galatea

Cervantes published *La Galatea* in 1585, only a few years after returning from captivity in Algiers. Using the pastoral setting as a frame for interpolated stories, discussions on love, love poetry, and a eulogy of poets, Cervantes appropriated for his first long work of fiction the model of the pastoral novel much in vogue since Montemayor published *La Diana* in 1559. *La Galatea*, with its cultured shepherds, distraught lovers, and bucolic backgrounds, looks very much like a pastoral novel. And yet, as every critic has recognized, the work varies greatly from its predecessors, challenging even the neo-Platonic world view that is their most salient common bond.[1]

A first reading of *La Galatea* produces, above all, a feeling of confusion. The length and complexity of the interpolated tales threaten the unity of the work, as if the space of the pastoral were too cramped to contain Cervantes' rich powers of invention. By contrast with the characters in the secondary stories, the principal characters, Elicio and Galatea, seem pale. They in fact have very little to do throughout the work other than to observe the many conversations, debates, poetry recitals, riddle contests, and love stories that unfold before them. What they see is a kaleidoscope of opinions, passions, and situations that seems to tumble in random patterns. No single attitude toward love and marriage emerges as a point of view safely attributable to Cervantes. And in the end, even the conflict that entangles the principal couple is left unresolved. Seen from the perspective of Cervantes' entire opus, *La Galatea* looks as much like a first example of Cervantes' famed ambiguity and difficulty with *dispositio* as an example of the pastoral.

La Galatea, precisely because it rejects the conventions of a stable plot, well-defined characters, and a clear set of themes, forces the reader in search of the book's underlying vision to use a different set of analytical tools in its presence. The disorder on the surface literally invites one to read across the current of the intended discourse and to recover in the process the unconscious unity of vision that is lost if each element is read naively.[2]

Several critics have noted the presence of antitheses in *La Galatea*[3] though the antitheses perceived are usually thematic in nature. Duality is more than a question of plot and theme; it is built into every aspect of the work. In *La Galatea* the pendular action oscillates endlessly between town and country, night and day, speaking and listening, peace and violence, advance and retreat. The shepherds involved in this swing between opposites, appropriately, make no progress toward a goal, as those in *La Diana* or *La Diana enamorada* seem to do. No one in *La Galatea* gets beyond the banks of the Tagus, and no magical person or place is discovered to release them collectively from their love problems.

The work mirrors the conflicts its shepherds experience. Theirs is the world of metaphysical desire par excellence that René Girard and Cesáreo Bandera have so well described.[4] It is a world in which love is coupled with hatred, peace with violence, and friendship with rivalry. If *La Galatea* fails as the priest said it did ("it sets out to do something and concludes nothing" [propone algo, y no concluye nada]),[5] it is because the work cannot escape from the contradictions of the neo-Platonism whose flaws it exposes so clearly. The pastoral romance, even as it protects itself from the "evils" of the world, participates in that world by maintaining a division between the "good" and the "bad." Although Cervantes does not launch a frontal attack on the tendency to so divide the world as he will in *Don Quixote* Part I, he does resist it:[6] through Erastro, he introduces a rustic character into a setting that had previously been the exclusive preserve of educated, courtly shepherds;[7] and through the interpolated tales, he restores to *La Galatea* the politics, city life, strife, and war that the pastoral traditionally expunged.

Cervantes' revisions of the pastoral have not escaped the notice of most critics of *La Galatea*. What has never been pointed out, however, is his unusual handling of the male and female protagonists. Earlier pastoral novels tend either to efface sexual differences, as in *La Diana*,[8] or to subordinate the woman to the male protagonists' projections of her. In *La Galatea*, however, Cervantes establishes a genuine polarity between the sexes that offers the possibility of escaping from the subjectivism so characteristic of the pastoral.[9]

Cervantes makes a great effort, as we shall see when we look closely at his handling of the characters, to present both the men's and the women's perspectives. Though the presentation of the female characters is not, in the last analysis, as well rounded as that of the male characters, Cervantes projects a fundamental acceptance in La Galatea; all the terms in opposition throughout the work are oriented toward a barely glimpsed totality rather than toward establishing a factional universe in which some terms are given preference over their polar opposites.[10]

To understand why the "harmony of the poeticizable cosmos," as Avalle-Arce calls it,[11] is not achieved in Cervantes' first work, we must distinguish among levels of opposition. Elicio, who despite his underdeveloped qualities is still the main protagonist, desires Galatea's love. Standing between him and Galatea, however, is the rustic, unlettered Erastro. The potential, highly understated competition between the two shepherds could pass as unnoticed by the reader as it is by Elicio if rivalry were not the basis of the two long interpolated tales Elicio hears. Both tales, Lisandro's and Silerio's, address the question of the same-sex opponent who threatens the lover's aspirations for his lady. The significance of the interpolated tales for the main protagonists is not so much that one ends tragically and the other happily but that the question of rivalry among men must be addressed before the lady can be won.

Elicio wants it both ways: he wants to continue happily to sing love duets with his "friend" Erastro and to have Galatea for himself. As Cervantes shows later in the interpolated story in Don Quixote Part I, "The Tale of Foolish Curiosity," the two impulses are mutually contradictory. The friend, once a lady has entered the picture, automatically becomes the rival, even if he might wish otherwise. How to overcome the barrier to the loved one that the friend of the same sex represents is something Cervantes worked out in a lifetime of writing fiction. The solution, when it finally comes, is unmistakable. But it requires passing through a clearly marked set of stages, the first of which is the recognition of the self in the same-sex other.[12]

For the characters in the main and secondary stories of La Galatea, two levels of opposition must be distinguished: the opposition between the rustic Erastro and the refined Elicio on the one hand, and the opposition between Elicio and Galatea on the other. Furthermore, the two levels that confront Elicio are mirrored by Galatea, who has a friend in Florisa and a potential lover in Elicio. The reader could ignore the four-sided configuration generated by the main characters were it not that the same configuration recurs in all four of the interpolated tales. A fourfold pattern appears, in fact, everywhere in *La Galatea:* there are four interpolated tales, four characters occupying the plane reserved for the main love story, and four major characters interacting within each of the interpolated stories. The presence of four in all of its symbolic permutations is strong in the ceremony at the end of the book that introduces the mystic experiences of Caliope. The number four, associated with the seasons and the four basic elements, is the traditional symbol of the material world and of the potential for psychic wholeness.[13] The surprising degree to which Cervantes remained faithful to the interrelations of the material world explains why his "pastoral" novel differs so greatly from those of his predecessors, whose view of nature was drawn from literary tradition and fantasy. The aversion to the superimposed preferences is also in keeping with his care to attend to all aspects of the society he introduced into his works.

The reading of *La Galatea* to follow will demonstrate, particularly by a close look at the homology between the main characters and the secondary characters, the way the fourfold structure that lies at the heart of the work challenges the very pastoral mode Cervantes had thought he was appropriating. The study, which will begin with a brief discussion of Elicio and the first interpolated tale and then move to Galatea and the second interpolated tale, will show to what extent Cervantes used the secondary stories to reveal aspects of the main characters that the pastoral novel tended to suppress.[14] Following the presentation of the two principal characters, the analysis will continue with a discussion of the remaining two interpolated tales and turn from there back to the fortunes of Elicio and Galatea as they function as a couple.

ELICIO

In an opening reminiscent of Montemayor's *La Diana, La Galatea* begins with the shepherd Elicio lamenting in solitude the hardheartedness of his beloved Galatea. He is very quickly joined by the rustic Erastro, who openly confesses his love for Galatea while acknowledging Elicio's superiority: "Allow me, good Elicio, to love her, since you can be sure that if you, with your skill and extreme grace and intelligence cannot soften her, much less can I with my simplicity" (Permíteme, buen Elicio, que yo la quiera, pues puedes estar seguro que si tú con tus habilidades y estremadas gracias y razones no la ablandas, mal podré yo con mis simplezas enternecerla [I, 23]). Elicio counters with a generous and equally self-effacing reply:

> It doesn't bother me, Erastro, that you love Galatea. . . . I hope that God gives the success to your desires that the sincerity of your thoughts deserve. From now on, do not stop loving Galatea on my account. I am not of such a corrupt nature that because I am unfortunate I wish others to be so also. Rather, I beg you, by what you owe to my goodwill toward you, that you don't deny me your conversation and your friendship, since of mine you can be sure, as I have said.

> (No me pesa a mí, Erastro, que tú ames a Galatea; . . . dete Dios tan buen suceso en tus deseos, cuanto merece la sinceridad de tus pensamientos. Y de aquí adelante no dejes por mi respecto de querer a Galatea, que no soy de tan ruin condición, que, ya que a mí me falte ventura, huelgue de que otros no la tengan: antes te ruego, por lo que debes a la voluntad que te muestro, que no me niegues tu conversación y amistad, pues de la mía puedes estar tan seguro como te he certificado. [I, 24])

Following their polite exchange, they sing a duet about the beauty and charm of Galatea and the unhappiness their love for her causes. Though the conversation between Elicio and Erastro seems entirely unrealistic, what follows immediately afterwards suggests that Cervantes was aware of the violence latent in such an exchange. In the middle of Elicio and Erastro's song, two shepherds break out of the mountains, one pursuing the other with a knife. The assailant stabs his victim to death, claiming vengeance for a Leonida, and then escapes back into the hills. Elicio and Erastro bury the dead stranger and then retire to their separate cabins for the night.

The scene may well be interpreted as Cervantes' effort to wrest the reader from absorption in the limitations of Elicio's conscious view of himself. Even before the murder, the narrator intervened in the story to counter Elicio's love complaints, showing that Galatea's actions toward Elicio were motivated not so much by disdain as by a desire to be polite:

> One must not imagine of Galatea that she despised Elicio, nor that she desired him. It is just that sometimes, almost as if convinced or obliged by Elicio's many attentions, she would raise him to heaven by some chaste acknowledgement. Other times, without even realizing it, she would spurn the ardent shepherd in such a way that he hardly knew where he was. . . . It seemed to Galatea that, since Elicio showed such respect for her honor in his love, that it would be too much ingratitude to not pay back his honest desires with some small token of recognition.

> (De Galatea no se entiende que aborreciese a Elicio, ni menos que le amase; porque a veces, casi como convencida y obligada a los muchos servicios de Elicio, con algún honesto favor le subía al cielo; y otras veces sin tener cuenta con esto, de tal manera le desdeñaba, que el enamorado pastor la suerte de su estado apenas conocía. . . . Parecíale a Galatea, que pues Elicio con tanto miramiento de su honra la amaba, que sería demasiada ingratitud no pagarle con algún honesto favor sus honestos pensamientos. [I, 17])

The narrator's dissociation from the lover's confusion takes us a long way from the typical pastoral novel in which the lover's complaints about his beloved stand as the only judgment upon her. From the very first pages, Cervantes establishes in *La Galatea* enough distance from the distraught lover to allow for the emergence of "unconscious" material—that is, material that Elicio "in his right mind" could never comprehend. The first interpolated story constitutes such unconscious material, since it introduces into Elicio's world the very rivalry and violence he so eloquently disavowed in his daytime encounter with Erastro. And, appropriate to that "other world," the atmosphere in which the story is told establishes numerous associations with the unconscious. Elicio hears the story at night, while Erastro is sleeping. This is how the narrator describes the nighttime journey that leads Elicio, unwittingly, to an enclosure where the murderous shepherd is hiding:

> . . . in the light of the beautiful Diana, who showed herself resplendent in the sky, he entered through the thickness of a dense forest in search of some solitary spot, where, in the silence of the night he

could, with more peace, give reign to his amorous dreams. . . . And thus, moving slowly on, enjoying the feel on his face of the mild breeze full of the sweet smell of the fragrant flowers that covered the green forest floor, enshrouded in a delicious robe of air, he heard a noise as if from one in deep anguish.

(con la luz de la hermosa Diana, que resplandeciente en el cielo se mostraba, se entró por la espesura de un espeso bosque adelante, buscando algún solitario lugar adonde en el silencio de la noche con más quietud pudiese soltar la rienda a sus amorosas imaginaciones. . . . Y así, yéndose poco a poco gustando de un templado céfiro que en el rostro le hería, lleno del suavísimo olor que de las olorosas flores, de que el verde suelo estaba colmado, al pasar por ellas blandamente robaba envuelto en el aire delicado, oyó una voz como de persona que dolorosamente se quejaba. [I, 30-31])

The passage might remind the reader of Don Quixote's celebration of the delights of chivalric literature with its invitation to dive through the lake of snakes to the sensous underwater world of beautiful damsels and fine castles. Concern with taste, smell, and touch is associated there, as here, with the unconscious. And there, as well as in the cave of Montesinos episode in *Don Quixote* Part II, the journey to the underground world is one that forbids as well as beckons.[15]

Elicio must pass through a thicket, not unlike the one Don Quixote goes through on his way to Montesinos' cave, in order to meet the suffering shepherd face to face and hear his story: "Breaking through the spiny brambles, in order to reach more quickly the place from which the voice issued, he came into a little round clearing which, like a theater, was surrounded by thick and intricate shrubs" (Y rompiendo por las espinosas zarzas, por llegar más presto a do la voz salía, salió a un pequeño prado, que todo en redondo, a manera de teatro, de espesísimas e intrincadas matas estaba ceñido [I, 34-35]). The theater in which the tale of violence and treachery unfolds is of difficult access, representing the resistance of the teller to incursions on his solitude and of the listener to the disturbances he has worked so hard to suppress. When Elicio tears through the thorn bushes he finds the murderer in a threatening pose. Elicio must show the frightened young man that he has come not simply out of idle curiosity but that he is inspired by sympathy with the shepherd's affliction. If he cannot convince the other of this, he risks being killed. The "other world" in which he finds himself is dangerous. He tells the shepherd: "Calm yourself, poor shepherd, for he who comes here brings a heart prepared to carry out your wishes. The desire of learning your misfortune has made him shed your tears and disturb the relief that you might have had were you to be alone" (Sosiega el pecho, lastimado pastor, que él que aquí viene trae el suyo aparejado a lo que mandarle quisieres, y quien el deseo de saber tu ventura le ha hecho romper tus lágrimas y turbar el alivio que de estar solo se te podría seguir [I, 35]).

The story Elicio hears at night under the moon while tormented by anxiety moves him and the reader far from the peaceful banks of the Tagus and the courteous discussions of love among rivals. Lisandro tells a tale of interfamilial strife inspired by envy. The hatred the two families feel for one another evolves through expressions of treachery, cruelty, and deception to its culmination in the murder Elicio and Erastro had witnessed in the afternoon.

Violence is a characteristic of the pastoral that has frequently been commented upon.[16] What is unusual in *La Galatea* is that the violence is not a random, unaccountable phenomenon. Instead, Cervantes carefully shows that murders and abductions are carried out by people who look just like the shepherds who live in apparent peace and harmony. The feelings that result in acts of violence grow out of desires all the shepherds experience. The place Cervantes chose for Lisandro's story suggests that he intended it to reveal the underside of Elicio's falsely idyllic friendship with Erastro. At night in a thicket inhabited by a menacing stranger, Elicio comes face to face with the passions his courtly, daytime demeanor cannot afford to recognize as his own.

Elicio, however, need not suffer Lisandro's fate. Having sought out the stranger and embraced him, he has taken the essential first step toward what Jung would call the integration of the negative contents of the personal unconscious.[17] By finding and listening to Lisandro, Elicio dispels this literal and metaphoric threat. Lisandro's story establishes a bond between teller and listener that releases Elicio from the dangers to which he would otherwise be exposed. An analysis of the time, place, setting, and circumstances surrounding Lisandro's tale reveals that it is more than simply an interpolated tale within a poorly organized text. The secondary tale here and throughout *La Galatea* is the vehicle through which the imbalances—psychological as well as social and political—of the pastoral mode are corrected.

LISANDRO'S STORY

Lisandro tells Elicio how he fell in love with the "impossible" woman Leonida, the daughter of his own family's most hated adversaries. Hoping somehow to dissolve the enmities that separated the two families, Lisandro made arrangements to marry Leonida secretly through the offices of go-betweens. While on the surface everything appeared to proceed smoothly, below the surface, neglected passions, represented by the scheming, jealous nature of the intermediaries, were working against Lisandro's good intentions.

Lisandro was too preoccupied with his own desire for Leonida to attend to the subterfuge growing up around him or to take seriously a dream that offered him a graphic warning of impending disaster. The dream came while he was sitting by the road in the woods at night awaiting Leonida who was to join him for their journey to another town to be married. In the dream a tree falls on his shoulders. As he struggles under its weight, a white deer emerges from the thicket offering help. The deer's inability to save him is dramatized by the sudden appearance of a lion, who bounds out of the thicket, pounces upon the deer, and drags it into the forest. When the dreamer escapes from under the tree, he finds the deer torn asunder in the woods.

Though the dream so affected Lisandro that he awoke from it in tears, he refused to associate it with his own situation. In retrospect, however, the dream's significance became clear, as he explained to Elicio: "I was beside myself when I reflected on what I had dreamed. But with the joy I expected to have on seeing Leonida, I paid no attention to the fact that my dream had revealed the very thing that was soon to happen" (Quedé fuera de mí, considerando lo que había soñado. Pero con la alegría que esperaba tener de ver a mi Leonida, no eché de ver entonces que la fortuna en sueños me mostraba lo que de allí a poco rato despierto me había de suceder [I, 48-49]). Shortly after awakening, Lisandro tells Elicio, he discovered that his bride-to-be had been murdered at night in the woods by her own brother, who had been tricked into the deed by a scheming, resentful adversary.

Lisandro's story, which functions as a dream for Elicio, contains a prophetic dream within it. Since Elicio also hears this story at night in the woods while preoccupied with amorous and anxious thoughts,[18] it is difficult to escape the conclusion that the story is intended as much as a warning to Elicio as Lisandro's dream was to him. Elicio is being forced to learn that it is not enough simply to desire the loved one and confidently expect that the obstacles to her will miraculously vanish. The obstacles are signs of internal weaknesses that must be attended to before the "impossible" loved one can become accessible. Elicio needs to take more seriously, apparently, the rivalry that the obscure, unrefined Erastro represents.

The question of rivalry and violence, however symbolically related to the fortunes of the main characters, remains nonetheless divorced from their daytime activities. Lisandro and his world of envy, resentment, and murder represents all that Elicio, as a refined shepherd in love, has renounced. And yet, as the ending to *La Galatea* makes clear, the moment finally comes, even to shepherds in their bucolic idyll, when the obstacle represented by a person of the same sex—a rival in the form of a friend, a father, or a brother—must be confronted. When Elicio resolves to take up arms if necessary to win Galatea, however, the novel ends. Direct combat, as *Don Quixote* and the *Persiles* will later make clear, is not a real solution to the dilemma the rival-plagued lover faces. To resolve the conflict between desire and fulfillment is, for Cervantes' characters, to begin a long journey into the unknown, but Cervantes' first hero, Elicio, is only able to take the first tentative step along the path. In *La Galatea*, nothing really *happens* to the major characters. All the "action" occurs in the secondary stories, at one remove from the lives of the main characters, who listen in rapt silence to the struggles and conflicts of "others" whom they only dimly perceive to be reflections of themselves.

GALATEA

Cervantes' narrator has already offered an explanation for Galatea's behavior toward Elicio that tempers Elicio's conviction that she is both hardhearted and all-powerful. Cervantes' unwillingness to side with Elicio against Galatea is further underscored in the second half of Book I, where narrative attention shifts to the world of the women. Only for an instant, in the middle of Book I, do Elicio and Galatea meet. There Galatea plays the prescribed role in the game of unrequited love in which she is an unwitting participant. When Elicio begs for just some small favor—a glance or a smile—she turns him away and goes to gather flowers with her friend Florisa.

The gulf that separates Elicio and Galatea appears, from their distinct perspectives or from that of anyone caught in the net of erotic love, unbridgeable. The poem each character sings in solitude reveals, however, that behind their postures of pursuit and flight lies another pattern that both understand perfectly, in which she is the tormentor and he the tormented. Galatea's song echoes the one Elicio sang in the opening pages of the book. The third stanza of Elicio's song said:

> I thought the flame which in my soul the winged boy
> Ignites, the rope with which he binds,
> The subtle net with which he takes the gods,
> And the fury and the vigor of his shaft,
> Would thus offend, as it offends me,
> The peerless subject who subjects me;
> But against a soul which is of marble made,
> No net, nor fire, nor noose, nor arrow can.

> (Creí que el fuego que en el alma enciende
> el niño alado, el lazo con que aprieta,
> la red sotil con que a los dioses prende,
> y la furia y rigor de su saeta,
> que así ofendiera como a mí me ofende
> al sujeto sin par que me sujeta;
> mas contra un alma que es de mármol hecha
> la red no puede, el fuego, el lazo y flecha. [I, 4])

The first quartet in Galatea's opening sonnet appears to reply:

> Away with the fire, the noose, the ice, and the arrow
> Of love which burns, binds, freezes, and wounds;
> Such a flame my soul wants not,
> Nor is it satisfied with such a knot.

> (Afuera el fuego, el lazo, el hielo y flecha
> de amor, que abrasa, aprieta, enfría y hiere;
> que tal llama mi alma no la quiere,
> ni queda de tal nudo satisfecha. [I, 57])

The verbal echoes in the two songs reveal that the same force intimidates both Elicio and Galatea; the fearful powers of the unconscious threaten to overwhelm consciousness. In later works—*El amante liberal* and the *Persiles*—both male and female characters will be exposed to the overwhelming forces of "strangers" or of nature, and both, before being "saved," will have to learn their way around in what I am calling here the world of the unconscious. In *La Galatea*, however, the principal female characters remain relatively free from the grasp of eros, thus trapping the male characters in their confusion and condemning them to the despair—madness or suicide—represented by Lenio and Galercio.[19]

Like Elicio, Galatea does not remain alone long. She leaves the adoring company of Erastro and Elicio in search of her companion Florisa. Florisa and Galatea appear subsequently throughout the novel, like Erastro and Elicio, as an inseparable pair. Yet it cannot be without significance that Galatea and Elicio first appear alone and that in their solitude each declares openly his or her conscious position with respect to the other. A comparison of the two allows us to see that, while the men and women in the novel receive nearly equal attention, they are handled separately because they begin from opposing conscious attitudes. A full analysis of the presentation of the sexes in this novel will reveal their inverse relation to one another. Their potential for union, however, exists in the presence of the alter ego, suggesting that each character has aspects that may yet be assimilated to make access to the other possible.

Elicio's opening poem expresses his sense of loss of being, while Galatea's shows a self-contentment that urges rejection of any threat to her internal balance. Galatea and Florisa are happy with one another's company and pass the morning collecting garlands of flowers with which to adorn themselves. But like their male counterparts earlier in the novel, they are interrupted in their pleasure by the appearance of a stranger in distress. After listening to the stranger's song of woe, Galatea and Florisa introduce themselves and encourage the reluctant young woman, whose name is Teolinda, to tell her story. The three shepherdesses find a quiet and enclosed place in which to engage in what will be the second interpolated tale of the novel.

Like that between Lisandro and Elicio, the similarity between Teolinda and her listeners cannot be ignored. Teolinda begins her story of unhappy love by relating her occupation before meeting her loved one. Her words recall those the narrator used to describe Florisa and Galatea's morning activities: "They began then to pick various flowers from the green meadows with the idea of weaving them into garlands with which to tie their hair, which hung loose about their shoulders" (Comenzaron luego a coger diversas flores del verde prado, con intención de hacer sendas guirnaldas con que recoger los desordenados cabellos que sueltos por las espaldas traían [I, 58]). Teolinda says:

> Oh, how many times, just to please myself and pass the time away, did I go from bank to bank, from valley to valley, picking here a white lily, there the purple iris, again the red rose, with the sweet-smelling carnation, making with these flowers a woven garland with which to adorn and tie up my hair; then admiring myself in the clear, tranquil waters of some fountain, I was so charmed with myself that I would not have changed my condition for any other!

> (¡Ay, cuántas veces, sólo por contentarme a mí mesma y por dar lugar al tiempo que se pasase, andaba de ribera en ribera, de valle en valle, cogiendo aquí la blanca azucena, allí el cárdeno lirio, acá la colorada rosa, acullá la olorosa clavellina, haciendo de todas suertes de odíferas flores una tejida guirnalda, con que adornaba y recogía mis cabellos, y después, mirándome en las claras y reposadas aguas de alguna fuente, quedaba tan gozosa de haberme visto, que no trocara mi contento por otro alguno! [I, 65])

Teolinda's story, exemplary as all the interpolated tales in Cervantes' works are, contains a warning, along with an opportunity for understanding. As a prologue, she tells her listeners that she spurned a friend suffering the distress of passionate love. Angered by Teolinda's rebuff, the friend cursed her with bad luck in love. Obviously, Galatea and Florisa are going to be better off for having listened sympathetically to Teolinda's story.

TEOLINDA'S TALE

The story that interrupts Galatea and Florisa's flower gathering takes place, like Lisandro's, in an enclave protected from the outside world by bushes. Though the story is told by day, it is associated with the siesta, allowing its homology with the dream to be sustained. Teolinda's story shows the instability hiding behind the self-sufficiency the female characters tend to display and its susceptibility to destruction by a "man from out of town"—the legendary handsome stranger. Her story is significant because it reveals, as Lisandro's did for Elicio, the underside of Galatea's personality. Lisandro exposed the passions of jealousy and hatred that lay beneath the surface of Elicio and Erastro's friendship. Teolinda shows how vulnerable to disturbance Galatea's narcissism is.

Teolinda's story also invites comparison with Galatea and Florisa since it deals with identity rather than with difference as Lisandro's story had. Teolinda has an identical sister, Leonarda.[20] Harsh-tempered Leonarda is out of town when Teolinda meets the stranger Artidoro during the preparations for religious celebrations. In a moment of collective activity, the young women (among them Teolinda) who are gathering flowers to adorn the temple are invited to join the circle of young men in the woods between their village and the river. The union of sexes is itself an event out of the ordinary, inspired by religious festival and carried on in the woods beyond the town limits. It is no wonder that the "harsh temperament" of Teolinda's identical sister is missing at that time. Only in her absence is Teolinda able to accept the presence of an "other" of the opposite sex.

At the sanctified time when Teolinda is caught in eros' net, all normal order is reversed. A wise old man, Eleuco, sends the men out to gather flowers. When they return, he urges each young woman to place a garland on the head of the shepherd of her choice. The established pattern encouraging a division of the sexes and the isolation of each has been broken.

The meeting of shepherds and shepherdesses offers a series of circle images. The shepherds have formed a circle that expands to include the shepherdesses when they arrive. The shepherds who go out to collect flowers come back, "each carrying a beautiful garland, coiled about his arm" (traía cada uno una hermosa guirnalda enroscada en el brazo [I, 70]). Teolinda expresses the feeling that the circle represents a bond when, after placing the garland on Artidoro's head, she asks her listeners: "What shall I tell you of what my inmost soul felt when so near to him who had stolen it from me, but that I would have freely given up anything I had desired for the liberty of putting my arms around his neck, as I put the garland around his head?" (¿Qué os diré yo de lo que mi alma sintió viéndome tan

cerca de quien me la tenía robada, sino que diera cualquiera
otro bien que acertara a desear en aquel punto, fuera de quererle,
por poder ceñirle con mis brazos al cuello, como le ceñí las
sienes con la guirnalda? [I, 71]).

The number six—six shepherds, six shepherdesses, six garlands—suggests the circle. The circle of Teolinda's self now
extends beyond her being, which is why she suddenly feels
lonely when parting from Artidoro: "I cannot imagine how in so
short a time I could transform myself into a different being, for I
no longer lived in myself, but in Artidoro" (Yo no sé cómo en tan
pequeño espacio de tiempo me transformé en otro ser del que
tenía; porque yo ya no vivía en mí, sino en Artidoro [I, 72]).

The sense of sanctity and expansion of the self intensifies as
the time of the ceremonies arrives. The religious rites extend
throughout the day and night and culminate in a sort of baccha-
nalia just before dawn. A dozen shepherdesses, including Teolinda, dance into the woods in a circle and are joined by a
company of shepherds. The two groups blend into a single
unit:

> The shepherds tuned their tambourines to the cadence of our
> oaten-pipe and with the same measure and dance came out to
> receive us, blending one with the other confusedly, and yet in
> time, and changing the instruments to the sound, we changed our
> dance, so that it was necessary that the women should disunite
> and give their hands to the men.

> (Los pastores del lugar, . . . acordando luego el son de un tam-
> borino suyo con el de nuestras zampoñas, con el mesmo compás y
> baile nos salieron a recebir, mezclándonos unos con otros confusa
> y concertadamente, y mudando los instrumentos el son, mudamos
> el baile, de manera que fue menester que las pastoras nos desasié-
> semos y diésemos las manos a los pastores. [I, 75])

After the dancing Eleuco again intervenes, the shepherds
and shepherdesses sit in a circle in the woods, and the old man
encourages Artidoro to sing. The day before, Artidoro had sung
of his flocks. Now he sings a song about love divided into six
stanzas of six verses each. The song completes the twenty-four-
hour period of religious festival and also ends the first segment
of Teolinda's story.

Were it not for Teolinda's distraught arrival at the banks of
the Tagus, one might be tempted to infer that her story is a

happy pastoral dream. But we know by now that Cervantes is
loath to allow such dreams to last. Just when all seems to be
going well in Teolinda's story, therefore, the three shepherdesses are startled by the incursion into their enclosure of a
rabbit pursued by a pack of hounds. The hunter is no other than
Galatea's father, Aurelio. That Galatea is able to rescue the
rabbit and that the dogs are under her father's control augurs
for a better balance among the forces of nature in Galatea's life
than the deer and lion of Lisandro's dream do for Elicio's. Still,
the father, as an image of authority, requires obedience and
symbolically disturbs, in his first appearance in the story, the
seclusion and self-contentment of the magic circle of shepherdesses that represents Galatea's condition. Though his nickname
"The Venerable" links him to Eleuco in Teolinda's story and to
the role of the wise old man, he enters the story in a limiting,
authoritarian rather than in a panurgic, facilitating fashion.
Galatea's father will encourage Elicio's union with Galatea not
by urging it, as Eleuco did with Teolinda and Artidoro, but by
imposing his authority to marry her to someone else.

The rabbit-chasing dogs that interrupt Teolinda's story recall
the lion and the white deer of Lisandro's dream.[21] In both cases
Cervantes reminds the reader that pastoral reverie is never
entirely removed from the world of authority and resistance.
Aurelio's dogs serve, furthermore, to link Teolinda's story to
Galatea's fortunes. For Teolinda's moment of romantic love also
belonged to a circumscribed, special time held apart from the
demands of the everyday. Both the story and the romantic love
it describes are subject to violent interruption.

Book I ends with the men and women briefly joined once
again as Elicio and the other shepherds accompany Galatea and
her friends back to the village. The apparent harmony, however,
is threatened by two individuals: Lenio, a fervent opponent of
love, and Galatea's father, Aurelio, who will later figure as an
obstacle to Elicio's aspirations.

Book I is a microcosm of *La Galatea* as a whole, expressing
both the parity and the inverse relationship that, while holding
Galatea and Elicio apart, form the basis of their potential union.
Elicio has been exposed, through Lisandro's story, to the world
of violence; Galatea, through Teolinda's, to the world of love.
Lisandro shows Elicio what he has suppressed in his simple
world of love and friendship; Teolinda, what Galatea has ignored

in her happy self-absorption. Both inset stories make clear that Elicio and Galatea, who listen to the voices of strangers, will be better off than the strangers themselves who refused to listen when they had the chance. Book I ends as ambiguously as the whole novel does. The group goes off together, anticipating a wedding. Yet they go off accompanied by characters who challenge the desired union.

Teolinda's story resumes in Book II in the village at night. In that setting Teolinda recounts the undoing of her love, which comes not from external forces but from within. Artidoro, who is as madly in love with Teolinda as she is with him, has promised to marry her. On the morning of their last meeting, however, he speaks to her identical sister instead of to her. Leonarda does not know the strange young man, having been out of town when Teolinda met him, so rejects him and goes home to denounce Teolinda and the young man to her father, who orders Artidoro's arrest. A young man fitting Artidoro's description is found and put in jail. Leonarda is called to identify him, but she discovers that though he looks like Artidoro, he is in fact Artidoro's identical brother, Galercio, with whom she falls in love.

Teolinda, meanwhile, has left home in search of the real Artidoro. The story she tells Galatea and Florisa ends without mention of Galercio. Teolinda only knows that Artidoro had come to her town in the first place in search of his missing brother. Not until Book IV, when the distraught Leonarda appears in person is her love for Galercio made known. Galercio, of course, loves not Leonarda but the harsh, unfeeling Gelasia, because of whom he attempts suicide in Book VI.

Teolinda's story, pieced together from several books in *La Galatea,* once again introduces a set of four characters—two women and two men—whose feelings of love cannot be stabilized in marriage. The obstacles here, however, are clearly internal. The identical pair Teolinda/Leonarda represents two unassimilated aspects of a single being, just as their masculine counterparts Artidoro/Galercio do. The brief union that Teolinda and Artidoro achieve is a magical one that takes place only when the "bad" brother and sister are absent. Once they return, which they do as soon as the religious festivities are over, the negative side of each character works to impede their marriage.[22]

Though the expression of failed love here may seem rather primitive, the insight the story provides into the causes of the failure is both profound and consistent with the strategy of the whole book. Before two people can be united in marriage, unity of each within himself or herself is required. Teolinda's story shows that the pubescent young woman's narcissism screens unrecognized negative qualities from view. If the young woman does not accept those negative qualities as a part of herself, they will intervene, as if arising from some other source, to impede the fulfillment of her love. Though in less-developed form, the story also shows that the young man needs to recognize such qualities in himself. If he does not—and that is the most common situation, especially in the pastoral romances—the young couple will continue pursuing one another forever in exact proportion to the degree to which each resists the other. The end of it all *can* be marriage—in Book V Leonarda, posing as Teolinda, tricks Artidoro into marrying her—but not the sort "made in heaven."

SILERIO AND TIMBRIO

If the first two interpolated tales tell of lovers who neglected to take account of their "friends'" resistance in their headlong pursuit of the loved one, the last two stories deal directly with the problems and dangers of rivalry. *La Galatea* began with Elicio and Erastro trying to rise above jealousy. The story subsequently told to Elicio, however, along with the one Galatea and Florisa heard, suggests that simply to disregard the threat of the rival is not to overcome it. Thus the question becomes: if one *does* confront rivalry, then what? The story of Silerio and Timbrio addresses this question. The solution, though an apparently happy one since Silerio and Timbrio marry sisters and remain friends, seemingly did not satisfy Cervantes. The problem got a different airing with quite a different result in *Don Quixote* Part I, as will be discussed in the next chapter. In *La Galatea,* the story begins in the late afternoon as Silerio, accompanied by Elicio, Erastro, and the courtly shepherds Tirsi and Damon, is walking toward town from the hermitage where he has taken refuge.

While Lisandro's story was grounded in discord, Silerio's reveals a friendship so deep that his whole life is oriented toward pleasing his friend. For Timbrio's sake, Silerio undertakes a long journey during which he has occasion to save

Timbrio from imprisonment and death. The physical tribulations Silerio undergoes for Timbrio prove to be nothing, however, compared to the emotional upheaval he experiences when, having been sent as a go-between, he falls in love with the same Neopolitan woman, Nísida, whom Timbrio hopes to marry.

As with Anselmo and Lotario in the "Tale of Foolish Curiosity," friendship takes precedence over love. Silerio says of Timbrio at the beginning of his story:

> Whether because of his great goodness or the influence of stars that made me gravitate toward him, I managed to make him my special friend by every human means; and heaven so blessed me in this that those who knew us, almost forgetting the name of Timbrio, and that of Silerio, . . . called us the two friends.

> (No sé si por la mucha bondad suya, o por la fuerza de las estrellas, que a ello me inclinaban, yo procuré, por todas las vías que pude, serle particular amigo, y fueme el cielo en esto tan favorable, que casi olvidándose a los que nos conocían el nombre de Timbrio y el de Silerio . . . solamente los dos amigos nos llamaban. [II, 128])

A full interpretation of each of Cervantes' interpolated tales requires attending to the elements surrounding it: its setting, the listeners, the time and place of its beginning and ending, and its interruptions. Silerio's story begins in Book II but is interrupted at the point of greatest complications. He finds himself pretending to be someone else for Nísida's sake and pretending to love someone else for Timbrio's sake. His tale of apparent confusion and disappointment, however, is interrupted by celebrants on their way to a wedding party. Teolinda's story, on the other hand, was interrupted at a point when her success appeared to be assured and all was in harmony. Her joyful moment in the narration was disrupted by the hunt and supplanted by Lenio's attack on love. The elements surrounding the narration bear noting, for they invariably reflect and comment upon the tale itself.

Silerio's story resumes in Book III, as Teolinda's had in Book II, in the village at night. The second part tells of the flowering of the love between Nísida and Timbrio that Silerio mediated. Silerio is about to describe a duel Timbrio is to fight to settle a question of honor when his story suffers another interruption. Outside the window Silerio and his listeners hear the sighs and lamentations of the shepherd Mireno, whom Silveria has rejected in favor of the rich Daranio. The five men listen to Mireno complain about fickle women and then Silerio resumes his story. The end of Silerio's story is also punctuated by concern over Mireno, who appears to be inconsolable, leaving town in despair just as the wedding festivities of Book III are about to begin. Again the interruption—the frame of the story—comments upon the events it interrupts. Mireno, in his despair, captures and amplifies on the mood of Silerio's story, which ends with Silerio believing that he has lost everything and must retire from the world.

Silerio explains his retreat to the hermitage saying:

> Tired by now and disillusioned with the things of this false world in which we live, I have decided to turn my mind toward a higher goal and to spend what little life remains to me in the service of Him who honors our wishes and deeds according to their merit. Therefore I have chosen this habit that you see, and the hermitage you found me in, so that in sweet solitude I may empty myself of my desires and direct my works toward a better end.

> (Cansado ya y desengañado de las cosas deste falso mundo en que vivimos, he acordado de volver el pensamiento a mejor norte, y gastar lo poco que de vivir me queda en servicio del que estima los deseos y las obras en el punto que merecen. Y así, he escogido este hábito que veis y la ermita que habéis visto, adonde en dulce soledad reprima mis deseos y encamine mis obras a mejor paradero. [III, 187])

But still a note of hope remains, for while Mireno, in the frame, complains of his loved one and writes her a letter attacking her faithlessness, Silerio, within the tale, blames only himself for his unhappiness, showing thereby a higher degree of self-awareness and suggesting that he will ultimately fare better than Mireno. In the hermitage Silerio hopes to free himself from what he calls his evil tendencies. Mireno, then, captures Silerio's sense of himself as an unwanted third in a love triangle and, consequently, as homeless and friendless. Silerio's self-restraint, however, contrasts favorably with Mireno's anger. Mireno drops out of the book at this point, while Silerio, as we shall see, stays to earn a dramatic turn of fortune. The entire second part of Silerio's story, including the two interruptions, takes place at night.

Though Timbrio and Silerio play complementary roles; Timbrio being more prominent and Silerio more retiring, each is subject to strenuous tests of character. Timbrio finds himself physically entangled in the world. He leaves home over an affair of honor, is captured by Catalan bandits, arrested as a supposed member of the gang by Barcelonan authorities, challenged to a duel—which he wins—and later confronted with storms at sea, naval battles, capture by the Turks, and eventual and miraculous release on the shores of Catalonia. The delicate and subtle negotiations of love were left to Silerio.

The happy end to Silerio's story begins when Elicio and his friends encounter a group of weary travellers resting by the bank of the river. The group includes none other than Timbrio, Nísida, and Nísida's sister Blanca, characters whom the shepherds recognize from Silerio's tale. The shepherds lead Silerio's friends to the hermitage, where, in the light of the full moon, the four are reunited and Timbrio completes the story Silerio left unfinished. Like Silerio, Timbrio undergoes purification through struggle. Nísida and Blanca, who accompanied him on his journey through storms, battles, and captivity, appear likewise to have been strengthened through adversity. By the time the four meet, all are theoretically in full possession of themselves. They therefore appear far more prepared than any of the sheltered characters of the pastoral to unite in marriage.

Still, the story is nothing more than a sketch for the later Byzantine solution to the problem of love and marriage that the *Persiles* develops at length. The marriages with which the Silerio/Timbrio story ends are nothing if not contrived. Nísida is scarcely developed as a character, and her sister Blanca seems to have been brought in as an afterthought. But the story is less concerned with marriage than it is with friendship; and less with friendship than with coming to terms with the complementary aspects of the self. Silerio, who seems to have gotten the worst deal, plays a role similar to Erastro's. In the *Persiles,* where all the complications of this problem are worked out, it is the Erastro figure—the lesser of the pair, socially speaking—who overcomes the rival. In *La Galatea,* the "winners" are the strong characters: the rich Daranio and the outgoing Timbrio. The solution, then, is no solution at all. It is the victory of the most powerful.

When Cervantes examines rivalry by matching equals (as in

"The Tale of Foolish Curiosity") or from the point of view of the weaker character, the results will be different.[23] In the *Persiles,* the victory of the younger brother is necessarily a spiritual one. Here, we have little better than the familiar "nice guy finishes last" syndrome, an outcome that does not reflect a higher development of consciousness.

ROSAURA'S STORY

Of *La Galatea's* four interpolated tales, the first and third are told to the shepherds, the second and fourth to the shepherdesses. The alternating pattern of male and female presentations, clearly visible in Book I, becomes more difficult to discern in later books as the narrative weave becomes more complex. Teolinda's and Silerio's stories undergo many interruptions and mingle with other events in the work in a way that Lisandro's did not. With Rosaura's story, the fourth in the sequence, the line between primary and secondary narrative units becomes difficult to discern. Rosaura's story does begin, like the others, with a tale of failed love narrated by the unhappy participant to a sympathetic band of listeners of the same sex. It is introduced, however, by a bit of dramatic action that Galatea, Florisa, and Teolinda witness as they are walking through the countryside. They see a veiled woman talking heatedly to a gentleman on horseback and hide in the bushes to watch as he follows her into the thicket.

The woman, Teolinda's friend Rosaura, threatens to commit suicide if the gentleman, Grisaldo, refuses to marry her. Grisaldo, yielding to Rosaura's hysteria, promises to settle matters so that the wedding can take place. Grisaldo proves to be a passive character and is really no match for the aggressive Rosaura. Though he was in love with Rosaura, his father convinced him that he should marry the rich and beautiful Leopercia instead, provoking Rosaura's threats overheard by the shepherdesses hidden in the bushes. After Grisaldo leaves, Rosaura tells her story.

Rosaura had spent much time with Grisaldo while he was visiting her father's house and becomes jealous when she hears about Leopercia. To test Grisaldo's resolve, she feigns attraction to another house guest, an Aragonese by the name of Artandro, who is also in love with her. The intended result is a triangle, with Grisaldo and Artandro both wanting Rosaura. Grisaldo, however, does not respond to the challenge of Artandro's interest in Rosaura. Instead he simply accepts his father's plan for him and agrees to marry Leopercia. Rosaura then finds herself, unwittingly, in the very situation she had hoped to avoid, struggling with the absent Leopercia for Grisaldo's affection.

The cycle of unrequited love that Rosaura's jealousy has created not only brings her into conflict with Leopercia and Grisaldo's family but also enrages Artandro, who now feels betrayed. The story ends in Book V with what, in another pastoral novel, would appear to be an abduction by a wild man. Artandro, who seems to come out of nowhere, storms the peaceful countryside with eight masked horsemen. They easily overcome Elicio's attempted resistance and then make off with Rosaura. As he leaves, Artandro announces: "Do not be amazed, good friends, at the seeming madness of my deeds, for the power of love and this lady's ingratitude have been their cause" (No os maravilléis, buenos amigos, de la sinrazón que al parecer aquí se os ha hecho, porque la fuerza de amor y la ingratitud de esta dama han sido causa della [V, 138]).

Once again Cervantes offers a violent interruption of the self-enclosed reverie of the shepherds. And once again he is careful to point out the victim's contribution to the violence. Artandro is carrying to its natural conclusion a series of events Rosaura engineered as a result of her jealousy. Rosaura's story is the obverse of Teolinda's, just as Silerio's was the obverse of Lisandro's. For whereas Teolinda's story focused on her relationship to Leonarda, Rosaura's concerns her manipulation of the two men who love her. Leopercia is the fourth figure in this story, as Galercio was in Teolinda's story. The concern shifts from the same-sex other in the first story the shepherdesses hear to the opposite-sex other in the second story.

In the men's case the concern moves in the opposite direction; the first story deals with the man's efforts to reach the woman, the second with his efforts to live harmoniously with his friend. As with so much else in this first work of Cervantes, the four interpolated tales reveal an effort to differentiate the sexes without subordinating the one to the other. Both sexes have weaknesses and strengths that complement one another. If each sees only himself or herself when looking at the other, these differences will result in confusion and violence rather than in harmony. If, however, either manages to escape from his or her hermeticism, the possibility of accepting the other as a complementary opposite is awakened.

THE INTERPOLATED TALES: A SUMMARY

I have given special attention to the four interpolated stories of *La Galatea* because they suggest a latent symmetry between the masculine and feminine components of this novel. I say latent because in fact the problems of men in love and the love stories told by men are longer by far than those presented by women. Nonetheless, the alternation between stories for and about male characters and stories for and about female characters reflects a tendency to extablish sexual polarities that distinguishes *La Galatea* from its pastoral predecessors. If marriage involves a union of opposites, both the masculine and feminine aspects of the union must be presented. What becomes clear, however, is that the erotic love that most of the characters experience involves a radical imbalance between the polarities. Whereas most pastoral romances are caught up in those imbalances, making the notion of marriage impossible,[24] *La Galatea* offers a pattern by which the imbalances, while being acknowledged, can also be corrected.

The process of correcting these imbalances involves first developing harmony within each side of the polarity, which is why the novel breaks down into a whole series not of dualities but of quaternities. Each interpolated story introduces a subquaternity through which various problems relating to the union of opposites can be examined. The collection of interpolated stories is in itself a quaternity, equally divisible into masculine and feminine halves; and the listeners to whom the four stories are narrated also form a quaternity, basically composed of the masculine pair Elicio/Erastro, and the feminine pair Galatea/Florisa.

Yet we must not give undue emphasis to the underlying structure, for what remains paramount in the work is not its order as much as its disorder. The dualities and quaternities are imbedded in a proliferation of apparently contradictory material that ultimately leads nowhere. Most of the stories, episodes, and songs deal not with union but with the failure to unite. I have uncovered the quaternities in the work only to show that *La Galatea* is in fact the forerunner to Cervantes' *Persiles* and to indicate the pattern through which erotic love and rivalry can finally be transcended in a marriage that is not a social convention but the symbol of a true union of opposing principles.

In *La Galatea* and in *Don Quixote* Part I, as in most Golden Age literature, erotic love functions as the enemy of marriage, which is seen as an institution imposed on young couples by parents, well meaning or otherwise. The larger implication of that enmity is that individual desires are perpetually and inevitably at odds with the needs of a well-ordered community. Fiction, as Bandera has shown,[25] becomes, in such a rift, the outlet for the expression of suppressed individual desires. The task Cervantes takes on is first to mediate and later to heal the division such a separation creates. In *La Galatea,* he mediates by alternating male and female perspectives; providing examples of love both as the instigator of refinement and as the generator of madness; allowing tales of murder and abduction to creep into the pleasantries of the pastoral; introducing husbands and fathers as well as distraught lovers; and leaving unresolved the question of Elicio and Galatea's love and marriage. What he produces is a cacophony of voices and situations. But beneath all that surface noise, as I hope to have shown, lies the structure of the natural order, a structure that refuses to cast out one set of values for the sake of the other. That refusal to take sides gives rise to a lot of confusion in *La Galatea.* In *Don Quixote,* it makes for Cervantes' famed perspectivism. In the *Persiles* it finally allows harmony to be established among previously warring entities.

ELICIO AND GALATEA:
FROM LISTENERS TO CHARACTERS

Galatea's father, Aurelio, whose hounds interrupted Teolinda's story in Book I, reappears in Book V to intervene more overtly in his daughter's affairs. There, finally, the forces of the external world impose themselves directly on the principal characters, as Elicio and Erastro learn that Aurelio has promised to marry Galatea to a Portuguese shepherd.

Elicio and Erastro fall into weeping and fainting when they hear the dreadful news. While Erastro resorts to prayer, recalling Silerio's function in the Silerio/Timbrio relationship, Elicio adopts a course of action. Elicio's challenge is represented by the episodes he witnesses immediately before and immediately after hearing of Aurelio's plans: before, he participates in an example of hopes fulfilled—Silerio's reunion with Timbrio, Blanca, and Nísida; after, he finds himself helpless when a "foreign" shepherd, Artandro, abducts Rosaura. The two episodes show Elicio's uncertainty and the confusion between success and failure that even Cervantes appears unable to resolve for his hero. Like Galatea, Elicio remains a weak and highly vulnerable character.

When Artandro abducts Rosaura, Elicio is speaking with Galatea in the countryside. After the abduction, Elicio, Galatea, Erastro, and Florisa, the four principal characters, leave the countryside for town. Along the road they encounter Silerio, Timbrio, Nísida, and Blanca, rejoicing in wedding attire. As the group proceeds, yet another optional resolution to the quandary of love and marriage confronting them emerges from the roadside, this time in the form of Lauso. Lauso is celebrating the restitution to his original self that he has achieved by finally recognizing the superficiality of the woman whom he had loved and by rejecting her once and for all. His is the other solution to the problem of love, and it is interesting that it should appear at just this moment. Lauso's sense of true liberation contrasts with Lenio's false and hysterical denunciation of love. Lauso's is presented as a credible alternative, leaving the question still open whether love is simply a madness, as Lenio asserts, or whether it can lead to a higher development of the self and eventually marriage.

As the group continues down the road, they encounter more of the shepherds and shepherdesses, and finally, the wise old man Telesio, who, as a priest, calls the shepherds in the area to gather for the annual ceremony in honor of the poet Meliso. Book VI takes place largely in the Valley of the Cypresses and contains much symbolic material that reinforces the novel's underlying organization into units of fours and twos that strive to transcend their separations. Although all the shepherds and shepherdesses gather at Telesio's bidding to honor the dead poet Meliso, those who figure most prominently are Elicio, Tirsi, Damon, and Lauso, who appear to have known Meliso best and whom Telesio asks to sing a song in his honor. The four later accompany Telesio to the mysterious flame that appears over Meliso's tomb at night. They watch as the flame divides to reveal the beautiful muse Caliope within.

Of the four sanctified characters—Elicio, Tirsi, Damon, and Lauso—whose participation in the mystic ceremony gives them a more elevated status in the novel, only Elicio has any true novelistic role. While Tirsi may lament the absence of his loved one, Damon cry over his loved one's rejection, and Lauso celebrate his freedom from love's illusion,[26] the women of whom they sing never appear. And when at the end of *La Galatea* Cervantes promises a second part to bring to a conclusion the unfinished love stories of the many characters who appear in the novel, he does not name Tirsi, Damon, and Lauso.[27] The most exemplary characters are apparently ethereal beings who are pure lovers and pure poets without the encumbrances of actual flesh-and-blood loved ones and struggles in the material world to contend with. Elicio is different, however. Galatea is present, and in Book V it becomes apparent that she is subject to the same human, social limitations that brought so many other characters squarely into the world of conflict and confusion.

In Book VI, Galatea, threatened by an unwanted marriage that would send her away from her friends, makes an overt appeal to Elicio. He has no choice now but to act. Aided by the advice of his friends, he decides to approach Galatea's father. If her father refuses him, he plans to resort to tormenting his Portuguese rival until he gives up his claim to Galatea. If that plan fails, he resolves to take action to prevent the marriage. In this he has the support of all the shepherds.

The novel ends at daybreak. Elicio is alone on a hilltop. As the sun arises he gazes down on the plains below and sees two squadrons of shepherds marching toward his cabin. He recognizes them as his friends and goes down to greet them. They meet at Elicio's cabin just as Tirsi and Damon are emerging. The company of shepherds offers him its services. Elicio informs them of the plans he has made with Tirsi and Damon: "And all went [toward the village] determined that if Tirsi's arguments could not move Aurelio to do what they asked, they would resort to violence instead" (Y todos llevaban intención de que, si las razones de Tirsi no movían a que Aurelio la hiciese en lo que le pedían, de usar en su lugar la fuerza [VI, 266]). The end comes just as Elicio is being asked to move from the world of dream into that of conflict. Since nothing appears available to bridge the gap between the pastoral idyll and the realm of

conflicting desires, Cervantes simply suspends the action, prom-
ising a continuation later.

Galatea, like Elicio, is surrounded by contradictory images at
the end of the novel. On the one hand there is Nísida, who
represents love fulfilled in marriage, but on the other there is
Gelasia. Two men, Lenio and Galercio, try to kill themselves
over Gelasia. In their presence Gelasia sings from atop a high
rock above the river:

> My loves both are, and have been, of the fields;
> Roses and jasmines are my chains;
> Free was I born, and in freedom am I grounded.

> (Del campo son y han sido mis amores;
> rosas son y jazmines mis cadenas;
> libre nací, y en libertad me fundo. [VI, 252])

In the series of songs about love that the shepherds and shepherdesses sing as they leave the Valley of the Cypresses, Belisa,
who is the last to offer her ideas, presents, in a minor key,
another example of female resistance to the lover's desires. The
last seven verses of the last stanza of her song go as follows:

> Let my free will govern thought in its own way;
> let my tender neck be exempt
> and neither permit nor consent
> upon itself the yoke of love
> which disturbs all calm
> and drives away all freedom.

> (Rija mi libre albedrío
> a su modo el pensamiento;
> mi tierna cerviz esenta
> no permita ni consienta
> sobre sí el yugo amoroso,
> por quien se turba el reposo
> y la libertad se ausenta. [VI, 239])

In the face of so many doubts, it is no wonder that Elicio is
apprehensive. Like the only successful lovers in the novel,
Elicio compares the dangers he faces to those of a journey
through rough seas:

> If from this boiling sea, and wild gulf
> that the tempest so violently threatens
> I save my life from so harsh an affront,

and reach land safe and sound,
Raising both hands in the air,
with humble soul and a contented will,
I will let love know and heaven feel
richly my gratitude for their goodness.

(Si deste herviente mar y golfo insano,
donde tanto amenaza la tormenta,
libro la vida de tan dura afrenta
y toco el suelo venturoso y sano,
al aire alzadas una y otra mano,
con alma humilde y voluntad contenta
haré que amor conozca, el cielo sienta
que el bien les agradezco soberano. [VI, 264])

CONCLUSION

The sea, like the moon, evokes the unconscious. The forests
and animals also stand for the unconscious to which the shepherds, confused by love, have retreated. All the stories, all the
songs, all the debates reflect Elicio's internal state as he undergoes the self-evaluation that his love for Galatea has prompted.
Yet, as we examine the songs, debates, and stories, we see that
irresolution remains. There is no clear-cut direction suggested
that will guarantee Elicio's success. Lauso shows that Lenio
could be right: love could easily be a delusion; the loved one
need not necessarily be an image of the divine. Union is not
guaranteed. In the ceremony in Book VI, the shepherds and
shepherdesses remain apart. The divine image of Caliope is
clearly of supernatural origin. Of the few cases of marriage, one,
that of Daranio and Silveria, is based on interest, and another
takes place beyond the reach of parents and society. In both
cases, or rather in all three, since Silerio/Timbrio produce two
marriages, the union carries with it a disappointed lover who
goes to the brink of despair.[28] A fourth marriage between
Leonarda and Artidoro is based on deceit, and the third party,
Teolinda, is left in misery.

In this world that remains split into male and female halves
from beginning to end, the majority of the male characters
suffer the rejection of their loved ones, and the majority of the
female characters remain aloof and protective of their freedom.
Those few female characters who do yield to love's bidding are

usually not exemplary and are unsuccessful in their efforts to bring about their own happiness.

While there are male characters in all walks of life represented in the work—wise and foolish old men, fathers, priests, young men—there are no mothers, wise old women, or priestesses. The only female who is not a desirable young shepherdess is Caliope, who is literally from another world. The absence of women as other than attractive young ladies may be, in fact, the key to the whole work: Cervantes appears unable at this point truly to present women in their variegated individuality as he is able, to some extent, to present men. Instead, he casts them all in a single mold, which must be understood as signalling the archetype of the lovely, inaccessible virgin—the Diana figure. Like Nísida and Blanca, they remain for the most part entirely passive, moons, as Blanca's name suggests, on which the male sees the image of his ideal reflected. Even when they are not passive, as Teolinda, Rosaura, and Gelasia are not, the ladies of Cervantes' pastoral novel act only in the context of the network of amorous desire in which they are caught and have no other novelistic role to play. Their effort is to sustain the image of inaccessibility and desirability in which they are cast.

The rational side of Cervantes, the observer of human life in its material manifestation, the distanced narrator who sees that women as well as men make mistakes and must develop beyond their weaknesses, makes ample room for a wide variation of human types, male and female. The unconscious side, however, which he explores through Elicio, still appears to be overwhelmed by the presence of the feminine, which remains largely unconscious and unassimilated, as the work he produces at this stage reveals.

The resolution, as the succeeding chapters will show, will come as the main male characters, having discovered their separateness from the unconscious, will finally have to relinquish the abstract image of the lady, as Don Quixote gives up Dulcinea. The process involves nothing less than the transformation of the hero, something that uproots all received ideas and inherited expectations and reflects back on the consciousness of an author who, from his earliest works, had built in the signals that would lead to his and his characters' conversion.[29]

The conflict between the rational and irrational is present in *La Galatea* in an unstated form. The lack of clarification of the issues makes for the work's overall inconclusiveness and ensures that Elicio and Galatea remain locked in a state of unfulfilled desire. In *Don Quixote* Part I, to be examined in the next chapter, the problem here represented in an unconscious manner will become the author's prime concern. The 1605 novel will be an exposition of the conflict experienced by a solitary male character who seeks to define himself in opposition to the boredom of the unconscious life prescribed for him as a country gentleman. Though Part I could not conclude any more than *La Galatea* could, since the terms in opposition remain untranscended, Part II offers a shift in orientation that provides an opening to resolution that the *Persiles* will explore in detail.

CHAPTER THREE

Don Quixote Part I

CONSCIOUSNESS AND THE
PATTERNS OF THE UNCONSCIOUS

As the chapter on *La Galatea* makes clear, Cervantes chose rather to disrupt the patterns established by literary tradition than to sacrifice the expression within his work of the natural order, however dimly that order was understood.[1] The natural order rejects the either/or formulation that arises when literature is used as an escape, affirming instead that the nonliterary world is composed of dualities that function as counterbalancing forces within a perfectly harmonious whole. The discrepancy in *La Galatea* between the conscious effort to assimilate the pastoral model and the unconscious resistance to it produced a work of apparent confusion and disorder.

Don Quixote Part I, like *La Galatea,* is at variance with the pre-established literary form it imitates, and its lack of apparent plan makes the work more akin to its forerunner than is generally recognized. The difference between *La Galatea* and *Don Quixote* Part I is that in the later work Cervantes takes an openly aggressive stance toward the literary models he appropriates. It cannot be simply incidental that the chivalric romances that are his principal focus of attack are themselves grounded in conflict. Whereas the pastoral romances seek to mask the conflictive world on which they rest, the chivalric brings strife among men to the forefront. Mirroring his models, Cervantes disguises his discomfort with the pastoral in *La Galatea,* while taking up sword and shield against the chivalric in *Don Quixote.*

The consciousness that produces pastoral romances, however, differs only in appearance from that which produces the chivalric. Most books of chivalry contain pastoral interludes, and even the tales of shepherds in love, as we have seen, never entirely

manage to avoid conflict and violence. The two literary forms
have in common the need, on the part of the author as well as
of the reader, to overvalue some characters, virtues, and experiences at the expense of others. Inasmuch as the romances
promote such over- and undervaluing, they participate in the
creation of a distorted simulacrum of the real world that is not
only fictional but ultimately destructive.

Cervantes' problem, as Cesáreo Bandera has so clearly demonstrated in *Mimesis conflictiva*,[2] is that to attack such fictions is
to take them seriously. They become real for the author as soon
as he allows them into his consciousness. Whether he enter-
tains them as a friend or as a foe is in the long run unimportant.
What matters is that he has entered their world, or they his.
And so, after all, *La Galatea* and *Don Quixote* have a lot in common.
Both works, for example, contain large amounts of secondary
material that is poorly integrated into the main plot. In both
works the formal subdivisions (into books, parts, and chapters)
do not truly organize or contain the onflowing narrative.[3] Both
main characters, Elicio and Don Quixote, suffer from the same
sense of distance between self and other that condemns them to
the frustration of their desires. Each work offers a wide variety
of literary styles. Neither comes to an ending that resolves the
problems the characters have generated. Cervantes' first two
long novels demonstrate, furthermore, a strange fidelity to their
own disorder. Character and text in both works resonate within
a system that affirms, beyond "literature" or the particularities
of individual desire, their foundation in truth.

Though they share certain characteristics that mark them
clearly as works of Cervantes, *La Galatea* and *Don Quixote* represent two very different phases in the author's development. In
Don Quixote Part I his attitude—on all fronts—is no longer
passive, as it was in *La Galatea,* but aggressive. Cervantes takes
on not only the chivalric novel but the whole lettered world,
and Don Quixote throws himself into the arena of his entire
society—the merchants, the sheep and cattle herders, the bar-
bers, the innkeepers, the clergy—and challenges them all. In
both works, the author's level of disconformity with the literary
model he has adopted is reproduced within the story in the
main character's attitude toward authority.[4] Elicio stops short of
challenging Galatea's father just as Cervantes avoids a head-on
confrontation with the assumptions and literary traditions of

the pastoral. Don Quixote, on the other hand, after years of quiescence as the retiring country gentleman Alonso Quijano, rips into every symbol of authority and power his compatriots hold dear, while he thrashes about in a text that claims to have declared war on the most popular literary forms of the day.

Don Quixote Part I can best be characterized by an attitude of aggression, permeating every aspect of the novel, toward the elements from which it is constituted. The attack begins in the Prologue, where Cervantes defends his book against the educated who would look for footnotes, quotes in Latin and Greek, and other signs of erudition.[5] The idea that the work is nourished from living founts and not from the inkwells of the world's lettered men is further emphasized when Cervantes' friend asserts that the book's intent is to destroy "the authority and influence which books of chivalry have in the world and among the common people" (I, Prologue, 30) (la autoridad y cabida que en el mundo y en el vulgo tienen los libros de caballerías [I, Prologue, 62]).[6]

Within the novel many forces work to undermine literary structure, the authority of words, and the sanctity of literary tradition. Most critics have pointed out the difficulty of finding ideas in *Don Quixote* that can safely be attributed to Cervantes.[7] Cervantes' play with words, along with his introduction of so many levels of discourse and so many literary styles, tends to break down whatever assumptions the reader might harbor about the fixed nature of literary language and the power of the word to assign meaning.[8]

The attack in *Don Quixote* Part I is directed not only at external targets but at itself as well. Don Quixote emerges as the conscious rejection of his former self, Alonso Quijano. The Arab scribe Cide Hamete chronicles the activities of an "enemy" Christian knight. The "Second Author," the reader who saves the book from extinction in Chapter 9, impugns the motives of the author whose book he is reading. The fictional landscape of *Don Quixote* Part I offers no place of repose in our search for certainty. The narrator denigrates his main character, the reader distrusts the narrator, characters clash with one another, the literary model the author follows is one he hopes to destroy, and the words with which he builds his house of fiction are shown to be as flimsy as cards.

Characters at their most eloquent—Don Quixote in his arms

and letters speech or Lotario when he tries to dissuade Anselmo from his plan to test his wife—prove incapable, however studied their rhetoric, of influencing events. The very text itself comes close to being sold as pulp. Most of the love poetry written by Grisóstomo goes up in flames, and Don Quixote's library is cast into oblivion in the twinkling of an eye. The written word is a fragile, faulty commodity in the world *Don Quixote* inhabits.

What needs to be examined here, however, is not the ample support *Don Quixote* Part I gives to those obsessed in our time with the inadequacy of the word, but rather the affirmation that is implicit beneath the spectacle it offers of self-destructive systems.[9] The affirmation is the same one it was possible to perceive underlying *La Galatea:* that terms in opposition reflect the balance of the natural world. Only when one is unconsciously identified with one side or another do the opposites become a source of conflict. *Don Quixote* Part I is the expression, par excellence, of the disruption of the natural order that results when each entity sees itself as isolated from every other. The work shows how conflicts multiply as more and more characters become swept up in the madness of isolation that Don Quixote brings with him into the world.

To study the structure of *Don Quixote* Part I, as with *La Galatea,* we must resist the tendency to read the work as a cause-and-effect sequence of events. When not caught up in the plot, the reader can observe how each character or situation that is off-balance calls its opposite into existence. The proliferation of terms in opposition makes the novel appear to grow out of itself, to be motored by its own internal contradictions. Don Quixote sees himself as knight-errant to counterbalance the overly sedentary Alonso Quijano; the text that appears destined for sale to the silk merchants finds within it a reader who rescues it; and when Don Quixote runs out of adventures, his horse chooses the path he is to follow. Passivity engenders activity; authors create readers who create authors; the unconscious (Rocinante) takes over when consciousness (Don Quixote's plan) falters.

The pattern in the apparently haphazard process by which *Don Quixote* was created can only be discerned when the reader disengages from Don Quixote's words, statements, ideas, and expectations and understands that each character's "novel" is not *the* novel. The truth of the novel belongs neither to Don Quixote, nor to Cide Hamete, nor to Sancho, nor to the priest. The novel is the interplay of these and other conflictive forces and voices within it, an interplay in which no one is "in charge," since everyone is, consciously or unconsciously, a partisan. *Don Quixote* Part I, as Cesáreo Bandera has shown so beautifully, is a battlefield of limited perspectives.[10] Cervantes makes the point clear by choosing a Moor as his fictitious author, a Moor accused by one of his most devoted readers of being not only mendacious by nature but envious of the very gentleman whose story he is writing.

But it is not enough just to perceive the conflict between narrator, reader, and character. We must appreciate that these conflicts are necessary, that Don Quixote, for example, *needs* his deflationary narrator to balance his own pretentions. Without Cide Hamete, Don Quixote could not exist, and not only because the Moor is his scribe. Cide Hamete is Don Quixote's own scoffing, sceptical voice that, if it were not splintered off into another character, would so stifle him that he would forever remain the long-suffering, inwardly raging Alonso Quijano. By embodying that internal resistance to Alonso Quijano's desire to go out and conquer worlds, Cide Hamete frees Don Quixote. In a like manner, the sceptical reader makes it possible for Cide Hamete to misrepresent Don Quixote. Were the reader to demand absolute fidelity to the facts, Cide Hamete would find himself saddled with constraints that would make the narration of his tale impossible.[11]

Once we recognize that the oppositions within *Don Quixote* not only generate but sustain one another, it becomes pointless to wonder whose side Cervantes is on. Cervantes was clearly able to back away from the whole spectacle of pretentions and deflations that constitute his novel to watch how they feed upon and reinforce one another.[12] It is another step entirely, however, to be able to transform the sets of conflicting polarities into a unified whole. By the end of *Don Quixote* Part I, the main character appears as convinced of the reality of his imaginary world as ever, and his neighbors as concerned about his madness as ever. Very little seems to have been done to restore order to the universe Cervantes set in motion, with all of its endless actions and reactions. The novel, as it was conceived in 1605, could not conclude for the same reason that it had secondary material not well integrated with the plot, that Rocinante was allowed to choose the path, and that Don Quixote continued locked in his vision of himself as knight: no one was truly in charge. The balance of opposites so clearly at play in the work was not consciously apprehended by the author.

The framework for a harmonious universe established in *La Galatea* continues intact in *Don Quixote* Part I. This framework, however, must be *consciously* embraced in order to be perceived as a basis for harmony. When this occurs, as it does in the *Persiles*, the author will no longer have to disparage his narrator, his narrator will no longer have to undermine his main character, and the main character will no longer suffer the eternal frustration of his desires. But in *Don Quixote* Part I, Cervantes, like his narrator and his characters, is still fascinated by fiction, even though he tries to repudiate it.[13] The fictional space in which all the opposing terms oscillate is nothing less than the consciousness of its author, reduplicated in each particle and perfectly mirrored in the whole.

Don Quixote, despite being the object of Cervantes' ridicule, is nonetheless the center of consciousness in the novel. To understand his significance, it is necessary to consider not his rusty armor and all the anecdotal material introduced to amuse and distract the reader but the essential role he plays and the constellation of characters his presence brings into the world. All the elements of the work cohere when considered in the light of the struggle between what is real and what is imaginary. Yet Cervantes, while understanding the illusory nature of Don Quixote's "truth," remains unable to grasp a reality that isn't just as limiting as his character's. For just as the whole novel reflects Don Quixote's consciousness, so Don Quixote reflects the consciousness of his author. The succeeding novels will show how that center of consciousness advances to the point where, in the *Persiles*, illusion is consciously manipulated by main characters who perceive themselves as fictional expressions of their real selves.

THE QUATERNITY IN *DON QUIXOTE* PART I

Don Quixote declares in his Golden Age speech in Chapter 11 that his mission as knight-errant is to defend women against the lustful advances that men in the present "age of iron" are wont to make. He seems to think Dulcinea is properly served when he sends his defeated enemies to Toboso to pay her homage. In Chapter 21, where he spins a fantasy of chivalric love to reassure Sancho about his promised island, he makes it clear that he wins the king's daughter through his military prowess more than through attention to a lady. Though he seeks union with the feminine, the route is through combat. In effect, the lady exists so that men may fight over her. She is won on the battlefield. Furthermore, Cardenio's story and "The Tale of Foolish Curiosity" will later show that when the lady is present, the men, no matter how strong their friendship, *will* fight over her. They fight over her because she is not real. She is a mirage generated from the imbalance between the masculine and feminine polarities. To the extent that the mirage is taken to represent reality, however, it will perpetuate—never resolve—the conflicts that the imbalance brings with it.

Don Quixote, like the heroes of the chivalric romances, sees the lady as a distant image of beauty and refinement, so distinct from the familiar world of men as to be not only unattainable but scarcely human. Dulcinea perfectly represents such a lady, though only slightly less stylized versions of her can be found throughout *Don Quixote* Part I.

The chivalric approach to the feminine is to put the woman out of sight and to engage in her name in a fascinating game of warfare with men. The chivalric consciousness, therefore, is heavily overbalanced on the masculine side. The pastoral approach, on the other hand, is to concentrate on the woman and to ignore, or try to suppress, the presence of conflict that male intermediaries represent. In the pastoral, the feminine is overvalued at the expense of the masculine.

The respective imbalances between masculine and feminine can be clearly seen in the words and actions of chivalric and pastoral heroes. The shepherd is continually complaining about his lady's cruelty and disdain. She is far too powerful, holding his very life in her hands. Conversely, the knight sees the lady as an object to be protected from the lustful designs of others. Both projections reveal the same imbalance and result in supplanting a real being with a false image of her. Both, therefore, guarantee the separation between masculine and feminine that is the hallmark of the pastoral as well as of the chivalric novels.

In this light is it easier to understand why Elicio in *La Galatea* listens to secondary tales of strife, while in *Don Quixote* Part I, the interpolated tales take up pastoral themes. In both works the inset stories serve as a counterpoise to an imbalance in consciousness on the part of the main character. The secondary tales are poorly integrated into the main story line in both works because they deal with precisely those aspects the main character has suppressed. Before taking a more detailed look at the secondary tales, we must consider how essential the suppression of the body, Alonso Quijano's chief characteristic, is to Don Quixote's self-construct.[14]

Alonso Quijano's entire obsession with reading may be an aspect of his fear of the body. At fifty he remains unmarried, living the life of an impoverished country gentleman on an estate that diminishes in proportion to the growth of his library. He shares his house with an unmarried niece and a middle-aged housekeeper. When he is not reading, he converses about literature with the barber and the priest who live in his village. Edward Said has associated novelistic beginnings with celibacy,[15] and Alonso Quijano is a fit subject for such a description.

Don Quixote, for all that he rejects what he thinks Alonso Quijano represents, carries with him into his chivalric world a mind determined to free itself from the confusions he feels in the presence of a marriageable niece, a superstitious housekeeper, and his own diminishing physical vigor. But as knight-errant he runs head-on into the world Alonso Quijano would have preferred to avoid. In the inns he keeps finding sexually active young ladies; on the road he imagines damsels in distress. His adventures, despite Fierabrás's balm, hasten his physical decline. His repasts are even less abundant than before, when as a country gentleman he could look forward to lentils and stew.

The fictional wall he builds to protect himself from the physical world is subject to continual and frustrating incursions by "enchanters" determined to tear it down. And so his increased identification with the domain of the intellect changes the name and appearance of the "enemy" forces over which he has no control but does not eliminate them. As Don Quixote, Alonso Quijano's flight from the unconscious—from engagement in life—simply takes a more active form.

In his Golden Age speech to the goatherds in Chapter 11,

Don Quixote deviates considerably from the traditional idyll by emphasizing to an extraordinary degree man's uncontrollable lust, and the dangers to which young women are subject in the present age. Formerly, he says,

> maiden modesty roamed, as I have said, wherever she would, single and solitary, without fear of harm from strangers' license or lascivious assault; and if she was undone it was of her own will and desire. But now, in this detestable age of ours, no maiden is safe even though she be hidden in the center of another Cretan labyrinth; for even there through some chink or through the air, by dint of its accursed persistence, the plague of love gets in and brings them to ruin despite their seclusion. Therefore, as times rolled on and wickedness increased, the order of knights-errant was founded for their protection, to defend maidens, relieve widows, and succour the orphans and the needy. (I, 11, 86–87)

> Las doncellas y la honestidad andaban, como tengo dicho, por dondequiera, sola y señora, sin temor que la ajena desenvoltura y lascivo intento le menoscabasen, y su perdición nacía de su gusto y propia voluntad. Y agora, en estos nuestros detestables siglos, no está segura ninguna, aunque la oculte y cierre otro nuevo laberinto, como el de Creta; porque allí, por los resquicios o por el aire, con el celo de la maldita solicitud se les entra la amorosa pestilencia y les hace dar con todo su recogimiento al traste. Para cuya seguridad, andando más los tiempos y creciendo más la malicia, se instituyó la orden de los caballeros andantes, para defender las doncellas, amparar las viudas y socorrer a los huérfanos y a los menesterosos. [I, 11, 155])

Consistent with his theory, Don Quixote finds menaced women everywhere: in Chapter 8 he fights a Basque man in "defense" of a lady he imagines is being taken off against her will; in Chapter 14 he marches into the woods in pursuit of any man who might dare attack Marcela; in Chapter 18 he fancies the rams and sheep as Moorish and Christian armies battling over a woman; in Chapter 29 he happily agrees to do what he can to help the "Princess Micomicona"; and at the end of Part I he charges upon a group of penitents carrying a statue of the Virgin because he declares they are abducting her.

Ironically, the only real virgin in need of protection in Don Quixote's life is the unmarried niece he has left at home under the care of his housekeeper. And since housekeepers in Cervantes' fiction are usually engaged in arranging—not preventing—

lovers' trysts, Don Quixote in his flight into madness has again made possible the very situation he feels called upon to prevent.

Throughout Part I, the image of Dulcinea is countered by the very real presence of prostitutes. Don Quixote's first meeting with women once away from home, in fact, is with inn prostitutes, whom he insists on calling princesses. Later, in Juan Palomeque's inn, he meets Maritornes whose ugliness and availability counterbalance the image of Marcela, whom Don Quixote had set out to pursue in Chapter 14. In the mountains he meets the nonvirginal Dorotea, whom he understands to be a damsel in distress. Just as Don Quixote creates Cide Hamete when he creates himself, he populates the world with erotically engaged women at the very moment when he sends images of Dulcinea out into the air. In a similar fashion, his own chastity and passion for literature call forth a host of illiterate, earthy men—headed by Sancho, but including less-friendly pig gelders, merchants' servants, goatherds, horse owners, muleteers, and police—many of whom deliver him merciless beatings.

What emerges from the dissociated knights and ladies Don Quixote brings into the world from books of chivalry is nothing less than the same quaternity seen in *La Galatea:* a quaternity in which the four cardinal points are as separate from one another as they can possibly be. *Don Quixote* Part I represents an advance over *La Galatea* in that the feminine half of the configuration has developed beyond its virtual state. The regressive side of the expression of the quaternity in *Don Quixote* is that, while developing the feminine opposition between the lady and the prostitute, the masculine opposition has intensified. The Erastro figure, when he emerges as a rough muleteer or an enraged pig gelder, is no longer the respectful friend he was in *La Galatea.*

In the secondary stories, the struggle on the masculine side of the quaternity will have the lady as its ostensible object. But in Part I, Don Quixote's clashes with men, including Sancho, reveal that other fictions are equally potent sources of conflict. At issue in all cases is the disorder that results when the creations of the intellect take priority over those of the real world. Reestablishing order means beginning first with what is closest at hand. Sancho plays an important role in forcing Don Quixote to listen to him. At Don Quixote's side, Sancho brings food, sleep, and the activity of the body into his master's consciousness. This results in Part II in a marked heightening of Sancho's presence and an equalization of their roles. The resolution of the opposition between the primary male characters, moreover, will bring with it an alteration in the projected image of the feminine, as the study of Part II will show.

For Part I the novel begins and ends with Don Quixote, however embattled, clinging to an imaginary world that casts the four sides of being to their furthest and most antagonistic points. But through this radical dispersion the voices of the disenfranchised are awakened. Marcela makes a far more developed statement in defense of her position than Gelasia was able to make in *La Galatea*. Maritornes, who has no real equivalent in the earlier novel, shows a great capacity to create havoc in Don Quixote's world, causing the multiple beatings of his first visit to Juan Palomeque's inn and stringing him up by the wrists from the hayloft chute during his second. Sancho also knows how to make his presence felt, insisting that he be allowed to speak, no matter what Don Quixote's books say about squires, and tying up Rocinante's feet if need be to keep his master from pursuing his knightly follies.

These "unconscious" presences—that is, the representatives of the aspects of Don Quixote that have no real place in his world—are not only destructive, however. The inn prostitutes are kind when Don Quixote is in need of help, and Sancho, though capable of disobedience and lies, is most notable for his loyalty to Don Quixote. The batterings that come from those less immediately involved with Don Quixote serve the important function of wearing him down so that, in his less well-defended state, other sides of his being can be heard.

Although Don Quixote continues throughout Part I to defend his consciously chosen position, the rhythm of the novel suggests that the unconscious forces are very much at work. The unconscious can make itself felt, as it does before Chapter 25 of Part I, through beatings, tramplings, failures, and a general upending of Don Quixote's invented world, or it can speak, as it does to an increasing degree after Chapter 25, through guile and dream. In the first twenty-four chapters, Don Quixote's own imaginative projections of the world by and large direct his journey. He seldom takes time to question or to assess his models. His wanderings lead him further and further from home, often taking him off the highway and into the wilds.

During this period Dulcinea serves only as a point of reference. Never does Don Quixote entertain the idea of communicating with her, directly or indirectly.

In Chapter 25, however, a whole range of events marks, quite literally, a turning point.[16] Having battled with Toledan merchants, windmills, the Basque gentlemen, the Yanguesans, the muleteer, the Holy Brotherhood, the herds of sheep and rams, the galley slaves, and Cardenio, Don Quixote retires in Chapter 25 to the wild heights of the Sierras to do penance. He has his models, of course—Cardenio, as well as Amadís—but most recent critics have followed Avalle-Arce in seeing his folly on Dulcinea's behalf as entirely gratuitous.[17] Indeed, Sancho himself sees it as such: "It seems to me, . . . that the knights who did things like that were provoked and had a reason for their follies and penances. But what reason has your worship for going mad?" (I, 25, 203) (Paréceme a mí . . . que los caballeros que lo tal ficieron fueron provocados y tuvieron causa para hacer esas necedades y penitencias; pero vuestra merced, ¿qué causa tiene para volverse loco? [I, 25, 300]). And Don Quixote agrees: "A knight-errant who turns mad for a reason deserves neither merit nor thanks. The thing is to do it without cause" (I, 25, 203) (Volverse loco un caballero andante con causa, ni grado ni gracias: el toque está en desatinar sin ocasión [I, 25, 300]). And yet, from the point of view of the structure of the unconscious, the act is an entirely appropriate one. When Don Quixote retires to the Sierra Morena, he does homage to a bit more of what he has neglected.

Of the four extreme positions for the masculine and feminine that enclose the novel, Don Quixote is conscious of only one. He tells the Canon of Toledo in Chapter 50 that since he became a knight-errant he has been "valiant, courteous, liberal, well-bred, generous, polite, bold, gentle and patient, and an endurer of toils, imprisonments, and enchantments" (I, 50, 442) (valiente, comedido, liberal, biencriado, generoso, cortés, atrevido, blando, paciente, sufridor de trabajos, de prisiones, de encantos [I, 50, 589]). Not only could Sancho well contest much of this self-description, but Don Quixote himself brings it into question shortly therafter by engaging in a furious fight with the goatherd Eugenio. The novel is filled to the brim with all that Don Quixote believes he is not. And the more actively he resists the impulses of the body that he refuses to accept, the more embattled he becomes. In the first half of *Don Quixote* Part I, Don Quixote loses his teeth and part of an ear; is beaten by the owners of the Yanguesan mares, the muleteer, and the galley slaves; and comes into contact with vomit and excrement far more than would have been seemly for a bookish country gentleman. By Chapter 25, when he retires to the Sierras in imitation of Cardenio, his conscious position has been severely battered.

It is not without importance that Don Quixote makes his first effort to send, through Sancho, a message to Dulcinea during his penance. In terms of the development of his psyche, the message is a significant step. In the same Chapter 25, furthermore, Sancho realizes for the first time that Dulcinea is Aldonza Lorenzo. The quaternity that has only existed in the abstract until now becomes, in this crucial chapter, identified with the names Don Quixote/Sancho/Dulcinea/Aldonza Lorenzo. The effort to conflate Dulcinea and Aldonza Lorenzo is the subject of *Don Quixote* Part II, but it clearly begins in Part I, Chapter 25, at a point when Don Quixote is at the highest reach of his journey and is the furthest from home.[18] In the wilds of the Sierras, he momentarily releases his hold on his self-created image. He discards his knightly attire, sends Sancho away on Rocinante, and gives himself over, for once, to direct concern with his lady. In the same chapter, he reveals a capacity for detachment from his role, allowing himself the freedom to pick and choose among literary models.

After Chapter 25, Don Quixote begins the process of return, making his way down from the mountains, to the inn, and finally home. The return journey is masterminded by "friends from home"—the barber, the priest, Sancho—and by a woman, Dorotea, disguised as the Princess Micomicona. In the journey home, a sense of total passivity, heightened by the long periods when Don Quixote is either absent or asleep, replaces the activity characteristic of Don Quixote in the first half. The relative inactivity of the second half of *Don Quixote* Part I gives rise to a series of secondary tales that involve union or the possibility of union.

The stories that suggest the possibility of recovery from the instability of romantic love—the Cardenio/Dorotea story, that of Doña Clara and Don Luis, and the Captive's tale—cannot be understood apart from Don Quixote's lapse into fatigue and dream in the return phase of his journey. That he had reached the furthest point of his chivalric fantasy in the Sierras and there began to focus upon the lady suggests that by Chapter 25 Don Quixote is vulnerable to the stirrings of the unconscious. During his second visit to Juan Palomeque's inn, the faint rustle of those stirrings—hinting at a revaluation of the feminine—will be heard. To understand properly the sleeping Don Quixote's relation to those stories of implied resolution, the reader must recognize that their respective heroes—Cardenio/Fernando; the Captive—meet at the inn with their ladies after arduous travels and trials that mirror those the exhausted knight-errant has undergone. The compensatory material their stories offer, however, remains secondary and unconscious, reflecting the stories' position and the inconclusive nature of the novel in which they are imbedded.

The sections to follow will take up the question of the interpolated tales: those in which Don Quixote takes an active part as listener and those which appear to pass over him unnoticed. The first and last tales—the Grisóstomo/Marcela story and that of Eugenio and Leandra—most closely parallel Don Quixote's conscious position, which appears not to change throughout the novel. The middle three stories—that of Cardenio/Dorotea; "The Tale of Foolish Curiosity"; and the Captive's tale—take a closer look at the masculine and feminine polarities and offer visions of both that Don Quixote is unable to fathom at this point, which is why they remain unintegrated either into the story or into the character of its protagonist.[19]

THE FIRST AND LAST INTERPOLATED TALES

Marcela/Grisóstomo

In Chapter 11, just after delivering his Golden Age speech to the goatherds with whom he is eating, Don Quixote hears the beginning of the first interpolated tale. The story, which continues the pastoral theme that the Golden Age speech introduced, offers further evidence of the violence and confusion simmering just beneath the placid surface of song and love that the literary pastoral promotes.

Grisóstomo, madly in love with the beautiful and distant Marcela, gives up possessions, status, sanity, and finally his life in her pursuit. A large portion of the story unfolds at his grave, above which the luminous figure of Marcela appears as Grisóstomo is being buried. She is described as "a miraculous vision —for such it seemed—which suddenly appeared before their eyes. For on the top of the rock in which they were digging the grave appeared the shepherdess Marcela, looking even more beautiful than she had been described" (I, 14, 107) (una maravillosa visión—que tal parecía ella—que improvisamente se les ofreció a los ojos; y fue que, por cima de la peña donde se cavaba la sepultura, pareció la pastora Marcela, tan hermosa, que pasaba a su fama su hermosura [I, 14, 181]).

Like Gelasia in *La Galatea,* Marcela is the object of many men's adoration and the ostensible cause of at least one man's demise. Her story, however, represents a considerable development over that of her earlier counterpart. She is of course beautiful and naturally disinclined to yield to any of her many suitors' importunings. She belongs very much to the Diana archetype that Gelasia embodied. But while *La Galatea* offered no information about Gelasia's life, the narrator of the Grisóstomo story devotes considerable time to a discussion of Marcela's childhood and upbringing. The effect is to humanize somewhat the mesmerizing figure that has so long held archetypal status in the pastoral and chivalric romances.

Marcela is an orphan; her mother died in childbirth and her father of grief shortly thereafter. Marcela grows up under the care of her uncle, the village priest. Beautiful and wealthy, she is overwhelmed by marriage offers by the time she reaches adolescence. Her uncle, however, leaves the decision up to her, and she refuses each young man who asks to marry her. She leaves home to become a shepherdess when it is no longer easy to justify her continued resistance to marriage.

Marcela's conversion to a shepherdess testifies to the role literature plays in filling the vacuum in one's life. Like Don Quixote, she is very loosely held by family ties. She is, in fact, Don Quixote's inverse, being the niece of a celibate uncle, while he, as celibate uncle, has an unmarried niece living in his house. The traditional pattern would require that the young woman either marry or enter a convent. Both courses, however, presuppose an authority that neither Don Quixote nor Marcela's uncle are capable of bringing to bear. In the absence of a real figure of authority, fictional authority takes over. Don Quixote abdicates his traditional role to become a knight, and Marcela evades hers to become a shepherdess.

Cervantes' rendering of the story makes it clear that Marcela, like Don Quixote, is not what she thinks she is nor what she appears to be to the men whom her beauty and inaccessibility move to madness. Believing herself to be untroubled by encumbrances of any sort, she is in fact controlled by them, spending her time running away from the constant threat to her "autonomy" that the flocks of adoring shepherds represent. She is an unwitting but nonetheless active participant in the game of predator and prey hidden in the chivalric and pastoral visions of romantic love. Her flight creates a vacuum that makes pursuit inevitable. In *La Galatea* the abduction of Rosaura by Artandro offers one possible ending; Lisandro's murder of Carino, another; and Galercio's attempted suicide, a third. What all three cases in *La Galatea* show is that an imbalance in the conscious position of any one character stimulates a compensatory imbalance in the position of all others with whom he or she comes into contact. By distorting the natural order, such an imbalance creates an instability that generates conflict and finally leads to the destruction of the participants in the game being played.

The Grisóstomo/Marcela story offers a virtual triangle, for Grisóstomo is accompanied into the countryside by his companion Ambrosio, who represents the whole flock of enamored shepherds said to be pining for her. Since in this case Grisóstomo's desperation is turned in upon himself, Ambrosio does not figure as a rival. The important point, however, is that the pattern of pastoral romance is a triangle. The essence of romantic love is increasing tension that finally leads to a release through death.[20]

Don Quixote is quite right to threaten those who listen to Marcela's words of defense from her heights above Grisóstomo's tomb with his "furious indignation" if any try to pursue her. He has accepted her speech as truth since it accords perfectly with the fragmented universe that he, like she, projects. He says of Marcela:

> She has shown with clear and sufficient argument that she bears little or no blame for Chrysostom's [Grisóstomo's] death, and how far she is from yielding to any of her lovers' desires. Wherefore it is right that, instead of being pursued and persecuted, she should be honored and esteemed by all good men in the world,

for she has proved that she is the only woman living with such pure intentions. (I, 14, 110)

(Ella ha mostrado con claras y suficientes razones la poca o ninguna culpa que ha tenido en la muerte de Grisóstomo, y cuán ajena vive de condescender con los deseos de ninguno de sus amantes, a cuya causa es justo que, en lugar de ser seguida y perseguida, sea honrada y estimada de todos los buenos del mundo, pues muestra que en él es ella sola la que con tal honesta intención vive. [I, 14, 184-85])

Having ordered the others not to follow Marcela, Don Quixote, not surprisingly, pursues her himself in order to offer himself up to her service. By following Marcela into the woods, he repeats the pattern established by Lenio, the "great enemy of love" in *La Galatea*, who cannot resist Gelasia because she declares herself to be as opposed to the claims of eros as he is. Fear and flight from life bind these characters to that which they hope to avoid. Marcela will be plagued by men to the extent that she spurns them, and they will hate her to the degree that she attracts them. Don Quixote, consciously admiring Marcela's independence, will unconsciously, like the other men in the fields, desire her.

What the pursuit of Marcela brings, however, is not the mutual admiration of disembodied spirits that Don Quixote might wish. Don Quixote does not find Marcela at all, in fact, and he and Sancho lie down to sleep by a stream after two hours of fruitless searching. While they sleep, Rocinante, who represents Don Quixote's unconscious, bodily self, suddenly takes it upon himself to "acquaint" some mares grazing nearby with his "needs" since he is free to wander without his master's knowledge. The "master's" suppressed eros finds its expression when he releases his control over it. The result, of course, is the famous fury of the mares' owners, a fury that turns into beatings, not only for Rocinante but for Don Quixote and Sancho as well.[21]

The imbalance occasioned by Marcela's beauty and inaccessibility does not stop there. It continues at the inn to which Don Quixote and Sancho repair in the following chapter in search of rest and food. There they find Maritornes, the inn prostitute who is clearly Marcela's obverse, who embroils Don Quixote and Sancho in a night of chaos and violence that perfectly counterbalances the serene daytime scene of Grisóstomo's burial and Marcela's reasoned self-defense.

Eugenio/Leandra

Eugenio's story of unrequited love in Chapter 51 is the only other interpolated tale that Don Quixote hears in its entirety and to which he actively responds. He has just finished relating his lengthy fantasy about the Knight of the Lake who finds beautiful nymphs in an elysian field beneath frightful serpent-infested waters, when the goatherd Eugenio appears, chasing after an unruly she-goat. The assembled, Don Quixote, the priest, and the Canon, invite Eugenio to eat with them, after which he agrees to tell the story of his pastoral frustrations.

Leandra, the desirable and desired female figure in the story, bears an uncanny resemblance to Marcela. The love problems in both tales originate in town and are inspired by the young woman's wealth and beauty. Like Marcela, Leandra has too many suitors, and like Marcela's uncle, Leandra's father leaves the burden of choice to the young woman, who is much happier spurning all who desire her. Also like Marcela, Leandra is vulnerable in a way that the men who are so fascinated by her cannot possibly perceive.

The unstated cause of this vulnerability may be, for both Marcela and Leandra, that they have no mother. Growing up in houses in which eros is suppressed makes them natural participants in the game of predator and prey. But whereas Marcela's capacity to become the predator when she is not seen as prey was never tested, Leandra's tale shows what happens when a young man as attractive and apparently self-sufficient as she comes into view. The young man is Vicente de la Roca, who arrives in town from his travels as a soldier to fascinate everyone with his multicolored costumes, his guitar, his poems, his stories of exotic lands, and the tales of his exploits:

> There was no country in the whole world he had not visited, and no battle he had not taken part in. He had killed more Turks than there are in Morocco and Tunis, and engaged in more single combats, according to his own story, than Gante and Luna, Diego García de Paredes, and a thousand others whom he named, and from every one of them he had come off victorious, without losing so much as a drop of blood. (I, 51, 447)

> (No había tierra en todo el orbe que no hubiese visto, ni batalla donde no se hubiese hallado; había muerto más moros que tiene

Marruecos y Túnez, y entrado en más singulares desafíos, según
él decía, que Gante y Luna, Diego García de Paredes y otros mil
que nombraba; y de todos había salido con vitoria, sin que le
hubiesen derramado una sola gota de sangre. [I, 51, 595])

In short, Vicente makes an attractive object of himself, revers-
ing the accustomed behavior of the young men in town. Leandra
falls in love with him before he even realizes she is there. She is
ready immediately to give him everything, and before long,
encouraged by his promises of marriage and high adventure,
she has left home with the young man, taking all her father's
jewels with her. There is no union, of course. Vicente makes off
with the jewels, Leandra is sent to a convent, and the young
men of the town move out into the countryside to continue
composing their songs of love and desperation to the beautiful
lady forever out of reach.

Leandra's actions are only understandable if she is perceived
as an unwitting participant in a situation over which she has no
control. As much a victim as victimizer, she is surrounded by
men who see her as an object of unconsummated desire. Without a mother to offer her another view of herself, she inhabits
a universe in which lover and loved one are forever locked
in a struggle of attraction and rejection.[22] She must reject what
is attracted to her and be rejected by what attracts her. She
and Vicente are made for one another, just as Grisóstomo was
made for Marcela, and Dulcinea was made for Don Quixote. All
these women are caught in appearances utterly dissociated
from the reality from which they spring. Eugenio and the other
goatherds love not Leandra but the mirage of beauty and perfection she offers them. And she in turn does not love Vicente,
about whom she knows nothing. She is dazzled by the image of
strength and worldly experience with which, through his stories, he covers himself. Beneath their respective shimmering
disguises hide a motherless young girl and a poor soldier of
fortune.[23]

Eugenio has apparently learned nothing from his story. He is
still bemoaning his fate and raging at the instability of womankind when he recounts his tale of woe to Don Quixote and the
others. And Don Quixote, who also appears to have learned
nothing, still offers his knightly services for the rescue of the
damsel in distress:

I promise you, brother goatherd, that were I in the position to be
able to embark on any adventure, I would immediately set about
bringing yours to a happy conclusion. I would deliver Leandra
from the nunnery, where there can be no doubt she is kept against
her will, in spite of the abbess and all who might oppose me.
(I, 52, 450)

(Por cierto, hermano cabrero, que si yo me hallara posibilitado de
poder comenzar alguna aventura, que luego luego me pusiera en
camino porque vos la tuviérades buena; que yo sacara del monas-
terio, donde, sin duda alguna, debe de estar contra su voluntad, a
Leandra, a pesar de la abadesa y de cuantos quisieran estorbarlo.
[I, 52, 599])

Eugenio has little sympathy for the strange figure who so much
resembles him, and in no time he and Don Quixote are locked
in furious battle, showing once again how easily beings separated from reality and caught in the net of illusion can be cata-
pulted into chaos.

The first and last interpolated tales that make up *Don Quixote*
Part I reflect and elaborate upon Don Quixote's one-sided consciousness. They reveal the contradictions of desire that remain
latent in the chivalric stories and the instability on which both
chivalric and pastoral tales feed. Leandra's story is, in a sense, a
complement to Marcela's, showing how easily the attracting
object can become caught in desire for the other. Together, the
two stories clearly illustrate the mechanism of romantic love
underlying Don Quixote's passion for Dulcinea and the violence
that such a passion creates.

THE MIDDLE THREE INTERPOLATED TALES

Between the first tale and the last fall a series of interpolated love stories that replace the triangular relationship with a
quaternity. The two stories that Don Quixote hears depict a
single woman—beautiful and out of reach—for whose sake at
least two, but conceivably an infinite number of men, leave
home and calling. In the Marcela story, Grisóstomo and his
friend Ambrosio go out to the fields to dream of the lady; in the
Leandra story, Eugenio goes out with his friend Anselmo. In
both tales, the woman is both remote and solitary, having no
female counterpart as the women in the middle stories will

have. Like Elicio and Erastro, the young men in love with the idealized ladies of their dreams seem content with one another's company and more inclined to rail against her or to console one another than to fight to possess her. In the middle collection of stories the male friends will still perceive the object of their desires as a single being, as beautiful as she is inaccessible, but the surrounding narrative material will reveal that in fact each woman has an alter ego. When the alter ego remains unrecognized—as will be the case with Leonela in "The Tale of Foolish Curiosity"—the triangle that excludes her will collapse on itself. However, when the fourth figure—the female alter ego—manages to bring herself into the consciousness of the male contenders, as Dorotea does, she will provide the means by which destruction can be avoided and harmony restored. The hidden fourth figure is always there of course—she appears as Maritornes in the Marcela story and as a she-goat in the Leandra tale—but in the first and last stories she remains outside the frame that contains the narrative and thus belongs entirely to the unconscious.

Cardenio/Dorotea

In Chapter 24 Don Quixote hears the beginning of another story of love. The wild man Cardenio whom Don Quixote finds in the mountains explains, at Don Quixote's insistence, that the cause of his present madness is embedded in a tale he is willing to relate only if Don Quixote promises not to interrupt him. Don Quixote of course agrees but forgets himself at the point when Cardenio mentions that his beloved Luscinda was an avid reader of books of chivalry. Don Quixote's interruption precipitates a battle not unlike the struggle with Eugenio at the end of the book, except that this one takes in all of the onlookers, turning the peaceful narration of a story into a melee of fists and stones.

Apart from demonstrating once again the madness and violence that absorption in fiction promulgates, the battle between Don Quixote and Cardenio also stops the story at the moment when all the relationships are about to change. From this interruption on, the stories no longer belong to Don Quixote. They are literally beyond his reach, being told in his absence.

The change that has occurred becomes clear as soon as Cardenio resumes his story in Chapter 27. In the portion of the story Don Quixote had heard, Luscinda was simply a beautiful woman whom Cardenio not only loved but also encouraged his friend Fernando to love. The story Don Quixote heard ended with both friends entertaining themselves by composing letters to Luscinda whose answers they would then read together.

But what Don Quixote could not hear and what Cardenio, to his downfall, could not heed was the woman, speaking in her own voice and urging the man she loved to action. The second part of Cardenio's narration *begins* with Luscinda's letter begging her young lover to ask his father's permission for them to marry. Cardenio stalls. He is afraid his father will say he is too young: "To be brief, I told him [Fernando] that I dared not ask my father, not only because of this obstacle, but because of other vague apprehensions which made me fear that my desires would never be realized" (I, 27, 227) (En resolución, le dije que no me aventuraba a decírselo a mi padre, así por aquel inconveniente como por otros muchos que me acobardaban sin saber cuáles eran, sino que me parecía que lo que yo desease jamás había de tener efeto" [I, 27, 330]).

Fernando, of course, is more than eager to fill the vacuum left by Cardenio's self-doubts. And Cardenio is just as ready to pile all the blame on Fernando's shoulders: "Oh greedy Marius! Cruel Catiline! Criminal Sulla! Crafty Galalón! Treacherous Vellido! Vindictive Julian! Covetous Judas! Cruel, vindictive, crafty traitor! What harm had this poor wretch done you, who so frankly revealed to you the secrets and joys of his heart? How had I offended you?" (I, 27, 228) (¡Oh Mario ambicioso, oh Catilina cruel, oh Sila facineroso, oh Galalón embustero, oh Vellido traidor, oh Julián vengativo, oh Judas codicioso! Traidor, cruel, vengativo y embustero, ¿qué deservicios te había hecho este triste, que con tanta llaneza te descubrió los secretos y contentos de su corazón? ¿Qué ofensa te hice?" [I, 27, 330]).

Fernando and Cardenio form a perfect pair. They had become fast friends, something the duke who sent for Cardenio had not expected. Something, in fact, quite out of order, since Cardenio was to have served Fernando's older brother. The friendship between Cardenio and Fernando is a spontaneous one: Fernando has the wildness of the *segundón*, the second son, that Cardenio admires but dares not emulate; Fernando is "free," while Cardenio feels himself bound; Fernando has money and takes pleasure in seducing young women. When Fernando turns his freewheeling love upon Luscinda, however, Cardenio is crushed. Despite urgent entreaties from Luscinda, Cardenio remains paralyzed in the face of Fernando's power and impulsive behavior. At the crucial moment, he hides behind a curtain at Luscinda's house and watches helplessly while his beloved marries his best friend. When Luscinda does not openly refuse Fernando at the altar, Cardenio loses all hope and runs away. He continues, suspended in his story, until the day, six months later, when first Don Quixote and later the priest and the barber urge him to tell it.

Out of the tale of triangular love that Cardenio recounts, an unnamed fourth emerges, taking bodily form in the person of Dorotea, whom the priest and the barber find washing her feet in a stream. Dorotea is the young woman Fernando seduced and then tried to avoid by leaving home. She enters Cardenio's story through the back door, for she literally has no place in it. As a farmer's daughter, she has no social standing to support her claims of value; as a seduced woman, she has forfeited her right to a place of honor in the world. She is in no-man's-land as her story begins—separated from her home and parents, dressed in her servant's clothing, and neither married nor maiden.

As the men are unaware of her, she represents their unconscious. And Cardenio, since he has nowhere else to turn, has no choice but to listen to her. Were he "at home" and "in his right mind," she would remain invisible. But in the wilds, her voice sounds the first note of hope, ending his entrapment within the confines of his story. Listening to her, as the author makes clear, is no easy task for Cardenio:

> No sooner did she mention Don Ferdinand's name then Cardenio's face changed colour, and he began to sweat and to show so much emotion that the priest and the barber looked at him in apprehension, fearing one of those attacks of madness which they had heard he was subject to. But he merely sweated and stayed still, staring hard at the farmer's daughter and reflecting who she might be. (I, 28, 240)

> (No hubo bien nombrado a don Fernando la que el cuento contaba, cuando a Cardenio se le mudó la color del rostro, y comenzó a trasudar, con tan grande alteración, que el cura y el barbero, que miraron en ello, temieron que le venía aquel accidente de locura que habían oído decir que de cuando en cuando le venía. Mas Cardenio

no hizo otra cosa que trasudar y estarse quedo, mirando de hito
en hito a la labradora, imaginando quién era ella. [I, 28, 346])

Overcoming his resistance to hearing another's story, he is rewarded by discovering that Luscinda did not betray him after
all.

When Dorotea finishes her story, Cardenio reveals, to her
surprise, that he knew her all along and that he even knows the
name of her father. The two discover, against all appearances to
the contrary, that they are parts of one another's stories. That
awareness makes them capable, finally, of restoring harmony to
their lives.

The trick is to understand that the story is a fabrication.
Dorotea's story forced Cardenio to see that his own—the part
he was capable of telling—was false. This realization is the first
step out of fiction and away from madness. Having seen themselves as belonging to a reality larger than either particular
story, Dorotea and Cardenio are then prepared to engage in fiction as a conscious rather than as an unconscious act.[24]

Dorotea's portrayal, in the next several chapters, of a damsel
in distress in order to bring Don Quixote out of the mountains
is not accidental. As Micomicona, Dorotea repeats the role she
played for the priest and the barber, but with a greater awareness of how that role is dissociated from her true self. She still
tells her own story, but by being forced, through Don Quixote,
to perform it in all of its absurdity and grotesque exaggeration,
she liberates herself from it at the same time. By the time Don
Quixote interrupts "The Tale of Foolish Curiosity," slashing the
wineskins in the inn and declaring the "giant" dead, Dorotea
has been well schooled in the limitations of literary roles and is
prepared to release herself from their grip.

Cardenio also participates in the second level of fiction, once
out of the wilds and his madness. No one has shown more
clearly than Cesáreo Bandera in *Mimesis conflictiva* how closely
"The Tale of Foolish Curiosity" resembles Cardenio's story and
how active Cardenio was in urging that the tale be read.[25] The
tale was in fact made for him, laying before him his own foolishness just as clearly as Dorotea's story of the giant revealed the
absurdity of her fears about Fernando. Seeing themselves in a
fiction from which they are separated gives Dorotea and Cardenio the opportunity to be "in the world but not of it." They
can see the errors and the consequences of those errors to

which, as participants, they were blind. Fiction can be dangerous when one is caught up in it, but it has a healing effect when one is able to see oneself beyond it.

Before discussing "The Tale of Foolish Curiosity" and its role in resolving the Cardenio/Dorotea story, we must briefly consider the absent members of the foursome. Luscinda, as Dorotea's story has made clear, has in fact resisted Fernando's efforts to marry her. She escaped to a convent, only to be later found and abducted by Fernando. They arrive at the inn, silent and masked, just as "The Tale of Foolish Curiosity" is ending.

The quaternity formed by the four major characters in this interpolated story repeats that of the primary narrative but brings the four cardinal points into closer harmony. Cardenio and Fernando figure as opposites because Cardenio represses the desires to which Fernando all too easily yields. Luscinda represents the pure, untouchable woman, while Dorotea stands for the accessible one. The foursome remains separated and in chaos because Cardenio feels inferior to Fernando and incapable of mastering his desires (represented by Fernando), and Luscinda, at the crucial moment, is apparently overcome by the social forces that have decreed her marriage. And so Cardenio, out of fear of ravishing the "impossible" Luscinda, goes to the countryside where, unconsciously, he "enjoys"—through Fernando—the accessible Dorotea, leaving Luscinda thereby open to the very abduction Cardenio hoped to avoid.[26]

In the foursome, it is the socially weakest member on whom the burden of restoration falls. Dorotea, fortified by her own conviction that something good will come of all this and instructed by the telling of her own story enough to separate herself from the role she is playing, succeeds in unmasking and silencing the "others," Fernando and Luscinda, to whom she and Cardenio "belong."

"The Tale of Foolish Curiosity"

The story the priest reads at the inn once again presents a triangle that is resolved when the hidden fourth participant makes her appearance. Anselmo and Lotario are the famous "two friends" who are inseparable until a woman comes into their midst. Though the two are equal in social status, Anselmo appears nonetheless to be the weaker member of the pair, never doing anything without first consulting Lotario. Lotario

acts as a go-between when Anselmo sets his heart on marrying
Camila and completely confounds Anselmo when, after the
marriage, he carefully stays away from the young couple's
house.

The equality between the two young men masks an imbalance that Anselmo, now on his own, very quickly reveals. He
tells Lotario that "he would never have married if he had
known that his marriage was going to deprive him of his [Lota-
rio's] . . . company" (I, 33, 283) (si él supiera que el casarse
había de ser parte para no comunicalle como solía, que jamás lo
hubiera hecho [I, 33, 398]) and begs him to "treat his house as
his own again, and to come and go as before" (I, 33, 283) (que
volviese a ser señor de su casa, y a entrar y salir en ella como de
antes [I, 33, 398]). When Lotario points out the impropriety of
such actions, Anselmo resorts to madness to bring his friend
"home" again.

The point is that Cardenio, who is listening to this story, may
have been correct in submitting to his unconscious resistance to
Luscinda. The obstacles that block the path from the man to the
woman are there for a reason. Were Cardenio to have fallen
automatically into the marriage everyone expected of him, he
might have discovered, when it would have been harder to do
anything about it, that Luscinda stood in his mind for two contradictory images of womankind, just as he was riven by a pair
of contradictory impulses over which he had no mastery. For
Anselmo, in "The Tale of Foolish Curiosity," the marriage was
too easy. He did not have to *change* to marry his lady, and so he
becomes obsessed by his warring views of her after the fact: Is
she pure? Is she seducible? Does she love me, or does she
really love Lotario?

Anselmo's plan to test Camila creates the triangle that should
have emerged during his courtship of her. In the period before
the marriage he could have fought his rival and won, in the
process, the confidence to meet her that he obviously lacked at
this stage in his development. The test would also have brought
out something of the real Camila that would have helped Anselmo glimpse her beneath the distortions that his imagination
supplied.

Lacking any sense of his own independent selfhood, Anselmo
can do nothing but reinstate Lotario as surreptitious master of
his house, while he hides, as Cardenio did in the previous story,

watching the seducer in helpless fascination. Camila, on whom the responsibility for restoring the balance of the household falls in Anselmo's absence, is equally lacking in self-awareness.[27] She appeals by letter to Anselmo, much as Luscinda appealed to Cardenio to rescue her from the advances of his rival. But, like Cardenio, Anselmo has already abdicated control over the situation, and hence he must leave Camila to her own devices.

Failing to find protection from the traditional source of authority in her house, Camila turns to the weaker protector and implores her maid Leonela to stay with her during her long dinners alone with Lotario. The story makes clear that Leonela represents an intimate, if unrecognized, aspect of Camila's being: "Camila went about surrounded by her man-servants and maids, particularly by her own maid, Leonela, of whom she was very fond. For they had been brought up together from their girlhood in Camila's parents' house, and she had brought her to Anselmo's when she married him" (I, 33, 298) (Siempre andaba rodeada de sus criados y criadas, especialmente de una doncella suya llamada Leonela, a quien ella mucho quería, por haberse criado desde niñas las dos juntas en casa de los padres de Camilla, y cuando se casó con Anselmo la trujo consigo" [I, 33, 415]). Leonela, however, cannot rescue her friend from her difficulties. Both Anselmo and Camila, having yielded control over themselves to another, must experience the consequences of their self-abandonment, the total destruction of the household over which no one has taken charge.

Leonela, like Lotario, follows her own impulses. "Camila gave her maid orders to dine before she did and never to leave her side. But the girl [Leonela] had no thought except for her own pleasure, and needed the time for her own affairs. So she did not always comply with her mistress's orders, but instead left them alone together, as if by instruction" (I, 33, 298) (Tenía orden Leonela que comiese primero que Camilla, y que de su lado jamás se quitase; mas ella, que en otras cosas de su gusto tenía puesto el pensamiento y había menester aquellas horas y aquel lugar para ocuparle en sus contentos, no cumplía todas veces el mandamiento de su señora; antes los dejaba solos, como si aquello le hubieran mandado [I, 33, 415]).

The symbolism of the lord who abandons his house expresses the central problem of the entire novel, and the consequences are spelled out in "The Tale of Foolish Curiosity."[28] The characters of novelistic significance in Part I have all left home. These characters lack an internal center; they operate out of and identify with a portion of their being but leave other parts unruled and unruly. Such a misapprehension of the self gives rise to all the confusion and lack of order that characterizes the novel with respect to both its content and its form.

Leonela, who, without knowing it, bears final responsibility for all the goings-on in the household, runs away when asked for explanations about the man Anselmo had heard in her bedroom. As she escapes through the window at night she pulls down with her the whole house of cards to which she was unknowingly attached.

The only profit that comes, within the story, from the undoing of the three principal characters is that Anselmo seems to recognize just before his death, his responsibility for all that happened. But more importantly, the listeners, principally Cardenio and Dorotea, are allowed to see reflected in the lives of others their own abandonment of responsibility for themselves and the consequences of that abandonment.

Only when the characters are seen as fragments of a disassembled whole can the sudden, otherwise improbable, appearance of Luscinda and Fernando at the end of "The Tale of Foolish Curiosity" be explained. Cardenio and Dorotea, who have listened to the story in rapt attention, are now able to face the sides of their characters that remained hidden and to release into the consciousness the "other" selves of which both were unconsciously afraid. The story-within-a-story structure, so often commented upon in discussions of *Don Quixote* Part I, offers the characters an increasing distance from what traps them—a distance made both necessary and possible by the stories they live, then tell, and finally observe carried to their logical conclusions in the laboratory of fiction that "The Tale of Foolish Curiosity" represents.

More than one critic has pointed out that the happy resolution to the love conflict has a magical quality about it, not unlike the magic that Cervantes criticized Montemayor for introducing in his novel.[29] There is, to be sure, some dissonance between the level of the plot, where a complete breakdown of the relations between the four main characters could easily take place, and the unconscious, magical level that, nonetheless, permits their union. The dissonance stems, however, not from a willful brushing away of the problems that the characters, in limited consciousness, have created for themselves, but from the affirmation that their larger selves, toward which their gradual disengagement from fiction allows them to move, are grounded in harmony.

In the final interpolated tale told to the company at the inn, Cervantes goes even further in the direction of bringing the limited, temporal selves of a captive Spanish soldier and his young Moorish fiancée within the orbit of their larger destinies.

The Captive's Tale

In the Captive's tale Cervantes comes as close as he can in *Don Quixote* Part I to representing the transformation process that will get its fullest expression in the *Persiles*. The process, which begins in this story as the hero leaves home and ends as he is returning to his paternal household in Leon, carries him out into a world of conflict and violence that tests his sense of selfhood at every level.

The first half of the Captive's tale recounts a process of disintegration of the self, as the main character is subjected to failure, imprisonment, and deprivation. During the period of progressive loss of self, when the hero is in the hands of enemy captors, he demonstrates his innate integrity by maintaining faith in his release and not succumbing to the temptation to join with the enemy as so many Spanish soldiers under similar circumstances did.

Halfway through the second of the three chapters devoted to his narration, the Captive finds himself in a prison yard in Algiers, from which he had tried to escape many times. When his fortunes appear to be at their nadir, the Captive and three other companions glimpse a white hand in the tiny window of a tower above the yard. The mysterious hand drops some money wrapped up in a note and indicates that the note is intended only for the Captive. After accepting the unexpected gift, he looks up to see in the same window a small cross of straw. The event occurs midway through the story, which continues to deal with the complex process by which the Captive is restored to his homeland and his freedom.

Alone among the interpolated stories in Part I, the Captive's tale takes the main character through a process of undoing and then leads him beyond it to a recovery, so that he returns enriched, like his two brothers who left home when he did. Because this story is unique, it is important to carefully examine some of its distinguishing details.[30]

The Captive begins his story with a long and seemingly extraneous explanation of how he and his brothers left home. His father's spendthrift habits were threatening to dissipate the family fortune; on his own initiative, his three sons now full grown, the father divides his patrimony equally among himself and his children, allowing each one, himself included, three thousand *ducados*. The action, symbolically, reduces the father to parity with his sons. The Captive, however, refuses to accept this arrangement and gives two of the three thousand he had been allocated back to his father. His brothers contribute one thousand each, so that in the end the father stays at home with seven thousand *ducados* and the three sons depart to seek their respective fortunes with the remainder.[31]

The Captive's action reinstates the father in his place of authority and serves from the outset to distinguish this hero from the many characters in *Don Quixote* who seem determined to challenge or ignore the symbols of authority in their lives. Throughout his travels at war and in captivity, the Captive continues to honor those things—country and religion—that those around him have undermined or shown to be faulty. The point is not that he is blindly religious or patriotic but that he demonstrates a sense of order and integrity in his life that reflects upon his own personality. Even under the adverse circumstances to which he is exposed, he does not lose his own centering. Unlike the Grisóstomos, the Cardenios, and the Anselmos, he does not alter his values in response to what others do or say to him.

Having retained rather than thrown away his self, the Captive is ready for the woman when she appears in his life. In the other love stories in *Don Quixote* Part I, when the woman appeals to the man for help, he turns out to be incapable of rendering it. When Luscinda begs Cardenio by letter to settle their marriage, he refuses. When Camila writes to her husband desperately urging him to return home and take charge, he also pays no heed. When the innkeeper's daughter asks Don Quixote to help protect her father, Don Quixote has a thousand reasons why he cannot. All of them are creatures of fiction because they believe their being resides in or depends upon someone apart from themselves.[32]

Zoraida, the woman who calls the Captive from her tower, is a true captive lady, the kind Don Quixote is always talking about freeing.[33] She is living the life of a Moorish girl against her will. Paradoxically, when she identifies her liberator, she participates in the process by which he, too, will be freed. The Captive, in taking upon himself the job of taking Zoraida to Christian lands, will combine his resources with hers to effect for them both an escape that neither alone could have made. They start from totally opposite situations, having neither language nor upbringing in common. She is wealthy, he is destitute; she belongs to Moorish society, he is their captive; she lives in a tower, he in a pit; she writes to him in Arabic, he knows only Spanish.

The differences between the two characters symbolize the opposition between the sexes that underlies their love story. From their opposite positions they are able to interact creatively rather than destructively because neither is seeking to capture the other. Starting from an already established bondage that holds each one separately, they combine their forces to bring about their release. The different attributes they offer reveal the potential for complementarity that opposition contains within it.[34]

Zoraida supplies the money for the escape, and the Captive, with the help of renegades, makes the arrangements. When they finally meet in Zoraida's garden, the story takes on all the earmarks of a courtly love romance. And yet it is much more. The reason the Zoraida/Captive story escapes the pattern of the courtly love story is their participation in a quaternity that promises union.

In early love stories by Cervantes the alter egos of the main character and his beloved represented unconscious negative factors that the main characters sought to suppress. Zoraida, however, consciously identifies herself with no less an alter ego than the Virgin Mary, whom her Christian nursemaid had taught her to love from an early age. From the very beginning of her contact with the Captive she tells him that she does nothing without Mary's guidance and that it is Mary who selected the Captive as her guide and who urged her to go with him to Spain. The Captive, also, consciously allies himself with God, who has been his only support during his long years of trials.

When the Captive answers Zoraida's first note he writes: "The true Allah keep you, dear lady, and the blessed Marien,

who is the true mother of God" (I, 40, 359-60) (El verdadero
Alá te guarde, señora mía, y aquella bendita Marién, que es la
verdadera madre de Dios" [I, 40, 489]). Mary's association with
God in the Captive's statement places their respective "alter
egos" in the tradition of the mystical marriage, which finds
expression in pre-Christian religion as well, with Isis and Osiris,
for example. The continuous mutual creation of the masculine
and feminine polarities that the image of Mary as the Mother of
God suggests surrounds the Captive and Zoraida in an atmosphere of union that transcends their limited selves and promises
their success.[35]

The journey, even so, is a perilous one, as the final chapters
of the Captive's narration make clear. Zoraida, like the Captive,
will have to relinquish her attachment to her material self, break
wrenchingly from her father, and have her jewels, money, and
fine clothes taken by corsairs. On the final leg of the journey to
Spain, she and the Captive are set adrift at sea on a moonless
night. There would be no better way to symbolize their total
abandonment to the hand of God/Mary. Without the support of
reason or a path to follow, they have to release themselves to
total trust of the unconscious, which the sea and the darkness
represent.

When they do reach shore in the morning, they find themselves at the foot of a steep mountain, which they climb up
together. Once again they are enacting a process of symbolic
recovery, now seeking through their own efforts to attain the
consciousness they had to abandon earlier. Their reward is the
discovery that they have in fact reached their destination.

The Captive's tale continues on into a fourth chapter, this
time narrated in the third person. The Captive has finished his
story when more travellers arrive at the inn. Among them is the
Captive's brother, who brings news of his own success and that
of their other brother, along with word that their father is still
alive and at home, awaiting his sons' return. The tale traces a
full circle and ends with the promises of family reunion and of
marriage. The protagonist grows in stature and wisdom and
returns to the point of origin with a beautiful woman and all the
signs of future happiness.

The Captive's tale is the only one of the collection of interpolated stories that is not interrupted, except at the end of the first

chapter (Chapter 39) when Fernando points out that the Captive's comrade in captivity was his brother. The story's relative integrity, when compared with the other interpolated tales, complements the integrity of the main character and narrator and the authority he has gained through his experiences. Though Don Quixote appears to be present at the story's telling, since his after-dinner speech on Arms and Letters immediately precedes it, he does not comment on it.[36]

Don Quixote does, however, twice engage in parodies of the tale, suggesting that he would like to have been able to imitate the Captive if he could. The first parody comes in Chapter 43, when Don Quixote hears a "damsel" call him from the grain chute ("which seemed to him to be a window") of the barn (which was of course a castle for him). The "lady," who is in fact Maritornes and the innkeeper's daughter, persuades him to give her his hand, which he does with great vainglory. Though the two girls humiliate him by stringing him up for the rest of the night, Don Quixote is led to his action by the homology between the situation confronting him and that of the Captive in his prison yard in Algiers. In Chapter 52 Don Quixote again undertakes a deed reminiscent, in a crude sort of way, of the Captive's, when he attempts to "liberate" a statue of the Virgin carried by penitents.

The two efforts to imitate the Captive only highlight the problem facing Don Quixote and most of the other characters in *Don Quixote* Part I. The imitative behavior they all engage in, whether consciously or not, binds them to appearances. They can all mimic what the other does or says, but they have no understanding of the motives behind the deeds and words of the other whom they seek to become through emulation. Divorced from the inner logic that gives the action of another its meaning, the mimetic characters become hollow, uncentered, and susceptible to destruction.

Leandra's is another case in point. How much her theft of her father's jewels might resemble Zoraida's! Had she heard the Captive's tale, she might even have justified her escape with Vicente de la Roca by citing the Captive's case. And yet, as her story makes clear, she lacked the invisible grounding in faith that guided Zoraida's actions, and her flight turned into yet another case of seduction and abandonment.

CONCLUSION

Don Quixote Part I offers, through the interpolated tales, two avenues by which characters can move from isolation into a fullness of being symbolized by the union of opposites. For those characters already trapped in the world of fiction, such as Dorotea and Fernando, the escape from their madness and violence comes through a progressive disengagement from their story/history. By telling it, they open themselves to a fuller understanding of their role in a situation much larger than they had understood it to be; and by hearing it told about others, they come to appreciate how catastrophic their abandonment of their own responsibility to themselves can be. Fiction, in this sense, can play a healing role in the lives of characters caught up in it.

The other means by which one breaks the web of fiction is presented in the Captive's tale. There the fiction is the more generalized idea that one grows up with—the sense that one is unique, separate from others. This fiction is broken down, in the Captive's case, through a violent tearing away of all comfortable assumptions. The process is very much like the kind of procedure the alchemists described so minutely in their writings.[37] And, as in the alchemical process, the end result is the royal marriage.[38]

But in *Don Quixote* Part I the process is not fully developed. The Captive and Zoraida are not raised up to the symbolic royal status of king and queen, and their union is only promised. In *Don Quixote* Part II the role of fiction as healer will be much more fully developed. In the *Persiles*, the transformation process will be much more thoroughly examined. In *Don Quixote* Part I these "solutions" to the problems Cervantes was surely feeling very acutely are only hinted at in a novel much more actively concerned with the foolishness and destructiveness of the mimetic behavior that Don Quixote brings into the world.

Don Quixote Part II

CHANGES IN ORIENTATION IN THE 1615 *DON QUIXOTE*

In Chapters 2 and 3 of this study we paid close attention to the secondary stories because they revealed the unconscious side of the main character. The analysis of *Don Quixote* Part II, however, requires a different approach. Here Cervantes so skillfully blends secondary stories with the actions of Don Quixote and Sancho that it is difficult to extricate the interpolations from the plot.

The poor integration of primary and secondary material in Part I of *Don Quixote* obviously troubled Cervantes, since he criticized the interpolated tales of the 1605 *Don Quixote* in the early chapters of Part II. Sansón Carrasco, the student from Salamanca, comments at length on the book published about Don Quixote, telling him:

> One of the faults they find in this history, . . . is that the author inserted a novel called *The Tale of Foolish Curiosity*—not that it is bad or badly told, but because it is out of place and has nothing to do with the story of his worship Don Quixote. (II, 3, 489)

> (Una de las tachas que ponen a la tal historia . . . es que su autor puso en ella una novela intitulada *El curioso impertinente,* no por mala ni por mal razonada, sino por no ser de aquel lugar, ni tiene que ver con la historia de su merced el señor don Quijote. [II, 3, 42])

Don Quixote, indignant at the thought of having been slighted in his own story, protests: "Now I believe that thè author of my story is no sage but an ignorant chatterer" (II, 3, 489) (Ahora digo . . . que no ha sido sabio el autor de mi historia, sino algún ignorante hablador" [II, 3, 42]). Later he adds: "I do not know what induced the author to make use of novels and irrelevant

81

stories, when he had so much of mine to write about" (II, 3, 490)[1]
(no sé yo qué le movió al autor a valerse de novelas y cuentos
ajenos, habiendo tanto que escribir en los míos" [II, 3, 43]).

To remove from the novel all material not clearly associated
with the major character, however, would require more than a
minor literary adjustment. Such a change would involve major
shifts in all the relationships the text establishes, affecting the
role of the narrator as well as that of the main character and
altering the way they see both themselves and each other. The
interpolated tales in the earlier two works were not mere fillers.
They served an essential function by compensating for the
limitations in the main character's view of himself and of the
world.

La Galatea's Elicio, in his pastoral idealism and pacifism,
could not imagine himself subject to the passions of jealousy,
vengeance, and envy that plagued the characters in the interpolated tales he heard. Don Quixote in Part I could never
accept the mad Cardenio or the woman-hating Eugenio as
reflections of himself. He either fought with the narrators of
such tales or did not listen to them at all. Only in Don Quixote
Part II is Cervantes able to offer a main character capable of
stepping outside of his chosen role to understand that he is part
of a larger picture. The resultant expansion of consciousness
allows the protagonist to engage in more extensive contacts
with others than was possible in earlier novels.

The 1615 Don Quixote awakens to find that the knight-
errant he struggled so hard to make real in Part I no longer
belongs exclusively to his imagination. The knight's deeds,
hopes, and dreams have fallen into the hands of a Moor, and his
name now crosses the lips of young and old. The book that
Sansón Carrasco brings to his attention further reveals that Don
Quixote is only one of a whole cast of characters and that the
Moor who is writing his story not infrequently pushes him into
the background for the sake of secondary tales totally extraneous
to his mission. These discoveries in the early chapters of Part II
transform Don Quixote, at least partially, into a passive observer
of his own creation, a creation that becomes, as Part II unfolds,
increasingly an object to be played with and elaborated upon
by others.

From his new vantage point in Part II, Don Quixote begins
not only to put his own story into perspective but to participate

in the stories of others. He mediates successfully, for example, between Don Diego de Miranda and his son. In Part I, when he tried to come between the boy Andrés and his master Juan Haldudo, he only aggravated an already bad situation. In Part II Don Quixote also successfully supports Basilio's claim to Quiteria at Camacho's wedding, and he later agrees to engage in combat for the sake of Doña Rodríguez's daughter. He makes a wise and kind companion to Roque Guinart and rejoices in Ana Fénix's reunion with her fiancé Don Gregorio. At no time in Part II does he totally withdraw from the stories swirling around him, nor does he attack the characters who are shown living out those stories. He tends to restrict himself to counsel rather than to act and is often effective, as he rarely was in Part I.[2]

The change in Don Quixote has radical implications for the entire network of relations that constitute *Don Quixote* Part II. Since the novel about him has already been written, Don Quixote is no longer compelled to struggle with Cide Hamete over how his image will be constructed. He was shocked to discover that he actually had an author and dismayed to learn that the author was a Moor. Though he expressed marked concern that his good intentions might be misrepresented in the book published about him, by Chapter 4 he clearly understands that the work on him has been completed. His image as knight-errant is abroad in the world, and the task he faces in Part II is dealing with the many ways in which that image comes back to him at the hands of others.

In Part II much of the action appears to be generated by characters who, like Cide Hamete in Part I, are fascinated by Don Quixote and moved to ridicule him at the same time. What none of them realizes, from Sansón Carrasco to Master Peter to the Duke and Duchess to Don Antonio, is that in the process of ridiculing Don Quixote, they themselves become ridiculous. More radically stated, they become, like him, creatures of fiction the moment they step into the world he has created.[3] The enormous joke of Part II is that the whole gallery of readers of Part I who jump in to play with Don Quixote unwittingly become his playthings. For he alone knows what it means to be a creature of fiction, and that knowledge distinguishes him in part from the fictional world to which he is attached.

In Part I it was already clear that Don Quixote's effort to redesign himself and the world had failed, but in Part II the author shows how generalized Don Quixote's delusions of power are and explains why real power is available only to those able to release themselves from exclusive reliance on reason and appearance. Don Quixote constantly encounters characters in disguise and situations designed to confound him. He puzzles over finding Sansón Carrasco's face beneath the visor of the Knight of the Mirrors and wonders throughout the novel whether what he saw in the cave of Montesinos was dream or reality. He meets actors in costume, bearded ladies, Merlin, enchanted heads, and the Devil in hell along his journey and continually asks himself about the truth of what he has seen. In Part II the whole world seems to have become enchanted, and while Don Quixote reels from one charade to the next in increasing frustration and confusion, he also plumbs the depths of fiction, seeking to discover its limits.

The narrator Cide Hamete, meanwhile, who was often associated with Don Quixote's supposed evil enchanter in Part I,[4] is no longer so concerned with belittling his main character. In the generalized atmosphere of deception and confusion over which he presides in Part II, Cide Hamete seems interested instead in demonstrating mastery over his material. In the new fictional world of Part II, Cide Hamete catches the reader time and again in the traps he has laid, showing how easy it is to be caught in illusion, and how much the reader belongs to the world Don Quixote inhabits.[5]

The reader in turn experiences a shift in alliances and sympathies in *Don Quixote* Part II. Much more often the reader is inclined to sympathize with Don Quixote, to stand with him as he puzzles over the strange apparitions that appear before him, and to suffer with him the humiliations experienced at the hands of those characters who delight in his supposed madness. The reader, who more than likely took part in poking fun at Don Quixote's madness in Part I, becomes a participant in Don Quixote's trials in Part II.

Reader, narrator, main character, secondary characters: the list of those elements in Part II that have shifted their position from Part I could go on and on. Sancho, about whom very little has been said so far, obviously changes enormously in Part II, as do Teresa Panza and Dulcinea. Don Quixote's goals and his approach to his adventures also change. Both the beginning and the ending of Part II mark a radical departure from Part I.

Though identifying a single underlying element that might account for all the changes is difficult, there can be no doubt that they have occurred. In the analysis to follow an effort will be made to relate the altered relationships in Part II to a shift in Cervantes' perspective that allowed for a more harmonious interaction between reason and the unconscious and that permitted him, in the *Persiles,* finally to create a main character who is both successful and credible.

The dissonances and disjunctions of *La Galatea* and *Don Quixote* have been presented here as signs of fullness of vision on Cervantes' part that no literary form available to him could neatly embrace. The problem, which surely belonged to Cervantes as well as to his characters and fictional narrators, was to find a vantage point from which fiction could be separated from reality and self from other. What *Don Quixote* Part I revealed, however, was the surprising degree to which reality was fiction and self was other. The more serious problem that *Don Quixote* Part II addresses is whether reality exists at all apart from the fictions that everyone invents in order to create an illusion of control over the self and others. And, correspondingly, whether a self exists apart from the role one adopts to get along in the world.

The effort to find a place outside of fiction, if successfully carried out, would signal the end of the novel and of Don Quixote. By Part II, Cervantes seems oriented not toward the endless spinning out of fictions but toward a discovery, through fiction, of truth. *Don Quixote* Part II takes its main character through the long and difficult process of seeing beyond his self-created world. The novel therefore constitutes an extended undoing of everything the main character built up in Part I.

In Part II those elements that the established order tended to suppress come into prominence. Allegory, magic, omens, dreams, and mysteries play a much larger role in Part II than they did in Part I. Women and servants reveal an autonomy in Part II they did not have in Part I, and both wild and domesticated animals intrude, often drastically, on the image Don Quixote established for himself in Part I. Many more adventures take place at night, and the whole structure of the 1615 novel has a circular, rather than a linear configuration. Finally, Don Quixote seeks not more adventures and more combat but Dulcinea, who obsesses him from start to finish.

All of these changes relate most directly to Don Quixote's

need to break through the limitations that knighthood has placed on his understanding of himself. For this reason, the analysis to follow will focus on the various stages in Don Quixote's struggle as he oscillates between embracing and abandoning the role he so painstakingly invented in Part I.

THE SEARCH FOR DULCINEA

In striking contrast to his first and second sallies, in Part II Don Quixote lingers at home a long time before setting out. In the first eight chapters both he and Sancho engage in extensive conversation with the womenfolk from whom they so stealthily and silently escaped in Part I. Home, throughout Part II, is a much more comfortable place for knight and squire, and their ears are better attuned to the talk of the women in them. When Don Quixote and Sancho finally do sally forth—inspired by the good omen of the sounds of Rocinante and Sancho's donkey[6]— they start out not at dawn with the open road before them but at night with a definite destination in mind.[7] Don Quixote, whose only effort to address Dulcinea in Part I took the form of a flowery letter sent through Sancho from the wilds of the Sierras, sets out in Chapter 8 of Part II with the sole idea of seeing his lady in person.

In Part I, Don Quixote was content with his imagined version of Dulcinea:

> I am quite satisfied, therefore, to imagine and believe that the good Aldonza Lorenzo is lovely and virtuous. . . . To make an end of the matter, I imagine all that I say to be true, neither more nor less, and in my imagination I draw her as I would have her be. (I, 25, 210)

> (Y así, bástame a mí pensar y creer que la buena de Aldonza Lorenzo es hermosa y honesta. . . . Y para concluir con todo, yo imagino que todo lo que digo es así, sin que sobre ni falte nada, y píntola en mi imaginación como la deseo. [I, 25, 309])

But in Part II, Don Quixote's private thoughts, for better or for worse, become manifest in the world. With book, author, and self all now materialized, he would also like to see in the flesh the woman whom he created. The search for Dulcinea with which Don Quixote begins the action in Part II forms the underlying motive for all that he does throughout the rest of the work.

In Part I, the episodes of Don Quixote's story were strung together as a sequence of chance encounters, transformed into adventures by his imagination. Nothing along the way suggested the end toward which he was heading. Each situation was simply enjoyed for whatever excitement and challenge it could offer. In Part II, on the other hand, a much more reflexive consciousness is at work. Situations are deliberately sought, and what is found is scrutinized for meaning. The journey to Toboso is not an event randomly chosen. For both its symbolic and its episodic value, the opening trip to Dulcinea's house warrants a close reading. It fixes the direction for the remainder of Don Quixote's adventures and perfectly represents the level of consciousness at which he finds himself in the 1615 novel.

Don Quixote and Sancho set out on what seems to be a long and unfamiliar path in the dark, entertaining themselves as they ride with talk of fame and eternal life. Suddenly the two main characters seem to be groping about in a different world, one in which reason and the senses no longer supply reliable information.[8] In the darkened atmosphere of Part II, the travellers need to rely on themselves and each other much more than in Part I and to consider the metaphysical implications of the journey on which they have embarked. Although the goal is Dulcinea—not God—she, in her perfection, inaccessibility, and difference, represents a desire for fulfillment on Don Quixote's part that is more challenging and more profound than what motivated him in Part I. Like Don Quixote, Sancho is caught up in the aspiration for a higher destiny. In their discussions, here and throughout Part II, Sancho proposes that they seek heavenly rather than earthly prizes.

> I mean to say . . . that we should set about turning saints. Then we shall get the good name we're aiming at sooner. . . . So, dear master, it's better to be a humble little friar, of any order you like, than a valiant and errant knight. A couple of dozen lashings have more effect with God than a couple of thousand lance-thrusts, even against giants, or hobgoblins, or dragons. (II, 8, 519-20)

> (Quiero decir . . . que nos demos a ser santos, y alcanzaremos más brevemente la buena fama que pretendemos, . . . Así que, señor mío, más vale ser humilde frailecito, de cualquier orden que sea, que valiente y andante caballero; más alcanzan con Dios dos do-

cenas de diciplinas que dos mil lanzadas, ora las den a gigantes,
ora a vestiglos o a endrigos. [II, 8, 80–81])

When the journeyers who travelled all night and the following day "without meeting anything worth mentioning" (II, 8,
520) arrive the day after that at Toboso, it is midnight. The town
is as unfamiliar to knight as it is to squire: "Have I not told you a
thousand times that I have never seen the peerless Dulcinea in
all the days of my life, nor ever crossed the threshhold of her
palace . . . ?" (II, 9, 522) (¿No te he dicho mil veces que en todos
los días de mi vida no he visto a la sin par Dulcinea, ni jamás
atravesé los umbrales de su palacio? [II, 9, 84]). To this question
of Don Quixote's, Sancho responds: "Since you say that you
have never seen her, neither have I . . . " (II, 9, 522) (Digo que
pues vuestra merced no la ha visto, ni yo tampoco [II, 9, 84]).
They are welcomed by the sounds of braying donkeys, grunting
pigs, and mewing cats. The only human being they encounter is
a stranger like themselves. Don Quixote takes the darkened,
sleeping town as well as the stranger's song about the defeat of
the French at Roncesvalles as a bad omen, as well he might,
since he will encounter all these signs from legend and the
animal world again as his journey leads him deeper and deeper
into his own undoing.

Don Quixote and Sancho find more than animals and a
stranger in Toboso at midnight. Don Quixote immediately takes
a large building looming in the darkness for Dulcinea's palace.
It turns out to be a church, and Sancho comments, "Please God
we haven't come for our burial. For it's not a good sign to be
wandering about graveyards at this time of night" (II, 9, 521)
(Plega a Dios que no demos con nuestra sepultura; que no es
buena señal andar por los cimentarios a tales horas [II, 9, 83]).
The church, which presides over eternal life, is appropriately
mistaken for Dulcinea's palace by Don Quixote.

Sancho, who has never been to Toboso and therefore could
not possibly know, tells Don Quixote, "If I remember rightly, I
told you that the lady's house is in a blind alley" (II, 9, 521) (Si
mal no recuerdo [he dicho] que la casa desta señora ha de estar
en una callejuela sin salida [II, 9, 83]). The "calle sin salida" is
an apt description for the road upon which knight and squire
are travelling. This road will bring them back exactly to their

starting point—back to Don Quixote's home in La Mancha. At the end of his journey Don Quixote will finally be able to say, "Dulcinea will not appear" (II, 73, 930) (¡Dulcinea no parece! [II, 73, 597]). But that dead-end street is very long. Along its barely perceptible arc, Sancho, and not Don Quixote, will be the guide.

In Chapter 2 of Part II Don Quixote defines the relationship between himself and Sancho as one of head to body: "As I am your lord and master, I am your head, and you are a part of me, since you are my servant" (II, 2, 482) (Siendo yo tu amo y señor, soy tu cabeza, y tú mi parte, pues eres mi criado [II, 2, 32]). Seven chapters later, however, Don Quixote literally forces Sancho to take charge, while he retreats to the woods outside of Toboso. Sancho tries to escape the burdens of his new position, since it will require him to continue to deceive Don Quixote about his trip to Toboso in Part I. But Don Quixote will hear nothing of it. When Sancho says he never saw Dulcinea, Don Quixote protests: "That cannot be, for you told me, at any rate, that you saw her winnowing wheat . . ." (II, 9, 522) (Eso no puede ser, que, por lo menos, ya me has dicho tú que la viste ahechando trigo [II, 9, 84]).

When Don Quixote alludes to Sancho's Part I description of his lady, he is saying, in effect, "better Sancho's version of Dulcinea than no Dulcinea at all." By capitulating to Sancho's version and refusing to accept the squire's avowal that he has never seen Dulcinea, Don Quixote forces Sancho to deceive him. In Chapter 8 of Part II he tells Sancho that he might have been able to see Dulcinea as one of the nymphs that Garcilaso described rising up from the Tagus, "were it not for the envy which some evil enchanter seems to display towards my affairs, in changing and turning everything which might give me plea-sure into shapes other than their true ones" (II, 8, 516) (sino que la envidia que algún mal encantador debe de tener a mis cosas, todas las que me han de dar gusto trueca y vuelve en diferentes figuras que ellas tienen [II, 8, 75-76]). With his master hidden in the thicket outside Toboso, Sancho's unwelcome task is to go forth at dawn and find the Dulcinea that neither one has ever seen. The head has given itself over to the body—reason has fallen into confusion. It is no wonder that Don Quixote's dominant mood in Part II is one of melancholy. He has yielded his strongest position and now, literally as well as figuratively in the dark, he wanders under the dominance of what he considers his inferior function.[9]

In his first adventure out on the road, Don Quixote symbolically grants Sancho the power to lead him and, thus, to deceive him. In Chapter 8, he tells him exactly how to do it, and in Chapter 10, he leaves him no alternative but to act as his master's "evil enchanter." Sancho's substitution of a peasant girl for the peerless Dulcinea throws Don Quixote into a state of confusion that will persist throughout Part II and will set the pattern for the other deceptions to which Don Quixote will be subjected as he proceeds through a world in which he has so lost his bearings that he will finally be led to exclaim in Chapter 29: "God help us, but this whole world is tricks and devices, one against the other. I can do no more" (II, 29, 661) (Dios lo remedie; que todo este mundo es máquinas y trazas, contrarias unas de otras. Yo no puedo más [II, 29, 264]).

Don Quixote's confusion is clearly of his own making. A symbolic reading suggests that during his journey in Part II the body, and not the head, is in charge. Sancho's prominence, success, unchecked garrulousness, and eventual attack on Don Quixote in Chapter 60 carry throughout the novel the symbolic transfer of power initiated in the first episode. Don Quixote's melancholy, self-doubt, irritability, and failure reiterate his loss of control. Only in Chapter 73, when Don Quixote finally realizes that the search for Dulcinea's house led him up a blind alley, is he able to see beyond the demise of his role as knight-errant to the true life disclosed to him in a dream revelation.

Don Quixote's travels in Part II begin with his search for Dulcinea and end with his renunciation of that search. The whole journey traces a circle away from and back to La Mancha, away from and back to his bed. The journey is synonymous with illusion; from beginning to end the main character's real self is obscured by his false role as knight-errant. Dulcinea holds out the illusory promise of perfection that renders all else unworthy by comparison. When she is not actively sought, as in Part I, she is dangerous because the dream of her incites men to conflict. When she leads them into a futile search for her, as in Part II, her dangers are not less but different. The search turns inward and challenges the very foundations of the self, producing an attitude of melancholy rather than aggression and leading to the death of the ego. Don Quixote's long dream of Dulcinea's unsullied perfection carries him further and further down the road of humiliation and degradation, and the dissipation of his dream represents his final undoing.

In a material sense, Dulcinea is a sham. The hero's pursuit of her does offer, however, the possibility of his discovering his true self, but only after his goal and all that is attached to it collapse. If Dulcinea is taken only as a sign of positive inspiration or only as a source of destruction, the value of her ambivalence is lost.[10] Dulcinea stands on the border between the ego and the unconscious, and she plunges those who follow her into its chaos and dangers. But she also symbolizes the seeker's highest aspirations, and when he stops associating them with her, he is capable of discovering these within himself. The sections to follow will trace the process by which Don Quixote continues to precipitate his own demise, with the dream of Dulcinea always in the background.

DON QUIXOTE'S SYMBOLIC UNDOING

In Part II Don Quixote only partially fills the role of knight-errant he constructed in Part I. The rest of him, hidden beneath his almost constant melancholy, is engaged in an intense reconsideration of his place in the world, as revealed both in his search for Dulcinea and in his extended conversations with Sancho about life and death, the meaning of existence, and the reality of appearances. In his new frame of mind, he tends to consider the outer world a manifestation of the inner world and not a series of discrete events, independent and autonomous. An explicit statement of Don Quixote's new orientation comes in Chapter 8, when he tells Sancho:

> It is for us to slay pride by slaying giants; to slay envy by our generosity and nobility; anger by calmness of mind and serenity of disposition; gluttony and drowsiness by eating little and watching late into the night; indulgence and lust by preserving our loyalty to those whom we have made ladies of our hearts; and sloth by travelling through all parts of the world in quest of opportunities of becoming famous knights as well as Christians. (II, 8, 518)

> (Hemos de matar en los gigantes a la soberbia; a la envidia, en la generosidad y buen pecho; a la ira, en el reposado continente y quietud del ánimo; a la gula y al sueño, en el poco comer que comemos y en el mucho velar que velamos; a la lujuria y lascivia,

en la lealtad que guardamos a las que hemos hecho señoras de
nuestros pensamientos; a la pereza, con andar por todas las partes
del mundo, buscando las ocasiones que nos puedan hacer y
hagan, sobre cristianos, famosos caballeros. [II, 8, 78-79])

The statement suggests that Don Quixote's new aim as knight-errant is to achieve victory over himself, to overcome his weaknesses.[11] The giants, who were envisioned as concrete beings in Part I, become symbols of passions that need to be tamed in Part II. Much of what Don Quixote does in Part II can be understood as an exercise in self-discipline: his resolution to leave Don Diego's comfortable house, his relentless travel, his reaction to Altisidora, his self-control in the face of Altisidora's accusations. Knight-errantry is seen by Don Quixote in Part II, and to some degree even by Sancho, as a means of achieving self-mastery rather than only as a way of gaining recognition and fame.

The reversal of values gives an oneiric quality to the events Don Quixote encounters—events whose truth is always subject to interpretation. Not only in the cave of Montesinos do Don Quixote's senses fail to verify the reality of the objects before him. The question of whether what he sees and hears is real permeates all his experiences in Part II, from his meeting with the false Dulcinea to his final encounter with the Knight of the White Moon. For Don Quixote, the world has become a complex series of signs that he has unconsciously brought into play and that he must try to decipher anew for each adventure. He cannot truly penetrate the meaning of what he sees, however, for beneath the glossy surface of the chivalric dream each event reveals the continued presence of all that the dream was designed to spurn. Were he properly to interpret the situations he encounters, he would cease to exist as Don Quixote. The opening adventure with Dulcinea shows that he prefers to hold fast to his illusions, since to give them up would mean relinquishing his invented identity.

When Don Quixote created himself in Chapter 1 of Part I he began by resuscitating the rusty armor of his forebears. He then saddled and named his bony horse, and gave the aging Alonso Quijano the name of Don Quixote. Before he finished his invention, he also converted the peasant girl Aldonza Lorenzo into Dulcinea and served notice on an unknown and unnamed scribe that he was on his way and that his story would have to be written. In Part II, working backwards from the last of Don Quixote's creations, each element in his self-portrait is stripped of its glitter. The process begins with Don Quixote's discovery that his author is a Moor and a proven "ignorant chatterer" who wrote what Don Quixote had hoped would be a noble, inspiring story, "blindly and without any method" (II, 3, 489) (a tiento y sin algún discurso [II, 3, 42]). The undermining continues in the episode immediately following when Sancho "enchants" Dulcinea, giving his master a rough and foul-smelling country woman in place of his beautiful image of her. After leaving Toboso, Don Quixote has three more encounters that directly reflect upon the self he has invented. Weaving in and out of all three episodes are conversations between Don Quixote and Sancho concerning the reality of appearances.

The Wagon of Death

Chapter 11, in which the wagon carrying the actors appears, opens with Don Quixote appearing despondent over the enchantment of Dulcinea. He feels responsible for her condition: "I alone am to blame for her misfortune and disaster. From the envy the wicked bear me springs her sad plight" (II, 11, 533) (De su desgracia y desventura yo solo tengo la culpa: de la invidia que me tienen los malos ha nacido su mala andanza [II, 11, 98]). But he also suggests that possibly only *he* sees her as ugly: "Against me alone, against my eyes, was directed the power of their venom" (II, 11, 533) (Contra mí solo y contra mis ojos se endereza la fuerza de su veneno [II, 11, 98]).

The discussion of whether Dulcinea is in fact ugly or only appears so is interrupted by a wagon driven by a Devil and packed with archetypal figures representing Death, an angel, an emperor, and Cupid as well as a knight in full armor. Don Quixote, who readies himself for another adventure when he sees the wagon, says that the coach "looks more like Charon's bark than an ordinary cart" (II, 11, 534) (más parece la barca de Carón que carreta de las que se usan [II, 11, 100]), once again revealing the extent to which his imagination is turned toward death.[12] The Devil, who is the driver and spokesman, explains that he and the others belong to an acting company. Don Quixote readily accepts the Devil's explanation saying, "When I saw this cart I imagined that some great adventure was presenting itself to me. But now I declare that appearances are not always to be trusted" (II, 11, 535) (Así como vi este carro imaginé que alguna grande aventura se me ofrecía; y ahora digo que es menester tocar las apariencias con la mano para dar lugar al desengaño [II, 11, 101]).

Up to this point, Don Quixote seems to have learned his lessons in Part II well. He demonstrates caution when confronting a new situation and a firm grasp of the illusory nature of appearances. The incident immediately following, however, reveals the instability of Don Quixote's self-control. One of the actors, in the guise of the Devil, jumps in front of Don Quixote, pretending to fence with him with a stick. He leaps to the sound of his bells and bangs the ground with ox-bladders. The narrator says: "This evil apparition so scared Rocinante that he took the bit between his teeth, and started to gallop across the field with more speed than the bones of his anatomy promised; nor was Don Quixote strong enough to stop him" (II, 11, 535) ([Esta] mala visión así alborotó a Rocinante, que sin ser poderoso a detenerle don Quijote, tomando el freno entre los dientes dio a correr por el campo con más ligereza que jamás prometieron los huesos de su notomía [II, 11, 101-2]). The Devil is not satisfied until he has thoroughly shaken up not only Don Quixote and Rocinante but Sancho and Dapple as well. When Don Quixote catches his breath and recovers from his fright, he is no longer the calm personage of the first conversation. Instead he has reverted to his role as knight-errant and threatens with great bravado to engage in battle with the entire stage company. Their aggressive response and Sancho's counsel, however, dissuade him. Knight and squire back off without a fight.

Although the incident ends peacefully, it does reveal that Don Quixote, despite his own best intentions, continues to rely on the model of the chivalric hero. While Don Quixote has achieved some intellectual understanding of the problems that concern him, his bodily self, as represented by Sancho and Rocinante, is far from having assimilated that understanding. The intellect exercises no control, in fact. When the Devil distracts Don Quixote, Rocinante takes the bit between his teeth and runs, leaving his "master" to hang on as best he can. Don Quixote has already announced, in the passage cited earlier, that his goal as knight-errant was to gain mastery over himself. The experience with the Devil suggests that Don Quixote's instincts still take charge of him time after time.

The Wagon of Death itself reflects Don Quixote's present state. At the onset of the adventure the narrator pointed out that the wagon contained, among the other actors, a knight in full armor. The driver, however, is none other than the Devil. On his first encounter after leaving Toboso, Don Quixote imagines himself as one of a whole cartload of actors, all dressed in papier-mâché and under the control of the Devil. The Devil-driven wagon portrays Don Quixote's state well, for the Devil represents those forces that, when systematically repressed, run rampant, causing the conscious personality no end of dismay and perplexity. The Devil feeds on the illusion-creating capacity of the unanchored ego, and with Dulcinea's enchantment, Don Quixote has clearly demonstrated that he prefers to be under illusion's sway than to relinquish the romantic dream the lady holds out to him. The attachment to illusion puts the Devil in charge and makes him, as he himself says, "one of the chief characters in the piece" (II, 11, 535) (Una de las principales figuras del auto [II, 11, 101]).

The symbolism of the Wagon of Death, with its figures of the knight, the emperor, Cupid, and Death, reveals that not only worldly power but romantic love and even death belong to the realm of illusion and of the Devil. It suggests furthermore that the Devil controls by fear and that escaping his influence is extremely difficult. Don Quixote, at this point in the novel, neither wants nor is able to let go of the false dreams that leave him at the Devil's mercy. His trials throughout the rest of the work result from the unconscious attachment to illusion that the Wagon of Death episode reveals.

The fear that keeps Don Quixote chained to his fiction is that without this fiction—the role he has invented—he is nothing. Without a Dulcinea, without the adventures of a knight-errant, there would be only emptiness for Don Quixote. The first figure on the wagon is the figure of Death. Don Quixote dubs the whole wagon the "Wagon of Death" and addresses the driver as Charon. The actors, indeed, perform a play called *The Parliament of Death*, which is clearly an allegory of man's life on earth since it is being performed to celebrate Corpus Christi week.

The feast of Corpus Christi so expansively celebrated in seventeenth-century Spain affirmed the doctrine that at the Eucharist the bread and wine become once again the body and blood of the living Christ. The miracle the church was celebrating in that week of July was one that Don Quixote was trying by his own will to reenact: to transform everyday objects into the image of the divine. Oblivious, apparently, to the church calendar or to the events of the collectivity with which he is associated, Don Quixote cannot bring forth from the base matter of Aldonza Lorenzo the exalted image of womankind that his imagination has supplied, nor can he become, of his own accord, the perfect, shining knight that he would like to substitute for the aging Alonso Quijano. His effort to recreate the world in his own image has succeeded in doing just that—in bringing up for his contemplation all the hidden fears and failures that constitute his unredeemed self. To be truly delivered from the bondage of his illusions—his love for Dulcinea, his dream of fame, his fear of death—requires divine intervention such as that required to transform the bread and wine. Until then, the actors will remain in costume, as they do in the episode of the Wagon of Death, their swords and crowns, though perceived as plaster, still holding office.

The Knight of the Mirrors

The opening chapters of Part II reveal to Don Quixote's horror that a hated Moor responded to his call for a scribe in Chapter 2 of Part I.[13] In his first adventure away from home, Don Quixote finds a peasant girl where Dulcinea was supposed to have been. In the following episode, the Wagon of Death shows him to be only one of many characters in disguise, all directed by the Devil. In Chapter 14, still another veil is briefly torn away from the world of knights and ladies to which Don Quixote is so attached. And once again, Don Quixote refuses to recognize beneath it the forces that really govern his life.

Don Quixote and Sancho are asleep in the woods when the new adventure comes upon them. The atmosphere in the episode reinforces the dreamlike quality that marks all the events in Part II and suggests once again that Don Quixote is meeting images from his unconscious. Don Quixote is awakened by the voice of a knight who, like himself, appears to be melancholy and in love. The Knight of the Woods (later called the Knight of the Mirrors) tells Don Quixote that he has travelled the world over, carrying out impossible feats at his lady's bidding. His most recent task was to make every knight-errant in Spain confess his lady the most beautiful and he the most valiant and enamored knight in the world. Among his conquests, he reports, is one Don Quixote. Don Quixote, stunned to hear himself named by the stranger as one who had been defeated in battle, asks for a description of the defeated knight. When everything seems to match his own appearance he becomes most confused:

> By the very exact and precise description of him that you have given me I cannot doubt that he is the same whom you conquered. On the other hand, I have the evidence of my eyes and hands that it could not possibly have been the same knight; were it not that he has many enchanters as his enemies. . . . For one of them may have taken his shape and allowed himself to be defeated. (II, 14, 552)

> (Por las señas que dél me habéis dado, tan puntuales y ciertas, no puedo pensar sino que sea el mismo que habéis vencido. Por otra parte, veo con los ojos y toco con las manos no ser posible el mesmo, si ya no fuese que como él tiene muchos enemigos encantadores . . . no haya alguno dellos tomado su figura para dejarse vencer. [II, 14, 122])

The episode of the Knight of the Mirrors offers an even more exact reflection of Don Quixote than the Wagon of Death did. Although Don Quixote generally seems changed in Part II because of his new tendency to observe the world while remaining detached from it, here, as with the Devil in the previous episode, he is forced out of his posture of equanimity and goaded into direct contact with the phantasms that appear before him. After trying to forestall the contest his challenger proposes, he finally yields to provocation and agrees to a duel.

Daylight reveals Don Quixote's alter ego and adversary as a fully armed knight dressed in a cassock resplendent with moon-shaped mirrors. Though the other knight is sturdily built, Don Quixote succeeds in knocking him to the ground when he is off his guard, thus winning the battle decisively and confirming once again the illusion of Dulcinea's beauty and his own prowess. The victory, of course, is a hollow one. The defeated knight's shining visor hides the face of none other than Don Quixote's friend and neighbor Sansón Carrasco. Don Quixote, and even Sancho, prefer to think the vision the work of enchanters, and Sancho suggests that Don Quixote run his sword through the sham knight's throat. Don Quixote, determined to preserve his illusion at any price, is ready to follow this suggestion when Sansón's false squire Tomé Cecial rushes up and tells Sancho:

" . . . beg and pray his worship your master not to touch, maltreat, wound, or kill the Knight of the Mirrors, who lies at his feet, for beyond any shadow of doubt he's the bold and ill-advised Bachelor Sansón Carrasco" (II, 14, 558) (pedid y suplicad al señor vuestro amo que no toque, maltrate, hiera ni mate al caballero de los Espejos, que a sus pies tiene, porque sin duda alguna es el atrevido y mal aconsejado del bachiller Sansón Carrasco [II, 14, 131]).

Don Quixote hears Tomé's cries and sees his neighbors' faces beneath their disguises, but he makes no comment and returns instead to the game that he is loath to abandon, especially because for once he appears to have emerged the winner. Though he does not kill Sansón, he continues to address the fictitious issues that prompted their duel and sends his challenger away defeated and in low spirits.

Once again Don Quixote refuses the evidence before him, consciously choosing his fictional self over his real one. This choice makes his later defeat inevitable, however. Sansón goes off vowing revenge, becoming, in the process, more deeply embedded in the fiction from which he thought he was extricating Don Quixote. The essence of the double is reciprocity:[14] the knight whom Don Quixote saw lying defeated on the ground was a reflection of himself, just as he, as victor, was reflected in the mirrors on his challenger's coat. In the episode of the Knight of the Mirrors, Don Quixote has written the script for his eventual downfall.

The Knight of the Green Coat

The episode of the Knight of the Green Coat that immediately follows Don Quixote's encounter with the Knight of the Mirrors makes it easy to understand why Don Quixote chose to continue in his fictional role rather than to recognize Sansón Carrasco behind the adversary's visor. To have accepted Sansón would have been to pack up his own costume as well and to return home. Nothing from the previous chapters suggests that he is ready to do that. He goes on, though his scribe has been revealed as an envious scribbler, his lady a rough peasant, and his whole enterprise a part of the Devil's charade. To stop the journey would be to revert to the quiet madness of Alonso Quijano, idling away empty hours in domestic chatter and the wild fantasies of his solitude.

A very discreet gentleman riding a mare and dressed from cap to spurs in green passes Don Quixote and Sancho while they converse about illusion and the enchanters who seem intent on turning their world upside down. The gentleman, expressing concern that his mare might upset Rocinante, would have gone on ahead had not Don Quixote insisted that he stay and ride alongside of him and Sancho assured him that "even if your mare brought him between two plates, our horse wouldn't so much as look her in the face" (II, 16, 564) (aunque se la den entre dos platos, a buen seguro que el caballo no la arrostre [II, 16, 138]). [15]

When the two men meet, Don Quixote is without helmet and visor. They look at one another in an amazement and fascination reminiscent of the meeting between Cardenio and Don Quixote in Part I. In describing the two gentlemen's studied appraisal of one another, the narrator moves between both of their points of view and so blends their perceptions that he finally has each one anticipating the other's reactions, as if each were simultaneously in his own and in the other's mind:

> The more the man in green stared at Don Quixote, the more did Don Quixote stare at the man in green. . . . His age appeared to be about fifty; his grey hairs few; his face aquiline. . . . But what the man in green thought of Don Quixote was that he had never seen anyone of that kind or anyone looking like him before. (II, 16, 564)

> (Si mucho miraba el de lo verde a don Quijote, mucho más miraba don Quijote al de lo verde. . . . La edad mostraba ser de cincuenta años; las canas, pocas, y el rostro, aguileño. . . . Lo que juzgó de don Quijote de la Mancha el de lo verde fue que semejante manera ni parecer de hombre no le había visto jamás. [II, 16, 138])

Don Quixote appears able to see himself through the eyes of the other gentleman: "Don Quixote observed the attention with which the traveller gazed at him and from his amazement assumed his curiosity" (II, 16, 564) (Notó bien don Quijote la atención con que el caminante le miraba, y leyóle en la suspensión su deseo [II, 16, 138]). From that newfound perception of himself from without Don Quixote volunteers: "I should not wonder if your worship were surprised at this appearance of mine, for it is both novel and out of the common" (II, 16, 565) (Esta figura que vuesa merced en mí ha visto, por ser tan nueva y tan fuera de las que comúnmente se usan, no me maravillaría yo de que le hubiese maravillado [II, 16, 138]).

After Don Quixote describes himself and his deeds, he insists that his interlocutor respond in kind. In a paragraph of almost equal length, the Knight of the Green Coat, whose real name is Don Diego de Miranda, gives an account of himself. He is a modest country gentleman who spends his time hunting, fishing, and reading. He owns some six dozen books, some devotional, some historical, but none chivalric. He describes himself as generous, disinclined to slander or to curiosity about the lives of others, devout, charitable, and free of hypocrisy and pride.[16]

Since the age, the station in life, the modesty, and the quiet, unobtrusive manner recall the Alonso Quijano out of which Don Quixote fashioned himself, Don Diego must represent the final step backwards in the symbolic deconstruction of Don Quixote that the first nineteen chapters of Part II have carried out. Don Diego rides a mare because he is associated with all the material, home- and tradition-bound aspects of life from which Don Quixote would like to have escaped. The mare can now safely ride alongside Don Quixote and his "steed" Rocinante because the masculine drives with which Don Quixote's horse is associated, and which appeared in Part I in the Yanguesan incident to which Sancho alludes, are no longer operational. Don Quixote has in fact, as the description of Rocinante and the appearance of Don Diego reveal, lost the impetus that drove him forward in Part I. His mad challenge to the lion in Don Diego's presence only further demonstrates his awareness of his loss of true aggressive power.

Don Quixote's similarity to Don Diego requires him to assert, or try to assert, his difference from him. To overcome a lion, the king of the beasts and the archetypal hero's opponent, would be to show the docile, passive self that Don Diego represents that he, Don Quixote, is the master.

Despite his bravado, Don Quixote undertakes the battle with the lion with an attitude of intense self-doubt. He hastily dons the helmet filled with cheese curds that Sancho has brought him and then suspects that his brains have melted when the curds ooze down over his face. Don Quixote's fears are echoed by Don Diego, ever in the background watching Don Quixote and wondering about his sanity. When Don Quixote challenges the lion, Don Diego murmurs, "Our good knight is giving us a proof of his nature. The curds, no doubt, have softened his skull and ripened his brains" (II, 17, 573) (Dado ha señal de quién es nuestro buen caballero: los requesones, sin duda, le han ablandado los cascos y madurado los sesos [II, 17, 148]). Throughout the several days he spends with Don Quixote, Don Diego never stops being concerned about his strange friend's mental state: "In all this while Don Diego de Miranda had not spoken a word, so carefully was he watching and noting every word and action of Don Quixote, who seemed to him a sane man turned mad or a mad man verging on sanity" (II, 17, 578) (En todo este tiempo no había hablado palabra don Diego de Miranda, todo atento a mirar y a notar los hechos y palabras de don Quijote, pareciéndole que era un cuerdo loco y un loco que tiraba a cuerdo [II, 17, 153-54]).

That Don Diego is the voice of Don Quixote's own uncertainty about his project is made clear by the regularity with which Don Quixote anticipates his companion's thoughts and tries to justify himself before them: "No doubt," he tells him after the episode of the lion, "your worship considers me both foolish and mad. And it would be no marvel if you did, for my deeds testify no less. But, for all that, I wish your worship to take note that I am not so mad or so lacking as I must have seemed to you" (II, 17, 578) (¿Quién duda, . . . que vuestra merced no me tenga en su opinión por un hombre disparatado y loco? Y no sería mucho que así fuese, porque mis obras no pueden dar testimonio de otra cosa. Pues, con todo esto, quiero que vuestra merced advierta que no soy tan loco ni tan menguado como debo de haberle parecido [II, 17, 154]).

The lion episode reflects Don Quixote's reduced vitality and consequent uncertainty. Rocinante has already been described by Sancho as past all sensuous stimulation. Far worse for Don Quixote's image of masculine aggressivity, the lion who has been extracted from the wilds and caged, like Don Quixote at the end of Part I, shows no interest in his challenger. Having sent Sancho and Rocinante away, Don Quixote meets the lion on foot, but the beast is only capable of yawning and returning voluntarily to his cage. The head—Don Quixote without the support of Sancho and Rocinante—knows that to subdue a lion at this point would guarantee his status as hero. But the beast he is to subdue has already yielded up its power. As if to underscore the emptiness of this gesture, Don Quixote has Sancho pay the lion keeper for the charade he has been allowed to perform.

Don Quixote is in his element in Don Diego's peaceful and

comfortable home. He converses wisely in the company of his host's family and especially enjoys discussing poetry with Don Diego's son Don Lorenzo. At the end of four days, however, he insists, to Sancho's dismay, that they take their leave of such pleasant surroundings, since "it was not right for knights errant to give up many hours to ease and luxury" (II, 18, 586) (por no parecer bien que los caballeros andantes se den muchas horas al ocio y al regalo [II, 18, 164]). The encounter with Don Diego, the last in the series of symbolic statements of Don Quixote's condition, makes it clear that Don Quixote will continue in his role as knight-errant despite his doubts, his boredom, and his fatigue. The alternative is the settled life whose demons of sloth, envy, lust, and pride seem too much for the aging and unmarried Alonso Quijano to overcome.

As a country gentleman, advanced in years and belonging to an idle, marginal class, Don Diego resembles Alonso Quijano in many respects. Sancho is so taken by Don Diego's self-description that he throws himself at his feet and calls him "a saint on horseback." Don Quixote, on the other hand, implies that he is a coward: "Pray go away, my dear sir, and see to your quiet pointer and good ferret . . ." (II, 17, 573) (Váyase vuesa merced, señor hidalgo . . . a entender con su perdigón manso y con su hurón atrevido [II, 17, 148]).[17] Don Diego is stodgy enough to resist his son's proclivity for poetry, yet openhearted enough to entertain Don Quixote and Sancho and to treat them with a respect they will not find later among those who have read the books of chivalry. He differs from Alonso Quijano in his assimilation of the feminine against which his guest struggles so painfully. Unlike all the characters to appear so far in the book, he is happily married, and his wife figures as a named character in the story. He enjoys hunting, but he also enjoys the comforts of his pleasant family estate house. Though Don Quixote, at this stage in his development, apparently sees Don Diego in the light of his own unsatisfactory experience as Alonso Quijano, the gentleman in fact resembles Alonso Quijano the Good, whom Don Quixote briefly becomes at the end of the novel.

The cluster of episodes examined in this section reveals Don Quixote's unconscious realization that the identity he has assumed is a sham, masking a quiet, peace-loving country gentleman concerned with the welfare of his soul. Don Quixote's defeat of the Knight of the Mirrors postpones, but also makes inevitable, his own defeat. The next time he meets the challenger —Sansón Carrasco again in disguise—he loses the battle and is forcibly stripped of his armor and identity. Then, after figuratively going through the hell prepared for him by Altisidora, he meets once more, on his deathbed, the gentleman whom he left behind so long ago and who appeared to him as Don Diego in Chapter 17 of Part II. In Chapter 73, however, all paths of escape now blocked, he experiences a revelation that unburdens him of his illusions. At the spiritual end of his journey he finally embraces his original self and, like Don Diego, seeks out books of devotion in place of the books of chivalry that previously so confused him.

THE CAVE OF MONTESINOS

The symbolic undoing of Don Quixote's self-image presented in the opening episodes of Part II is fully captured in Chapters 22–24, in Don Quixote's descent into the cave of Montesinos. The journey into the cave represents an extension of the continued attraction to the feminine that motivates Don Quixote's actions in Part II. The cave belongs to a whole cluster of images associated with the irrational forces pulling at Don Quixote in Part II. It represents depth rather than forward progress, darkness rather than light, concern with origins rather than with results, and thus opposition on every level to the linear direction of Don Quixote's exploits in Part I.

Don Quixote's vision in the cave, though it introduces him to a world apparently different from the familiar one aboveground, reproduces to an astonishing degree the confusions and doubts that have become his daily fare. When he sets out toward the cave after relaxing for four days in the "marvelous silence" (II, 18, 586) of Don Diego's house, he leaves with two goals in mind: the one—to discover the source of the Lakes of Ruidera—corresponds to his attraction to the unknown; the other—to participate in the jousts at Zaragoza—perpetuates the masculine ego ideal that his transformation into knight-errant has always represented.

Both Don Quixote's need to establish a destination and his plan to participate in the jousts suggest an emptying of his image of himself as knight-errant. His failure to plumb the depths of the cave both expresses and anticipates his analogous failure fully to experience success in his guise as knight-errant. The feminine component of his psyche, while apparently distinct from the masculine side, is nonetheless a reflection of it. Don Quixote's dual goals upon leaving Don Diego's house, his very need to reject the comforts it offers, his later only partial descent into the cave, the dream he has while sleeping there, and his inability properly to interpret the dream when he later tells it to his skeptical companions, all reiterate the same theme: Don Quixote is struggling unsuccessfully to harmonize the aspirations of his conscious mind with the demands of his unconscious.[18] With each refusal to see the everyday and ordinary aspects underlying and sustaining his fantasy world of knights and ladies, Don Quixote condemns himself to greater confusion.

Don Quixote is accompanied to the cave by Sancho and a young "humanist" scholar devoted to collecting odd facts and publishing them as wisdom. The humanist appears necessary as a counterweight to Don Quixote, whose new interest in caves, omens, and dreams requires an unimaginative literalism for balance. The literal-minded humanist not only complements Don Quixote, however. He also reveals an essential, though hidden, aspect of the knight's character. Although aboveground Don Quixote appears wild, brave, and out of the ordinary, he is in fact best understood in conjunction with the companions who wait for him outside the cave. When Sancho later says "tell me what company you keep and I'll tell you who you are" (II, 23, 621) (dime con quién andas, decirte he quién eres [II, 23, 210]), he is saying more than he thinks.

Once alone within the cave, Don Quixote abandons his venturesome guise, coils up the rope intended to ensure his return, and goes to sleep. In his dream he meets the knights who have so stimulated his imagination, only to find them old, tired, and confused like himself, having followed to the letter but to no avail the text they were given to enact. Don Quixote has brought with him into the cave, and into the crystal palace it becomes in his dreams, the limitations represented by the friends who keep vigil at the surface. When he meets himself in the dream image, he finds Sancho, the humanist, and Dulcinea's fallen beauty all there too. It is no wonder, then, when he recounts his "adventures" in the cave, that his friends subject its wonders to skepticism, ridicule, and an empty gathering of "factual" information, for that is all that Don Quixote's rational mind can handle from the underground world that he himself has so superficially visited.[19]

Don Quixote's literalism, understood in the light of all that has preceded this scene, is clearly a defense. The cave represents a force that is as terrifying as it is attractive. Not only does Don Quixote approach the cave armed with Sancho *and* the humanist, but he brings with him a rope to ensure his safe return. The cave's mouth is covered with briars so thick that Don Quixote must slash them away with his sword to enter. His actions disturb the sleeping spirits of the night—the crows, jackdaws, and bats—who awaken and fly out at Don Quixote with enough speed to knock him over. Despite the difficulty and fearfulness of the approach, Don Quixote continues, determined to enter the cave. Before entering he offers a silent prayer to God and a voiced petition to Dulcinea for protection. The terrifying nature of Don Quixote's adventure is further underscored by the prayers and entreaties Sancho and the humanist offer on Don Quixote's behalf.[20]

The epic hero must descend to the underworld, and the journey must be a perilous one designed to show his courage in the face of all sorts of monstrous apparitions. In this sense the cave of Montesinos episode, like the earlier episode with the lion, fits into the mock-heroic pattern Cervantes established for his novel. In both cases what makes Don Quixote absurd is the gratuitousness of his undertakings. He approaches both the lion and the cave with apparently frivolous motives in mind. Like the jousts, the hero's tasks that Don Quixote takes upon himself are all for show.

The episodes may still be taken seriously, however, as indices of Don Quixote's character. The lion's indifference to Don Quixote's challenge expresses Don Quixote's own collapsed vitality. Don Quixote's descent into the cave shows the futility of his literal enactment of the epic paradigm. After returning from the cave, he will feel as confused as the enchanted knights therein, who did everything according to the letter and still found themselves caught in the web of unfulfilled desires they called Merlin's enchantment. When Sancho hears Don Quixote's tale of Montesinos and Durandarte he comments: "Your worship goes about with the enchanted who watch and fast. It's no wonder, then, that you didn't eat or sleep whilst you were in

their company" (II, 23, 621) (Andase vuestra merced con en-
cantados ayunos y vigilantes: mirad si es mucho que ni duerma
mientras con ellos anduviere [II, 23, 210]). Sancho comes even
closer to recognizing Don Quixote's affliction as one of enchantment when he adds:

> I believe . . . that this Merlin or these enchanters, who bewitched
> that whole crowd your worship tells us you saw and talked with
> down below, crammed all that rigmarole you've told us into your
> head, and what remains to be told as well. (II, 23, 621)

> (Creo . . . que aquel Merlín o aquellos encantadores que encan-
> taron a toda la chusma que vuestra merced dice que ha visto y
> comunicado allá bajo, le encajaron en el majín o la memoria toda
> esa máquina que nos ha contado, y todo aquello que por contar le
> queda. [II, 23, 211])

Montesinos, Durandarte, Belerma, and all the characters Don
Quixote sees in the cave repeat once again the story of his
failure, the story he wants to understand but cannot accept, no
matter how often he hears it. The same chivalric paradigm that
prompts him to follow his quest also prevents him from perceiving the truth when he finds it. The state of suspension in which
he finds himself in Part II is beautifully represented both in the
approach to the cave and in the dream he has while there.

Don Quixote stops his downward journey, having used less
than half of his rope, on a shelf in the cave into which light from
above still falls. This ledge soon becomes the theater in which
the tattered remains of his chivalric dream are dramatized.
Through the mediation of the dream, the stone ledge becomes a
beautiful field, in the middle of which stands a crystal palace.
An old man with a long white beard and a black hat, a purple
cape falling behind him, and a green satin sash tied across his
chest, comes out to greet Don Quixote. The old man is none
other than Montesinos, one of the French heroes of the battle of
Roncesvalles about whom the stranger in Toboso sang in Chapter 9. Montesinos greets Don Quixote as the savior for whom he
has been waiting—the savior who will break the spell of five
hundred years that has kept him and his companions in unabat-
ed misery and confusion. Montesinos leads Don Quixote into
the palace and introduces him to his dear friend Durandarte,
who died at Roncesvalles. Durandarte lies on a marble tomb,
his right hand covering his heart.

Though the heroes of the Carolingian romance address him and even honor him, Don Quixote figures in this part of the dream primarily as an observer. In his presence Montesinos and Durandarte reenact a scene that reveals their mutual incomprehension and despair. Durandarte, who, though of flesh and bone, resembles a stone carving as he lies atop his catafalque, repeats in mournful tones the verses from the ballad about him:

Oh, my cousin Montesinos!
It was the last thing I asked you,
That as soon as I was dead
And my spirit had departed,
You should bear my heart to where
Fair Belerma dwelt and waited,
Cutting it from out my chest
With a sword or with a dagger. (II, 23, 617)

(¡Oh, mi primo Montesinos!
Lo postrero que os rogaba,
que cuando yo fuere muerto,
y mi ánima arrancada,
que llevéis mi corazón
adonde Belerma estaba,
sacándomele del pecho
ya con puñal, ya con daga. [II, 23, 206])

Montesinos, repeating an action performed over and over again during the five hundred years of their enchantment, falls to his knees before his friend and swears that he has carried out his wishes to the last detail:

I tore out your heart as best I could, and left not a fragment of it in your bosom. I wiped it with a lace handkerchief. I set out with it on the road to France, . . . with enough tears to wash my hands clean of the blood-stains they had got from groping in your entrails. . . . At the first place I came to after leaving Roncesvalles, I threw a little salt on your heart so that it should not smell bad. (II, 23, 617)

(Yo os saqué el corazón lo mejor que pude, sin que os dejase una mínima parte en el pecho; yo le limpié con un pañizuelo de puntas; yo partí con él de carrera para Francia, . . . con tantas lágrimas, que fueron bastantes a lavarme las manos y limpiarme con ellas la sangre que tenían, de haberos andado en las entrañas. . . . En el primero lugar que topé saliendo de Roncesvalles eché un poco de sal en vuestro corazón, porque no oliese mal. [II, 23, 206–207])

Here is Don Quixote's own literalism—found aboveground in Sancho's concern over what kind of dagger was used to cut the heart out, in the humanist's interest in the antiquity of playing cards, and in Cide Hamete's question about the truth of what Don Quixote had told—repeated below in the very heart of the chivalric myth. The mysteries of the depths simply reflect the banalities of the surface, for both belong to Don Quixote, whose confusion arises from his inability to force experienced reality into the narrow mold of the chivalric pattern.[21]

The two friends from the Carolingian epic whom Don Quixote meets in the cave express Don Quixote's conflicting attitude toward his enterprise. Durandarte has given up hope, lingering eternally in the penumbra between death and life. When Montesinos introduces Don Quixote to him as the hero who will revive the ancient art of chivalry and perhaps rescue them from their enchantment, Durandarte manages only to respond in a faint whisper, "and if that should not be . . . if that should not be, cousin, I say: patience and shuffle the cards" (II, 23, 618) (Y cuando así no sea . . . cuando así no sea, ¡oh primo!, digo, paciencia y barajar [II, 23, 208]), before turning on his side and reverting to his customary silence. Montesinos, on the other hand, remains upright, unflagging in his effort to prove that he has performed his duty as knight properly and alert for an opportunity to find an escape from enchantment.

The image of despair and hope, engaged in an endless and fruitless exchange of accusation and self-justification, tells the story of Don Quixote's own melancholy and fitful efforts to revive his chivalric ardor. The split in the image, furthermore, which no amount of explanation can repair, is repeated in each character separately. Durandarte is both dead and alive, yet really neither. He hears but does not listen; he responds but does not believe. Montesinos, in his dress, represents a similar combination of opposites in disharmony with one another: his white beard contrasts with his black hat; his flowing purple cape clashes with his constricting green sash. He is suspended between the certainty that he did what Durandarte asked of him and the confusion that arises from Durandarte's continued despair. In their enchanted state, the chivalric heroes age, though they neither eat nor sleep. They are, like Don Quixote, neither in the world nor of it: they have neither the satisfaction of material success nor the consolation of spiritual fulfillment to relieve their miseries.

The failure on the masculine side of the chivalric melodrama that Don Quixote witnesses in his dream is of course repeated on the feminine side. Belerma, the loved one to whom Montesinos took Durandarte's heart, follows her part in the enchanted ritual by parading four times a week in a funeral procession of maidens dressed in mourning past the room in which Durandarte lies. A glass wall—translucent yet impermeable—separates the men from the women. Like her lover, Belerma has lost her youth and beauty. She carries Durandarte's mummified heart— now dried and shrivelled—in her hands as she weeps the ritual funeral dirges over Durandarte's body.

Belerma and Montesinos both focus their despair on the body of their lover and friend Durandarte. Belerma bewails his death, while Montesinos tries to stimulate his recovery. Montesinos recalls his large fresh heart; Belerma possesses its shrivelled remains. Belerma wears a huge white turban on her head and dresses in black, while Montesinos wears a black hat and a long white beard. She is accompanied by many maidens, he stands alone. Like the others in the scene, Belerma endlessly repeats her ritual of despair. Though in some ways she represents Montesino's opposite, she duplicates him in her failure to live up to the chivalric ideal. The chivalric ritual, which Durandarte is condemned to see reenacted for eternity, provides neither the beauty nor the heroism the books about it promised.

It should not be surprising that Don Quixote, in the second portion of his dream, sees the "enchanted" Dulcinea, who, with her round face and flat nose, resembles the Belerma of the earlier dream segment. Like Belerma, Dulcinea is seen beyond the glass confines of the crystal palace, and Montesinos advises Don Quixote that any effort to go after her would be in vain. Dulcinea, however, is not unaware of Don Quixote, as one of her emissaries makes clear. The lady's companion tells him that Dulcinea needs money, which she asks of Don Quixote in exchange for a new cotton slip. Though Dulcinea's elusiveness, ugliness, and poverty already reveal the failure of Don Quixote's powers, since she represents the image of his soul, his inability to supply her with what she asks only further underscores his weakness.[22] Confronted with such failure, Don Quixote can only fall back on the chivalric rhetoric that has come to sound hollow even to his ears:

You will say to her . . . that, when least she expects it, she will hear
that I have made an oath and vow, like that which the Marquis of
Mantua made to avenge his nephew Baldwin when he found him
on the point of death in the midst of the mountains. . . . So too
shall I swear; not to rest, and to travel the seven portions of the
earth more diligently than did Don Pedro of Portugal, until I have
released her from her enchantment. (II, 23, 623)

(Diréisle . . . que cuando menos se lo piense oirá decir como yo he
hecho un juramento y voto, a modo de aquel que hizo el marqués
de Mantua, de vengar a su sobrino Baldovinos, cuando le halló
para espirar en mitad de la montiña, . . . y así le haré yo de no
sosegar, y de andar las siete partidas del mundo, con más pun-
tualidad que las anduvo el infante don Pedro de Portugal, hasta
desencantarla. [II, 23, 213-14])

Before prancing off, Dulcinea's emissary notes, "All that and
more our worship owes my lady" (II, 23, 623) (Todo eso, y más,
debe vuestra merced a mi señora [II, 23, 214]).

Throughout the remainder of the book Don Quixote will
seek to disenchant Dulcinea, though his increasing melancholy
reveals the degree to which doubt erodes his intentions. The
cave dream is situated at the end of an opening sequence of
episodes in Part II, all of which symbolically tell of Don Quixote's search for and simultaneous refusal to accept the truth
that lies behind the chivalric mask. The dream offers an X-ray of
Don Quixote's psyche and reveals his suspension, self-doubt,
and the confusions that spur both his melancholy and his
bravado as he follows his journey to its end.

DECEPTION

The assault upon the chivalric world to which Don Quixote
is subjected in Part II, combined with the sympathy his unhappiness arouses in the reader, has often created the belief among
critics that Cervantes is presenting, through Don Quixote, a
generalized attack on the power of reason and of the senses to
produce understanding. Don Quixote says in bewilderment of
his experience in the cave that it must really have happened
since he saw everything there with his own eyes and touched it
with his own hands. When pondering the presence of Sansón
Carrasco's face behind the visor of his fallen adversary, Don
Quixote searches for a reason why his friend and neighbor

would want to fool him. Was Sansón his enemy? Had he ever wronged him in any way? As the novel progresses, Don Quixote becomes increasingly confused as sense perception and reason fail to explain the many strange incidents that befall him. To protect his sanity, he more and more frequently calls upon the evil enchanters, on Merlin and on omens and magicians, to help explain what seems incomprehensible.

The novel makes clear, however, that reason and sense data are not lacking. Instead, the patterns that custom, or literature, impose on the world are what distort it. Cervantes releases in Part II the power of all those elements that Don Quixote's limiting and unitary view of the world twist out of shape or abolish. Teresa Panza, the niece, the housekeeper, Sancho, and the animals assert themselves with increasing fervor as Don Quixote's chivalric world breaks down. Between the nullifying rigidity of a fixed world view and the chaos that threatens when the forces of the natural world rise up, Cervantes offers the mediating figure of the trickster.[23]

Cervantes' fascination with deception as a weapon against oppression and stupidity is apparent in many of his works and is especially visible in the *entremeses* and some of his *comedias*.[24] Escape from the restrictions of a power that has abused its authority is, by its very nature, comic and is also associated with the literary genre of romance.[25] Both in its comic and in its romance expressions, the overturning of authority is accomplished by characters schooled in the art not of force but of fraud.[26] Fraud, from the wife who deceives her husband to the younger brother who marries his elder brother's fiancée, is the weapon of the less powerful—the women, the poor, the servants, the younger sons—and its effects can be amusing or inspiring. In either case, deception appeals to an order that escapes the notice of the centers of power who in turn become the butt of the joke or the losers in the contest.

Inasmuch as Don Quixote represents a character locked into a preestablished way of looking at the world, he is the trickster's natural target. *Don Quixote* Part II, which abounds in magicians, cheats, and deceivers, cannot be properly understood by focusing solely on the undoing of the main character. Side by side with Don Quixote's decline are demonstrations of power and control available to those who, unlike Don Quixote, are able to stop being controlled by established patterns of behavior, fixed ideas about the way the world is, and false expectations.

The theme of deception, which is associated with the feminine, accompanies Don Quixote throughout his journey in Part II. The two prime deceptions, the ones that will determine Don Quixote's activities throughout the novel and ultimately cause his downfall, are carried out by Don Quixote's "friends from home"—Sancho and Sansón Carrasco—and are both directly connected to the women in his life. In Chapter 15 Cide Hamete explains to the reader that Sansón Carrasco became the Knight of the Mirrors after Don Quixote's housekeeper implored him in Chapter 7 to help her master return to his senses. Further association with the feminine is established in the mirrors and moon of Sansón's disguise.[27]

As has already been discussed, Sancho was compelled by fear and Don Quixote's obstinate desire to see Dulcinea to carry out his fundamental deception early in Part II. The kind of deception in which Sansón and Sancho engage is contaminated and undermined by their own weaknesses. Sancho's fear of Don Quixote's ire and Sansón's obvious delight in mocking knight-errantry catch both in the thicket of their own confusions, and they pay in frustration and humiliation for their failures. Their behavior early in the novel anticipates the later, and far more reprehensible, types of deception the Duke and Duchess and Don Antonio practice on Don Quixote. All of them wind up caught in the syndrome of the "deceiver deceived" about which so much has been written.

The novel offers another type of deception, however, one motivated by love and the struggle for survival that demands far greater concentration and self-mastery than are needed for whimsical or cowardly deceptions. Just as Don Quixote is offered, in the opening episodes, a series of images designed to reveal the limitations of his self-image as knight, so is he confronted with several situations that demonstrate the value of seizing control of the image and learning how to use it to his own advantage.

Don Quixote himself introduces the theme in Chapter 16 while discussing poetry with Don Diego. He points out that, though the poet is born with his talent, "the natural poet who makes use of art will improve himself and be much greater than the poet who relies on his knowledge of the art . . . for art is not better than nature, but perfects her" (II, 16, 569) (el natual poeta que se ayudare del arte será mucho mejor y se aventajará al poeta que sólo por saber el arte quisiere serlo; la razón es porque el arte no se aventaja a la naturaleza, sino perficiónala [II, 16, 144]). Although Don Quixote's words echo a familiar Renaissance topic, they also address a point that will later be demonstrated. The student fencers, Basilio, and Master Peter will show to what degree artistry is capable of subduing the powers of the natural world.

Basilio (Camacho's Wedding)

Don Quixote hears about Basilio from two students whom he meets along the road between Don Diego's house and the cave of Montesinos. As in his encounter with the Wagon of Death, Don Quixote is introduced by the students to a situation not of his own making. All the other episodes—the enchantment of Dulcinea, the battle with the Knight of the Mirrors, the challenge to the lion—have to do directly with Don Quixote's chivalric madness. The students, and Camacho's wedding to which they guide him, however, represent a world very little associated with Don Quixote. What they offer, not only in their separation from him but in their general orientation, is another view of the world. The actors in the Wagon of Death evoked, both by their costumes and by their association with the Feast of Corpus Christi, the recollection that the world is a stage and that what appears to be one thing may in fact be another. The students' demonstration is designed to point out that what is required on that stage is study and artistry.

Don Quixote watches as the students quarrel about fencing. The one, who is apparently very strong, tells the other that all his intricate study of fencing techniques is for naught. They engage in an exquisitely narrated match in which the fencing student reduces his fierce challenger to a shambles of frustration. The two immediately become friends again when the loser confesses that success in fencing comes from skill and not physical prowess. The students' duel is about dueling: neither love, nor jealousy, nor anger intervene to convert it into the means to some other end. What little passion there may be in the fight is compensated for by the mastery of the one who has studied the intricacies of his art. The fencers do not become confused about the fight, clearly understanding that it resolves a theoretical question that bears only on itself.

Basilio, whose story the students tell Don Quixote on their way to Camacho's wedding, makes the same point, using the archetypal tale of the love triangle of which Pyramus and Thisbe is the prime literary example. Though a handsome and gifted young man who has loved the beautiful Quiteria since his youth, Basilio appears to have lost his beloved to Camacho, one of the richest men in the village. Their triangle represents the incompatibility of love and marriage that has been a basic theme in Western literature. The separation between heart and head, individual desire and social convenience, signals a breach between consciousness and the unconscious that is the main topic of *Don Quixote* in Part I as much as in Part II. To offer, through Basilio, a means of transforming individual desire into a socially acceptable expression of love and creativity, is to signal a fundamental shift not only in the main character but in the background from which he emerges.

Basilio's success is grounded in trickery, plain and simple. Earlier examples of love becoming the basis for marriage depended on a large dose of coincidence and the intervention of divine will. In Chapter 21 Part II of *Don Quixote*, however, Basilio falls back on his own skill and self-control. Significantly, he is the *inferior* of the two pretenders on a material level. Earlier Cervantine characters in such a position—e.g., Mireno in *La Galatea* and Cardenio in *Don Quixote* Part I—gave up in despair when confronted with the rival's overpowering claim to the lady. Basilio, however, who stages a mock suicide in imitation of the literary examples that formed everyone's expectations of him, turns his disadvantage into an opportunity. When some in the crowd shout, "A miracle, a miracle!" upon seeing him recover so quickly after Quiteria has officially become his wife, he replies, "No miracle, no miracle, but a trick, a trick!" (II, 21, 606) (¡No "milagro, milagro", sino industria, industria! [II, 21, 191]).

Basilio plays the role of the trickster, who, as Jung and others have pointed out, functions as an agent of the divine.[28] The trickster's job is to make a mockery of the powers that appear to control the human consciousness. Basilio shows how little power money has for the person who refuses to accept the dominant value system. Without having recourse to violence, he assumes for himself all the attributes intended for Camacho. Like the student fencers who introduced the episode—which is itself filled with staged events of explicit allegorical significance—

Basilio turns the possibility of real violence into theater. The winner is the one who manipulates the world as a stage and remembers where fiction ends and reality begins.

What Basilio wins is as significant as how he wins it. He harmonizes the masculine and feminine polarities by showing that he is able to operate at a level of consciousness that, while taking reason and sense perception into account, allows him to perceive the hidden truth from which they emerge. Escaping his "given" role he performs through trickery a real miracle, the union of love and marriage.

Camacho's wedding immediately precedes Don Quixote's descent into the cave. Don Quixote, who sided with Basilio and even moved to defend him in case Camacho's supporters wanted to object to his maneuver to win Quiteria, once again reveals by his actions that his instinctive drive in Part II is to bring himself into harmony with the feminine side of his being. The dream in the cave, however, reveals the extent to which he remains divorced from the feminine: both Belerma and Dulcinea appear unattractive, alienated, and in need of something he cannot provide.

Master Peter

Following the cave episode, Don Quixote is once again presented with a demonstration of trickery, in the form of the travelling puppeteer Master Peter. Whereas Basilio mastered a single trick for a specific, limited goal, Master Peter is a professional master of illusion. Don Quixote could safely observe Basilio but is caught by Master Peter, who transforms him, symbolically, into a puppet. This encounter anticipates later adventures in which he will again fall into the hands of people whose only desire is to fool him and therefore marks a turning point, as does the cave episode, in Don Quixote's journey through Part II.[29]

Master Peter represents a considerable advance over his alter ego, Ginés de Pasamonte, the writer and outlaw whom Don Quixote released from chains in Chapter 22 of Part I. Ginés was caught between two mutually contradictory situations that were nonetheless inextricably linked. As outlaw, he survived by sleight of hand and thievery. When the law caught up with him, he turned writer. Outlawry, therefore, created both the opportunity and the subject matter for the writer. But as in all the interpolated stories of Part I, the moment of action was separated from the moment of reflection. Ginés was simply another storyteller caught up in the trap of his own past like Cardenio, Dorotea, Doña Clara, Eugenio, and all the other first-person narrators of Part I.

In Part II, however, where theater replaces narrative as the dominant mode for the secondary stories,[30] Ginés juxtaposes action and reflection, becoming both author and main character in his chosen role as Master Peter. Moving action and reflection onto the same plane transforms the character from victim of his past and passions to master, liberating both body and mind from the chain of misfortunes to which they are bound by their disharmony. When action operates independently from reflection, the mind is forced to puzzle over the apparently incomprehensible and certainly uncontrolled actions of the body. When the two are coordinated, a master self takes charge and can direct events as he chooses. Master Peter reveals the extent to which Don Quixote is out of harmony with himself. With his mind functioning on one level and his emotions on another, the knight of La Mancha makes easy prey for Ginés.

Ginés' advantages over Don Quixote are apparent from the start. He immediately recognizes Don Quixote when the two meet at the inn, while Don Quixote (like the reader) has no idea that the celebrated puppeteer with the patch over his eye is in fact the cross-eyed galley slave of Part I. Exploiting his victim's gullibility, Ginés has Don Quixote pay him for information he already possesses. The trained monkey Ginés uses for the transmission of his supposed divinatory messages symbolizes the lowered state of consciousness on which Ginés' trickery feeds.[31]

Don Quixote initially distrusts Master Peter's talking monkey: "It is clear that this ape speaks in the style of the Devil, and I am astonished that he has not been denounced to the Holy Office, and examined, and had it squeezed out of him by whose virtue he divines" (II, 25, 637) (Está claro que este mono habla con el estilo del diablo; y estoy maravillado cómo no le han acusado al Santo Oficio, y examinádole, y sacádole de cuajo en virtud de quién adivina [II, 25, 230]). But Don Quixote nonetheless allows himself to consult the beast on the question that is uppermost in his mind: whether what he saw in the cave was true or not. Although the answer offers little satisfaction ("the ape says that part of what your worship saw or experienced in the said cave is false and part true" [II, 25, 637] [el mono dice que parte de las cosas que vuesa merced vio, o pasó, en la dicha cueva son falsas, y parte verisímiles (II, 25, 231)]), Don Quixote finds enough in it to quote later in support of his vision. Don Quixote's question as well as his repetition of the monkey's answer show how deeply his intellect is mired in events from the past. By offering his inmost preoccupations to the monkey he declares, in symbol and in fact, that his rational powers have been given over to his body.

As the puppeteer, Ginés further reveals Don Quixote's subjugation to his unconscious. Master Peter's performance starts out comfortably enough; Don Quixote's comments show that he is fully aware that what is happening on the miniature stage is make-believe. Before long, however, Don Quixote loses all perspective on the events taking place on the puppet stage and leaps up to assert his will upon them.[32] This incident, for which Don Quixote's greater sensitivity, intelligence, and patience in Part II leave the reader ill-prepared, perfectly demonstrates the hidden control the dream of knight-errantry continues to exercise over him. Although Don Quixote knows in theory that art perfects nature in the making of a poet, that skill overcomes force in the game of fencing, and that power comes from becoming conscious enough of one's assumed role to manipulate it in the presence of others, his reaction to Master Peter's puppet show reveals that he is too deeply involved in the emotional satisfactions that the chivalric ideal offers him to step away from his role and to see it as others do. Correctly spotting an easy victim, Master Peter deftly pulls the strings of the knightly mannequin that Don Quixote has allowed himself to become.

Based on the Carolingian cycle of tales that produced such characters as Montesinos and Durandarte, Master Peter's puppet show pushes Don Quixote perilously close to the brink of the cave from which he has just emerged. The narrator of the show tells of Melisendra, Charlemagne's beautiful daughter held captive by Moors in Zaragoza. The captive-lady motif, which determined so many of Don Quixote's exploits in Part I and has become Don Quixote's central problem in Part II, is bound to stir up dangerous feelings in him. Zaragoza, where Don Quixote is heading, further links him to the tale, associating him with Gaiferos, Melisendra's husband, who finds himself obliged to go there to free his wife.

The lackadaisical Gaiferos, who hangs around Paris gambling while his wife remains captive to the infidel, recalls Don Quixote's dream image of Durandarte and his indifference to the excitement of the heroic. The staged presentation of Gaiferos being forced from his pleasures at the gaming table by the emperor places before Don Quixote the drama of his own struggle in Part II to keep away from the pleasures of good food and conversation that were offered him at Don Diego's house and Camacho's wedding and that will continue to figure prominently in his adventures at the Duke's palace and Don Antonio's home. Don Quixote, who often confesses to hunger and fatigue in Part II, is obviously attracted to the comforts showered upon him in Part II and is only driven out onto the open road again by the puppet emperor within who insists that the lady must be freed. Gaiferos' reluctance to go to Zaragoza reiterates the image of chivalric decay so evident in Don Quixote's earlier dream vision of Montesinos and Durandarte.

Prodded into action by his irate father-in-law, Gaiferos compensates for his former idleness and unconcern with a great show of bravura, boasting, as Don Quixote often has on similar occasions, that he is "capable of rescuing his wife alone, even though she were imprisoned in the deepest bowels of the earth" (II, 26, 639) (él solo es bastante para sacar a su esposa, si bien estuviese metida en el más hondo centro de la tierra [II, 26, 235]). The reference to the lady imprisoned in the deepest bowels of the earth further cements the connection between the drama in Don Quixote's heart and the one presented on Master Peter's puppet stage, by unmistakably evoking the image of the enchanted Dulcinea.

In Zaragoza, the puppeteer shows Melisendra being forcibly kissed by a lascivious Moor, a scene surely designed to awaken Don Quixote's horror of lust as revealed in his Golden Age speech and his several battles on behalf of "assaulted" ladies in Part I. Gaiferos arrives to rescue his wife from her tower, but in the escape her slip catches on an iron bar and tears. Wasting no time, Gaiferos places her on his horse "astride, like a man" and makes off for Paris. The abuse of the woman, her torn slip, and her manner of riding the horse, all find echoes in Don Quixote's deepest concerns, experiences, and dreams regarding the enchanted Dulcinea.[33] The whole thing, when put together, produces nothing less than the skillful recreation of Don Quixote's inner drama enacted on a puppet stage by a sagacious trickster who has already primed Don Quixote's vanity by calling him an "illustrious reviver of the now-forgotten order of knight-errantry" (II, 25, 634) (resucitador insigne de la ya puesta en olvido andante caballería [II, 25, 228]). Don Quixote would like nothing better than to believe that and allows himself, under the puppeteer's sway, to abandon his lethargy.

Up to the point where Gaiferos rescues Melisendra, Don Quixote behaves very much like a spectator, commenting on the way the show is being presented and recognizing that Master Peter is a puppeteer who produces plays for a profit. But when the boy who narrates the show describes the horde of drum-beating and trumpet-playing Moors who pursue the fleeing French couple, Don Quixote suddenly finds himself on stage, declaring that he is a knight-errant and raining blows down on the heads of the "puppet heathenry." In the light of so many failures it is no wonder that he is near despair when he explains: "I assure you gentlemen that all that has passed here seemed to me a real occurrence. Melisendra was Melisendra; Sir Gaiferos, Sir Gaiferos . . ." (II, 26, 643) (Real y verdaderamente os digo, señores que me oís, que a mí me pareció todo lo que aquí ha pasado que pasaba al pie de la letra: que Melisendra era Melisendra, don Gaiferos don Gaiferos [II, 26, 241]). After the incident of the enchanted boat, which follows this episode with the puppets, Don Quixote will come to the end of his rope and will never again undertake a gratuitous act of knight-errantry.

The fury Don Quixote demonstrated when fighting the puppets, like that of the student who lost the fencing match, is without art or order. His sword winds up cutting through "friend" and "foe" alike, chopping off Emperor Charlemagne's head and leaving Melisendra minus her nose and one eye. Beyond demonstrating the indiscriminate nature of unchecked violence, Don Quixote's outburst also puts him at the mercy of Ginés, who emerges from behind the puppet stage to play the bereft puppeteer for all it's worth. As he did in the lion episode and as he will in the episode of the enchanted boat, Don Quixote winds up paying for his folly. Master Peter goes off the next day with his disguise intact and his pockets full of money, while Don Quixote continues the series of humiliations that constitute the long journey ahead.

Both on and off the puppet stage, Master Peter shows himself to be fully in charge. Only when the puppeteer has left the inn does Cide Hamete step out to unmask Ginés de Pasamonte. In so doing, Cide Hamete carries the image of control one step further, demonstrating that while Ginés may be a master of illusion, he is still a character within a book. The "real" man in charge is Cide Hamete, who exploits his readers' gullibility just as Master Peter had. Cide Hamete tricked the reader about Sansón Carrasco's disguise, Basilio's "suicide," and Ginés de Pasamonte, only explaining the deception involved *after* each event. In Part I, where deceptions were poorly handled and infrequently used, both the primary and secondary stories offered an image of events going out of control, of a world in which no one was in charge. Cide Hamete also showed little awareness of the overall trajectory of his narration. In Part II, however, where deceptions and staged events abound, the narrator makes his control over his material abundantly evident. The high level of skill required to accomplish a trick such as those carried out by Basilio and Ginés is duplicated in the role of the narrator, who makes it clear in Part II that he knows exactly who his main character is and where he is going and that he has chosen to exercise control over his readers' understanding.

As the novel progresses in Part II, deception will become more and more common. From Chapter 30 on, however, the deception will be directed almost entirely against Don Quixote and Sancho, who inspire the Duke and Duchess to unheard-of heights of imagination in their endless creation of illusion. But the desire to deceive is something the Duke and Duchess have a hard time containing. Their servants, Altisidora, and the townspeople at Barataria all begin to join in the fun, and the Duke and Duchess often find themselves trapped in their own illusions. Unlike Master Peter or Basilio, they are not truly in charge. Their control, not based on self-awareness, is easily overturned.

CHAOS AND REVELATION

The episode with Master Peter reveals the degree to which Don Quixote's conscious mind continues to fall victim to the powers of the unconscious. Master Peter, though he exposes the rift in Don Quixote's being, is not for that reason either superior or exemplary. He simply plays the role of trickster and disappears. Functioning only to challenge the imbalances that he finds in Don Quixote, he provokes his victim to find a solution.

After Don Quixote leaves the inn, he encounters the villagers about to engage in combat. The aldermen of one village have learned to bray like donkeys, and the townspeople of the other have insulted them. Like the talking monkey, the aldermen who take pride in imitating donkeys reflect the generally lowered consciousness that is Don Quixote's condition in Part II. Don Quixote's speech to them, however, suggests that such an atmosphere, while inviting chaos, also promotes healing. His words appeal directly to the spirit and anticipate the final revelation in Chapter 73 that will release him from his madness. He says, in part:

> The taking of unjust vengeance—and no vengeance can be just— goes directly against the sacred law we profess, by which we are commanded to do good to our enemies and to love those who hate us, a commandment which may seem rather difficult to obey, but which is only so for those who partake less of God than of the world, and more of the flesh than of the spirit. For Jesus Christ— God and true man—who never lied, nor could, nor can lie, being our law-giver, said that His yoke was gentle and His burden light, and therefore He could not have commanded us to do anything impossible to perform. So, my dear sirs, you are bound to keep the peace by law divine and human. (II, 27, 650)

> (El tomar venganza injusta, que justa no puede haber alguna que lo sea, va derechamente contra la santa ley que profesamos, en la cual se nos manda que hagamos bien a nuestros enemigos y que amemos a los que nos aborrecen; mandamiento que, aunque parece algo dificultoso de cumplir, no lo es sino para aquellos que tienen menos de Dios que del mundo, y más de carne que de espíritu: porque Jesucristo, Dios y hombre verdadero, que nunca mintió, ni pudo ni puede mentir, siendo legislador nuestro dijo que su yugo era suave y su carga liviana; y así, no nos había de mandar cosa que fuese imposible el cumplirla. Así que, mis señores, vuesas mercedes están obligados por leyes divinas y humanas a sosegarse. [II, 27, 249-50])

In the long journey through the palace of the Duke and Duchess, to Barcelona, and back home to La Mancha, Don Quixote shows increased loss of control over his circumstances and at the same time greater patience, humility, and meekness.

As the knightly image undergoes its unrelenting battering, the practice of the beatitudes brings Don Quixote closer and closer to the Alonso Quijano the Good whom his attackers are unwittingly shaping. The revelation in Chapter 73 appears sudden, yet it is being prepared from the very earliest discussions in Part II, when Don Quixote and Sancho speak of their efforts to win the kingdom of God and how best to go about it.

The Feminine

Crucial to the argument of this study is the understanding of the role the feminine plays in releasing Don Quixote from his madness. The feminine is evoked in the images of night, moon, Dulcinea, the quiet house of Don Diego and Doña Cristina, the mirrors, the cave, the deceptions, the women who function autonomously, the servants, the townspeople, the animals, the sea, and death. All of these elements stand in the penumbra of Don Quixote's conscious desire to go out and conquer and be recognized as a hero. And all of these will eventually claim him so entirely that he must finally give up on that goal. When he does, it becomes clear that the chivalric has blocked, not promoted, his good.

Since all of the novel can be read as a reflection of Don Quixote's character, what goes on in the background represents what is occurring in Don Quixote's own unconscious. In Part I, women appeared almost exclusively in the role of nubile creatures disputed over by the men. In Part II, however, women are no longer subject to the desires of men. The change is noticeable from the beginning, when Don Quixote's niece and housemaid engage in a long conversation and enter into schemes designed to bring the wayward gentleman out of his madness. Teresa Panza also takes on a new significance in Part II, arguing furiously with her husband about his adventures with Don Quixote and later entering into his fantasies. In Part I she did not even have a fixed name, much less a voice of her own. Even Dulcinea, through her emissary, shows more activity in Part II, making demands on Don Quixote and riding a horse free, beyond his control. She also appears to him as she is and not as he would have her be.

Later, in the hallucinatory events conjured up by the Duke and Duchess, the Duchess plays the prominent role. She is the first to meet Don Quixote and does most of the talking and planning relating to Don Quixote and Sancho's visit. At the

Duke and Duchess's palace women play a major role in tormenting Don Quixote. The kitchen maids decide to wash Don Quixote's beard and make great sport at his expense. Altisidora, in her mock love for Don Quixote, reverses the traditional order by initiating the courtship, serenading her loved one, and tormenting him for his disdain toward her. Doña Rodríguez approaches Don Quixote on her daughter's behalf, and when her gossiping with the knight is discovered, she and Don Quixote are beaten, not by muleteers and police, as in Part I, but by women. The elaborate story of the Countess Trifaldí deals with her handmaids' participation in facilitating the young lady's encounters with her lover. In punishment for their complicity, all her handmaids are given beards, a symbolic acknowledgement of the masculine role the women in general have assumed in the absence of strong male characters in Part II. Even Teresa Panza's daughter Sanchica gains prominence in Part II, in contrast to her son, who was alluded to as a member of Sancho's family, but who never appears.

On Sancho's island women are shown to be strong, active, and curious. One of Sancho's first tasks is to judge the story of a woman who claimed to have been raped. Sancho so handles the case that the woman herself demonstrates her power over the man who was supposed to have assaulted her, thus proving not only her superior strength but her equally potent sexual desires. In another case on the island Sancho discovers a girl dressed as a man. She wears the disguise because her father has not allowed her out of the house. Burning with curiosity to experience the world for herself for once, rather than vicariously through her brother, she persuades him to exchange clothes with her for a night so that she can get out.

When Don Quixote and Sancho leave the Duke's palace, they encounter still more ladies engaged in fantasy or in behavior not directed toward their survival. These are the group of young ladies who have read *Don Quixote* and are enacting the life of the shepherdess in their false Arcadia. When Don Quixote and Sancho are subsequently captured by Roque Guinart, they have a chance to hear the story of Claudia Jerónima, who comes to the Catalan bandit for help. Claudia, suspecting her lover's infidelity, has gotten her vengeance by stabbing him to death. In Barcelona Don Quixote and Sancho witness another love story in which a woman takes on the active role, but this one has a happy ending. Ana Fénix first appears dressed as a man and is about to be killed as a Turkish soldier. Her lover, Don Gregorio, on the other hand, remains in Algeria in a harem, disguised as a woman. Ana resolves to free him by sailing to Barcelona and recovering a family fortune left in Spain when her Morisco family was forced to leave. This story makes an interesting parallel to the Captive's tale in Part I and again shows how the role once occupied by a man has been assumed by a woman. Also in Barcelona, it is women who dance with Don Quixote until he is so exhausted that he must be carried to his room. On Don Quixote's final journey home, Altisidora, dressed as a dead woman, further torments Don Quixote. Women are far more prominent, active, and efficacious in Part II than they were in Part I.[34]

Sancho also becomes more autonomous in Part II. Not only does he create the most important deception in the work, but he shows from the beginning a desire for adventure that surpasses that of his master. Representing Don Quixote's instinctual self, he both keeps his "master" and takes on, though unwillingly, the burden of freeing the enchanted Dulcinea. Sancho's Barataria experience repeats, in miniature, the journey his master is taking, and his development culminates in Chapter 60 when he becomes angered by Don Quixote's insistence that he beat himself to free Dulcinea, forces Don Quixote to the ground, and threatens to beat him up if he doesn't leave him alone. This startlingly explosive episode, about which very little is generally said, reveals the truly fragile position of Don Quixote's disassociated ego and represents the culmination of the assertion of the body over the head, a theme that began in the opening search for Dulcinea.[35]

The World of the Animals

Far less potentially disruptive but of equal significance, are the attacks Don Quixote undergoes from the animal world, which are but another manifestation of suppressed materiality invading a too limited consciousness. Don Quixote sees Master Peter's monkey as an expression of the Devil, the Devil being the inheritor of all that the rational mind rejects. The monkey represents a very early stage in the lowering of consciousness, however, and offers not wholesale destruction but rather a parody of the disembodied intellect. It indicates a reversal of order, making the man the servant of the beast, the mouthpiece for an intelligence incapable of speech. The episode of the braying aldermen that both precedes and follows the Master Peter story depicts a similar degeneration of the independent intellect, presenting symbols of order and authority who pride themselves on their ability to imitate donkeys. Here the animal does not even pretend to collaborate with the intellect but inspires the language-making beast to reduce its capabilities to the mere imitation of sound.

In the rarefied air of the Duke's palace and the false Arcadia, where all effort to integrate ego and nature is abandoned, the beasts are both more prominent and more dangerous. The wild boar, though pursued for sport, inspires terror. Cats, through Altisidora's malevolence, claw Don Quixote's face. Bulls later trample Don Quixote as he guards the false Arcadia. While the boar and the cats at least act out of self-defense, the bulls in Chapter 58 reveal neither discrimination nor intention, moving by herd instinct alone. The final phase in the beasts' undermining of the intellect occurs in Chapter 68 when Don Quixote is run over by pigs. Having none of the power and vitality traditionally associated with the bull and known mostly for their voracious and indiscriminate appetite, the pigs represent the final phase of Don Quixote's undoing.

In the next chapter, Sancho catches a rabbit whom hunters have been pursuing. In the hunters' failure, Don Quixote sees his own and thus is able, for the first time, to remove himself from the endless game of the hunter and the hunted that represents his and the dominant social attitude toward the relation between men and women.[36] This scene, the final stage on the return home, continues the release of the captive image of the feminine and the use of a nonrational method of perception. Taken together these events sum up what has been explored here—the circular nature of the journey; the enlightened return to the center; the emergence of the feminine as an independent force; and the release of illusion that allows the hero finally to understand the truth of his situation.

In a process that repeats the symbolic acts in the initial episodes of Part II, Don Quixote has in fact relaxed his hold on each of the various levels of ego construction created so systematically in Chapter 1 of Part I. In the final chapters of Part II, Sansón

Carrasco actually divests Don Quixote of the sword and armor that are his outermost image, pigs trample Don Quixote and Rocinante, Don Quixote trades in his chivalric name for a pastoral one, and Altisidora, as the lady, stages a mock death and descent into hell in which all vestiges of the chivalric construct and the literary world from which it grew are broken down.[37] If in the first chapters of Part II the structure created in Part I was threatened from the bottom up, it was nonetheless preserved by the false perpetuation of Don Quixote's persona as knight-errant. At the end of Part II, however, the structure finally collapses. This time the erosion from within is matched by destruction from without. Don Quixote must face the world of matter bereft of his defenses. By the time he enters his house of origin he possesses nothing of his dream. Thus cleansed of ego constructs, he is finally open to revelation and dies redeemed, restored to his sanity and to his sense of participation in a natural cosmic order that transcends his limited ego-consciousness.

The important point in the undoing of the hero described in Part II is that Don Quixote becomes exemplary not because he insists on the chivalric identity he has created but because he does not resist the chaos that his role eventually stirs up. By deepening his own virtues even as he suffers his dismantlement as Don Quixote, he allows the unconscious elements he tried originally to deny to rise up and conquer him. And when he finally succumbs, he awakens only to find that he has triumphed.

CHAPTER FIVE

The *Persiles*

PRELIMINARY REMARKS

The *Persiles* is a difficult book to discuss in an orderly fashion. On one level it follows a clear linear pattern, tracing the fortunes of the two main characters as they travel from northern lands of ice and snow through rough seas to Portugal, Spain, and France on their way to Rome. The two characters, however, are not really two but four, and everything they do has a double meaning. Ostensibly the pair are a brother and sister, called Periandro and Auristela, on a pilgrimage to Rome. Very early in the work it becomes clear, however, that Periandro is not really a poor wandering pilgrim—or at least that he is not only that. Beneath the tatters of his pilgrim's garb stands a king's son, Persiles, who is in love with—not brother to—Sigismunda, the young woman disguised as Auristela with whom he travels. Daughter of Queen Eusebia of Frislandia, Sigismunda is heir to a kingdom, which, like Persiles', is at war.

Periandro and Auristela, in addition to each having a dual identity, have a dual goal. As pilgrims, the two seek instruction and illumination in the faith. They respond to the call of the Heavenly City in its jubilee year from the dark and cold of their war-torn homelands, undergoing tremendous hardship to reach their destination. But hero and heroine also have another motive for their journey. As disguised lovers, they look to Rome as a refuge, for Persiles loves the same woman his older brother Magsimino wants to marry. Magsimino, who is off at war, knows Sigismunda only from her portrait. Since Persiles, who has remained at home, is growing ill from love, his mother, Queen Eustoquia, counsels him to leave for Rome with Sigismunda on a pilgrimage.

Throughout the work the young couple experience conflict

from the mixed motives for their journey: as pilgrims, Periandro and Auristela make a noble image of devotion to God; as runaway lovers, the two appear engaged in subterfuge and concerned only with their personal desires. On their way toward Rome, they encounter reflections of their higher and lower selves, between which they struggle for their very survival.

Truly to understand the *Persiles* one must perceive two planes of action simultaneously in play throughout the work. On one plane, a young couple avoids a threatened interdiction to their marriage by escaping to Rome. On another plane, the novel describes the intricate and dangerous process by which the self is transformed

The *Persiles*, in other words, has allegorical as well as novelistic dimensions.[1] The allegory, however, is a subtle one. Cervantes has so blended the two planes on which he is working that the reader can never safely neglect one for the sake of the other. Periandro is both a character in his own right and, as his name suggests, an image of every man.[2] Both on the material and on the psychological plane he is credible, and yet he is also a bona fide hero. Cervantes takes care not to give his characters supernatural powers, just as he prevents them from being totally swallowed up in the subhuman. Suspended between heaven and hell, between their godlike and their bestial inclinations, the hero and heroine of the *Persiles* undergo for every reader the series of confusions and trials that are the lot of all humankind, demonstrating how their apparent failure and constant fear can be transformed into fulfillment.

The *Persiles* is no chivalric romance or tale of idyllic love, and Cervantes does not minimize the difficulties his characters face. Periandro and Auristela's path is cluttered with examples of failure. Both suffer loss of heart at one time or another. They are often pushed to the limits of their faith and are also asked, on occasion, to misrepresent themselves or their intentions for the sake of their survival. They combine, as no other Cervantine heroes have, the deceptive skills of a Ginés de Pasamonte or a Basilio with the search for the highest in themselves of the Don Quixote of Part II. In the *Persiles*, the trickster is one with the hero, and his artistry is oriented not toward any secondary goal but toward life itself.[3]

It should not be surprising that Cervantes all but abandoned his ironic voice in his last work, for the *Persiles*, unlike *Don*

Quixote, celebrates the achievement of harmony not only among the characters but between character and narrator, dream and reality, fiction and truth. If the main thesis of this study is correct—if an evolution can be discerned in the sequence of works Cervantes produced—Cervantes would no more be able to resurrect the scoffing voice of Cide Hamete than the false heroics of Don Quixote. The *Persiles* has been called a "potboiler," although the opposite is true.[4] The *Persiles* was possible because Cervantes did not simply turn out works according to a formula. His new hero, who blends the passivity and devotion of an Elicio with the aggression and determination of Don Quixote, cooperates with and complements his narrator. Narrator and hero interact with such accord that Periandro takes over the narrative for many chapters in Book II, filling in information from his past that the narrator, with his in medias res technique, has omitted.[5]

Freed from Cide Hamete's fascination with the negative qualities of his character, the narrator of the *Persiles* intervenes frequently to offer general commentary on life and the work. He speaks about jealousy, virtue, honor, love, disappointment, anger, vengeance, and God's will, as Don Quixote and Cide Hamete both did to some degree in Part II of *Don Quixote.* The narrator's frequent commentary contributes to the interplay of time and timelessness that is a basic element in the structure of the work, Persiles' exemplarity providing the material example of the truths the narrator is wont to discuss in the abstract.[6]

The temporal structure of the *Persiles* perfectly complements the characters' dual roles and their relation to the narrator. Following neo-Aristotelian precept and the model of Heliodorus, Cervantes begins the *Persiles* in the middle of the action.[7] The reader, like the main character, finds himself on page one in the thick of a totally confusing situation. Not until halfway through the book does it become clear that the work's beginning coincides with the midpoint in the heroes' journey from Thule to Rome. And only on the very last pages of the work do the events that prompted the heroes' journey emerge. The story, then, works backwards as the characters advance forward, so that in the end, what is truly revealed is the beginning. It should not be surprising that a book whose contents are occupied—psychologically, symbolically, metaphorically, and theologically—with the theme of rebirth would be so structured.

Unlike his earlier long works of fiction, Cervantes' *Persiles* ends both happily and conclusively, bringing all the planes and doubles together without destroying their particularity. It represents a perfect blending of the secular with the religious, since Persiles and Sigismunda want both to immerse themselves in the mysteries of the church and to get married in Rome. The two goals are distinct and yet mutually dependent, as an examination of Book IV will show, for each goal alone fails to bring fulfillment. Only when the religious lessons have been learned and the couple agrees to marry does everything come together.[8] The main characters' marriage also represents the miraculous union of two distinct beings. Periandro and Auristela's long temporal journey restores them to their true selves. They marry not as pilgrims in disguise but as king and queen, recovering at the end their heritage as heirs to kingdoms in peace.

The marriage of Persiles and Sigismunda at the end of the *Persiles* corresponds to the alchemical symbol of the royal pair, the signal of the highest stage of development of the self, whose natural prelude is the stage of the brother-sister pair.[9] The perfect consonance between the orthodox and the imagery of the occult further reveals the power of the insight that informs Cervantes' last work.

It is no wonder that Cervantes considered the *Persiles* his masterpiece. The work not only succeeds from a structural, psychological, and religious point of view but also fulfills the neo-Aristotelian prescription for a modern prose epic. Since the work of W. C. Atkinson, E. C. Riley, and Alban Forcione, students of Cervantes have been aware of the importance of neo-Aristotelian literary theory in the work of Cervantes. Not for nothing did Cervantes boast that the *Persiles* could compete with Heliodorus, whose works the neo-Aristotelians held up as classical models for the prose epic.[10] As early as *Don Quixote* Part I Cervantes dreamed of writing such a piece of fiction as the neo-Aristotelians proposed: a work, as the Canon of Toledo described it in Chapter 47, that would offer a wide variety of actions within the trajectory of a single, coherent plot; one that would excite a sense of the marvelous without awakening the skepticism of an incredulous intellect; one, in short, that would wed the flights of the spirit with the imperfections of a matter-laden world.

To know of such a theory, even to approve of it and to want

to execute it, is one thing. To bring it off is something else altogether. Cervantes' final work culminates the effort of a lifetime and was made possible only by successive attempts to reconcile the opposites in a world whose every expression—personal, political, literary, and even religious—testified to their inevitable disunion. In the more detailed study to follow, the four books that make up the *Persiles* will be examined in order. Although it will not be possible to study every element of this rich and complex work, it can be shown how each of the four books marks the growth of the main characters, at the same time that it moves them another step forward in their journey to Rome. At each level the characters encounter the same problems: temptations of the flesh, temptations of the spirit, jealousy, violence, and treachery. As they advance toward Rome, their trials become less and less overwhelming, signalling an increase in their own powers and a corresponding weakening of the powers of others over them.

BOOK 1

The Symbology of Rebirth and Union

The *Persiles* begins with a scene rich in the imagery of rebirth. The book opens as the still-unnamed character, Periandro, is hauled into the light of day from a cave into which he had been thrown two days earlier, along with many other captives. This new hero is surrounded by unfamiliar sights and voices, helpless and immobilized as he comes forth from the bowels of the earth. The natural world into which he is born is one prepared to condemn him to death: barbarian arrows are aimed at him from the moment he steps into the light; the sea nearly drowns him; and fire threatens to consume him. But Periandro is more than mere natural man. He comes out of the cave looking skyward and giving thanks. His radiant beauty, which the barbarians can perceive even beneath the grime of his face, saves him from the instant death that was to be his destiny.

Periandro's attitude clearly establishes, on the first page of the work, the vertical axis—from hell to heaven, from death to rebirth—that is an essential component of the story.[11] The events that occur along the horizontal axis will all acquire, because of the vertical dimension, a symbolic overlay that accompanies them along the story line. The tumultuous experiences suffered by the main character seem less overwhelming as a result.

Periandro survives a storm at sea that drowns his captors to be rescued by Arnaldo, Prince of Denmark. Arnaldo is the first of a series of challengers who will test Periandro's ability to remain fixed on his goal and to avoid the world of conflict that his true rival, Magsimino, represents. Arnaldo captains a pirate's ship and sails about in search of his beloved, Auristela. For most of Books I and II and a large part of Book IV, Arnaldo accompanies the hero and heroine in their travels without realizing that Periandro is also in love with Auristela until the end.

On Arnaldo's ship Periandro learns that Auristela may be on the Barbarous Island from which he has just escaped. In order to find out, Arnaldo plans to sell Auristela's maid Taurisa to the barbarians. Periandro offers to go in Taurisa's place, however, saying that Auristela is his sister. Arnaldo, who shows no inclination to doubt Periandro's word, agrees, and soon Periandro is back on the island, this time dressed as a beautiful woman.

On the island Periandro finds Auristela in men's clothing about to be executed by the natives. When Periandro and Auristela first meet, therefore, in the work that will be devoted to their adventures and ultimate marriage, they embrace, each one in the costume of the other. The meeting between the lovers is as important symbolically as was the opening scene where Periandro was raised up into life. Periandro and Auristela's embrace not only prefigures the union they have set out to achieve but reveals how necessary to that union experience in the role of the opposite sex will be.[12]

In *La Galatea* women remained by and large separated from men, though both were shown to be similarly afflicted by weakness and limitation. Elicio, who was not even aware of his rivalry with Erastro, could not begin to comprehend the deeper realms of the psyche in which the feminine resides. In *Don Quixote* Part I the hero is thoroughly engaged in fending off the rival, inventing giants and abductors whom he attacks in defense of his imaginary lady. In Part II, having largely tamed his impulse to destroy the masculine challenger, Don Quixote comes face to face with the feminine, not as he would like to have her, but as she insists on appearing to his resisting consciousness. To compensate for the lovely lady whom his one-sided intellect has established, the feminine he meets in Part II is rough, ugly, and coarse.

Periandro represents another stage in the evolution of the hero that Cervantes' works trace. Fully conscious of the power and danger of the rival, who now appears not as an inferior or an equal but as an older brother or a prince, Periandro takes charge of his situation by avoiding conflict, like Basilio in Part II of *Don Quixote,* without relinquishing his claims to his loved one. Having renounced force as a means of attaining his goal, Periandro adopts a consciousness traditionally associated with the feminine.[13] This new posture for the male hero is represented symbolically by the lady as companion and by Periandro's wearing women's clothes. Periandro, unlike Don Quixote or Elicio, has befriended the feminine, who responds by loving him as he loves her. For the first time in the long works of Cervantes, the hero is presented with a female counterpart with whom he travels in harmony.[14]

The reciprocity between masculine and feminine is shown in the initial encounter between hero and heroine in Chapter 4 of Book I. Auristela dresses as a man to show that she is loyal, even to death, to her vow to remain a virgin until she reaches Rome with Periandro. Periandro dresses as a woman to prove his willingness to find Auristela at all costs. The change to the opposite-sex role is both an expression of devotion and a sign that each is able to cross the barrier separating the masculine from the feminine.

Although the couple symbolically achieves union and rebirth on the opening pages of Book I, theirs is still a *history* that must unfold in time. Their travails represent a continuous battle with their lesser selves, a constant temptation to follow a path that will end the discomforts of their suspension, landing them solidly—or so it would seem—in heaven, or even, for the apparent certainty of it, in hell. As the work develops, both Periandro and Auristela will seem to yield, at one time or another, to the temptations they repeatedly encounter.

In the *Persiles* one can easily trace the psychological process that leads from darkness and confusion to fulfillment, for everything in the work contributes to the expression of that process. In Book I, the "bringing to life" of the main characters from the mouth of the cave that held them captive illustrates, on the vertical axis, their participation in the cycle of rebirths that mark their journey to God and to each other.[15] On the horizontal axis, their "birth" on the opening pages symbolizes their psychological infancy. Throughout Book I their vulnerability will make them subject again and again to attacks that nearly take their lives. It is grace, explicitly alluded to, that saves them every time.

The infantile nature of Periandro and Auristela in Book I is apparent not only in their confusion, disorientation, and vulnerability but in the character of their adversaries. The barbarians into whose hands they have fallen reveal the primitive state of consciousness at which they themselves exist. Though they are rich in material possessions, like Periandro and Auristela, the barbarians are motivated by a desire not for gold but for power. A tribal shaman has told them that a child of theirs could become ruler of the world. To produce such power, the barbarians need to mate one of their men with the most beautiful foreign woman their gold and diamonds can buy. The man chosen to father the future king of the world should be able to consume a powder made from the hearts of murdered foreign men without showing any signs of disgust.[16]

Buried in the myth of power that inspires the barbarians' behavior is the wild fantasy of the *segundón*, the less-privileged younger brother who would take the "foreign" woman by force and through her inherit the world. The fantasy, as Auristela and Periandro's experience shows, is both dangerous and destructive, based as it is on a totally alienated image of the feminine other through whom the power would be acquired. The fantasy masks, furthermore, a complete lack of control over the passions. It is indulgence, pure and simple, and arises from a sense of impotence. The savages themselves demonstrate the hopelessness of the fantasy. When confronted with the beauty of Periandro and Auristela, they begin squabbling; many hope to have one of the two for themselves. Their fighting quickly escalates, drawing others into the conflict, and ends with the conflagration of the island. Periandro, Auristela, Auristela's nursemaid Cloelia, and a translator barely escape with their lives. Fire will also destroy those who threaten Auristela and Periandro in Books II and III. It represents the cataclysmic destruction that occurs when the passions burn out of control, as well as the cleansing that permits successive rebirths.[17]

The Interpolated Tales

A stranger appears to Periandro and Auristela as they stand engulfed in the flames. Explicitly identified as an agent of grace, the savior is a half-barbarian, half-Spanish young man named Antonio. Antonio leads the captives to a cave where he lives with his sister Constanza and their parents, Antonio and Ricla. There Periandro and Auristela are restored to safety, hear the first of three interpolated tales that will give insight into their destiny, and learn of the temptations that will plague them on their journey.

Antonio the father tells the travellers a story of inflated honor and quick temper. Having been exiled from Spain for his untamed anger, Antonio got into further trouble while at sea, with the result that his shipmates cast him overboard in a small raft. After drifting several weeks at the mercy of the elements and entrusting his fate entirely to God, he ran aground, nearly dead, on the shore of the Barbarous Island, where Ricla found and cared for him. With Ricla, Antonio started his life anew. They have two children whom Antonio has instructed in Spanish and the Catholic faith.

Antonio and Ricla, in their faith and natural prosperity, resemble Adam and Eve. Their adolescent children, an actual brother-sister pair, represent the image that Auristela and Periandro are trying to emulate. Symbolizing the fruits of the original wedding of spirit and matter, Antonio and Constanza are apt companions for Auristela and Periandro and will travel with the two, becoming pilgrims themselves on their journey to Rome.

Antonio and Ricla urge the group to leave the still-smoldering island. Antonio wants to return home to Spain to make peace with his former enemies and to see his parents. They flag down a trading ship carrying other escapees from the island. Though they will still suffer cold and the vicissitudes of a tempestuous sea, Periandro and Auristela's journey away from the barbarians marks a step toward a higher level of control. No longer captives, they find themselves instead in the company of repentant Christians, all of whom have a story of sin and redemption to tell.

The second of the interpolated tales in Book I comes from an Italian dancing master named Rutilio. Like Antonio, Rutilio had landed, near death, on the Barbarous Island. He spent many years there dressed in animal skins and pretending to be a deaf-mute. In his native Sienna he had fallen in love with a wealthy young pupil. Though her family had already promised her to a young man of higher social standing, she ran off with Rutilio to Rome. The police intervened and threw Rutilio in jail where a witch offered to arrange his escape. Demanding that he renounce his faith and marry her in exchange for his freedom, the witch transported him by magic to Norway where she herself was transformed into a she-wolf. Terrified of the wolf in the dark and cold of the strange country, Rutilio killed the witch. Speaking perfect Italian, a rescuer, not unlike the young Antonio, appeared shortly thereafter. This man, the son of an Italian man and a native Norwegian woman, took him home and taught him a trade. Later, at sea, a shipwreck drove him to the shores of the Barbarous Island.

Rutilio's story sets the stage for one of the principal struggles in the work—the desire for a young lady that will tempt Periandro and a host of rivals throughout the journey. It also focuses on an aspect of Periandro's prehistory, exaggerating, in dream fashion, his inferior status as younger brother and the baser intentions of his flight with Sigismunda to Rome.

Rutilio remains with the pilgrims during the first two books of the *Persiles* and seeks throughout to master the desires that caused him so much trouble. It is not accidental that he reappears in Rome in Book IV, just when Periandro is undergoing his final test before marrying Auristela, for he represents a significant facet of Periandro's journey, as the analysis will show.

A third story is told by a Portuguese nobleman, Manuel Sosa de Cotinio, whom the pilgrims find adrift in a small boat. If Rutilio's error was undervaluing the lady by reducing her to an object of lust, Manuel's problem was deifying the young woman he loved. So exalted was Leonora in Manuel's imagination that he dared not even approach her. When he met her at the church on the day of their arranged marriage, he fell to his knees before her, exclaiming that he could never be worthy of one so beautiful as she, even if he were emperor of the whole world.

Trapped in the belief that no man was her equal, Leonora declared on her wedding day that she had decided to become not Manuel's wife but the bride of Christ. Hearing that, Manuel ran from the church in despair, cast himself into the sea, and died a few weeks later, shortly after telling his story to Periandro and Auristela. The pilgrims discover in Book III that Leonora also died a few days after learning of Manuel's death.

Periandro and Auristela are offered, in the three interpolated stories, three images of male-female relationships. Only Antonio and Ricla's story ends in union and prosperity. The other two show how the young woman degenerates into a witch and she-wolf when pursued only for her beauty and how her inaccessibility leads to madness and death when she is deified. Imbalances of matter or of spirit, the stories seem to say, promote disharmony.[18]

Separation and Near Death

In Book I the characters are hard-pressed literally to keep their heads above water. At the beginning of the book, Periandro nearly drowns; at the end, the ship Auristela is on sinks. The oceans in which they drift typify their submission to the powers of the unconscious, just as the sparse and far-flung islands on which they land from time to time stand for their precarious achievements of conscious control.

Some advances, however, are clearly made in the watery world of Book I. The island of Golandia, where the pilgrims land in Chapter 11, has a port and an inn accommodating travellers from such recognizable places as Denmark and the British Isles. Through the characters the pilgrims meet there—Mauricio, Transila, Ladislao, Rosamunda, Clodio, and Arnaldo—Cervantes introduces a theme that will become much more important in Books II and III: individual response to social corruption. In the first ten chapters of Book I, all the attention was focused on personal weaknesses. In Chapter 11, travellers from Britain show the effects of society on the self.

Mauricio, astrologer and guide for the travellers, is a covert Catholic living in Protestant Britain. When his daughter Transila is to marry Ladislao, he is forced to come face to face with the jus primae noctis custom that he abhors but dares not combat.[19] Transila, seeing her father's and fiancé's cowardice, takes her defense in her own hands and escapes her homeland by ship.[20] Rosamunda and Clodio, who disembark from the same ship that carried Mauricio and Ladislao, arrive chained to one another. Rosamunda, former mistress of kings, represents female attractiveness exploited for the sake of power. Clodio, her perfect male counterpart, has gained control over others in the past through gossip and slander. Thriving on the corruption that Rosamunda's actions fostered, Clodio earned his living by spreading stories of evil doings.

Through the new secondary characters, Periandro and Auristela once again meet images of themselves. By behaving as a man, Transila has defended her honor just as Auristela did, though in a different way, on the Barbarous Island. Her husband-to-be, Ladislao, follows her. But their image of noble behavior is counteracted by Clodio and Rosamunda, who spend their time hurling invective at one another for excesses of which both are guilty.

Arnaldo also catches up with the pilgrims once again on Golandia. As the handsome young prince in open pursuit of Auristela, Arnaldo is Periandro's double and rival. He represents the desires that Periandro cannot yet express. But Periandro's journey represents a growth process. Learning to spiritualize his desires gives Periandro a depth that Arnaldo lacks. Arnaldo's superficiality makes him easy to fool. He succumbs to Clodio and Rosamunda's appeals for release, for example, and never sees through Periandro's disguise as Auristela's brother. Although he is a fundamentally good character whose story has a happy end, Arnaldo represents natural man, who is neither engulfed in evil as Clodio and Rosamunda are, nor drawn to a higher plane of development as Auristela and Periandro are. His inadequacy is revealed by his quick degeneration from prince into pirate when seized with desire. The young woman traveling with him, Auristela's former companion Taurisa, becomes so ill in his company that Arnaldo is forced to give her to some other pirates, in whose care she dies. Arnaldo's symbolic relation to the feminine reveals the inadequacies that will finally make him the loser in his pursuit of Auristela. Taurisa represents the neglected inferior creature who is left to die while a more beautiful and inaccessible being is sought after. She is the rejected fourth whose death dooms the lover's aspirations to failure.

Arnaldo's weakness is also symbolized by his relationship to the sailors who make his ship function. Mauricio, the astrologer, predicts that treachery on board ship will bring about catastrophe for the travellers, all of whom are in Arnaldo's ship at this point. Just as Mauricio foresaw, the ship breaks in two and sinks, the result of a conspiracy by two of Arnaldo's sailors. The sailors hoped to save only Auristela and Transila, whom they could then enjoy for themselves. The plan, of course, does not work. Both sailors die, while the travellers collect in two lifeboats and float to safety.

The disruptive desires brought to the surface by two sailors conspiring in secret in the hull of Arnaldo's ship clearly illustrate the nature of Periandro's "journey." Mauricio, who predicted the catastrophe, also counselled against trying to avoid it, saying, "it will be better for us to meet this danger, since it does not affect our lives, than to wait for some other which may prove more fatal" (mejor es arrojarnos en las manos deste peligro, pues no llega a quitar la vida, que no intentar otro camino que nos lleve a perderla [I, 18, 130]). The implication is that the hidden passions, however dangerous, must be brought into the light of day. The whole tempestuous journey is a metaphor for just such a lowering of consciousness through which the noxious powers can be exposed and released.

As in *La Galatea*, the attention in Book I shifts to the women at some point. After the shipwreck, the company of travellers splits into two groups. The remainder of Book I focuses on the lifeboat carrying, in addition to all the women, the aged astrologer Mauricio and the younger Antonio. This group lands on a snowy island that offers neither shelter nor food. There Auristela witnesses the death of two of the most negative expressions of the feminine. Rosamunda, who tries to seduce Antonio, commits suicide when he violently rebuffs her. Taurisa, who had been Auristela's handmaiden on Arnaldo's ship and who withered to nothing in his care, arrives on the island at death's door borne by two pirates who kill each other doing battle over her. The pirates who fight for possession of Taurisa demonstrate what could happen should Auristela lose her power to influence Periandro: the result would be a paling of the feminine in him and a return to the combative, aggressive mode in which struggle between men takes on more importance than alliance with the feminine.

To ensure Periandro's devotion, Auristela must not fall into the trap that Rosamunda represents either—using her capacity to inflame passion to manipulate men. The deaths of these two characterizations of the feminine on the barren island express both the state of Auristela's soul at this perilous moment in her journey and her rejection of the two methods by which she might be tempted to resolve her problems.

If Book I began with an exploration of Periandro's problems, it ends with a consideration of Auristela's. To leave the barren island, she boards a ship on which she learns that she too has a rival. She discovers that during the two years of separation, while she was in Arnaldo's hands, Periandro lived on an island where he was loved by a woman called Sinforosa. Auristela's jealousy of Sinforosa nearly overwhelms her, and literally provokes yet another storm at sea. Cervantes' handling of the elements makes it clear that they are to be undestood as manifestations of psychological upheavals.[21] In Book II, which begins with Auristela and her companions' near death on the very island where Sinforosa lives, the action will focus directly on the problem of jealousy as it afflicts both hero and heroine.

BOOK II

Amplification of the Theme of Jealousy

Like Periandro's smaller ship at the beginning of Book I, the ship Auristela is on sinks at the beginning of Book II. Providence, however, again does its work: "merciful Heaven, which helps the unfortunate, ordered that the vessel be cast ashore" (los piadosos cielos, que de muy atrás toman la corriente de remediar nuestras desventuras, ordenaron que la nave, . . . a la orilla del mar [diese] en una playa [II, 2, 162]).[22] The resurrected passengers find themselves alive on the same populated and civilized island about which Auristela had heard at the end of Book I. The same desires for dominance and possession that the barbarians revealed in Book I are expressed in Book II through more socially advanced characters who are nonetheless still dangerous. The increased level of social organization represented in Book II, combined with the more secure habitat that island offers the pilgrims, suggests that they have advanced to a higher level of consciousness.

Book II, when stripped of the polite veneer of good intentions the hosts show toward their guests, is surprisingly similar to

Book I. In both, the hero and heroine independently land on an island whose most powerful inhabitants desire to possess them. Both times the hosts' desires result in burning the island and forcing the heroes to seek escape. The first two books of the *Persiles* are designed to highlight the struggle both main characters experience when faced with the image of their desires. Each confronts the possibility of open conflict with the rival, and each is saved by adopting an apparently pliant attitude toward those who threaten them.

In Book I Periandro had to master his jealousy of Arnaldo. In Book II Auristela meets a rival who, like Arnaldo, is free to express her desire openly. Sinforosa, daughter of the island's ruler King Policarpo, is in love with Periandro and does not hesitate to confide to Auristela that because of his previous stay on the island she likes, loves, and adores him ([le] amo, quiero bien, adoro [II, 3, 169]). Sinforosa's guileless expression of love hits Auristela when she is especially vulnerable. Like Periandro when he encountered his rival in Book I, Auristela has recovered from almost drowning. Sinforosa voices feelings that Auristela dares not express, just as Arnaldo did for Periandro in Book I.

The identity rival and lover share could not be clearer, for Periandro as much as for Auristela.[23] Arnaldo and Sinforosa, like Persiles and Sigismunda, are prince and princess in their respective realms. Like Sigismunda, Sinforosa has a younger sister. The difference, one that the narrator insists upon, is that the kingdom to which Sinforosa is heiress depends on the goodwill of the populace for its continuation. At the allegorical level of the work, the populace represents the unconscious, and the island's method of governance reveals that King Policarpo is subject to the power of the unconscious as the true king should not be. Sinforosa, then, is an unstable image of Auristela, a shadow figure over which she must assert her control.

Though Auristela is ill and filled with consternation over Sinforosa, she is able to see herself in the other: "Her [rival's] fault," she reasoned, "was the same as her own, her wishes the same. She could not condemn the princess without finding herself guilty of the same crime" (su culpa era la suya, sus pensamientos los mismos que ella tenía, su intención la que ella traía desatinada. Finalmente, no podía culparla, sin que ella primero no quedase convencida del mismo delito [II, 3, 173]). Auristela agrees to speak to Periandro on Sinforosa's behalf.

The exercise has the positive effect of forcing her to express her love for Periandro, for Auristela's problem, as Book IV will make clear, is her unconscious resistance to Periandro.[24]

Like all the tests the main characters undergo, that involving Auristela's jealousy is fraught with two potential errors. On the one hand, she could oppose the rival rather than try to understand her. On the other, she could give in to the rival entirely. When she first approaches Periandro as Sinforosa's emissary, Auristela appears to have relinquished all claim to him. She suggests that Periandro remain on the island and marry Sinforosa while she continues the journey to Rome alone, telling him:

> Here they are offering you abundant wealth, not in promises but in fact, and a noble and extremely beautiful woman. . . . We are far from our home, you hounded by your brother, I, by my bad luck. Our road to Rome becomes longer and more difficult the harder we try. My intentions have not altered, but they are trembling, and I would not want death to catch me among these fears and dangers. For that reason I plan to end my life in religion, and I would like you to end yours in a comfortable station.
>
> (Aquí se te ofrecen riquezas en abundancia, no en promesas, sino en verdad, y mujer noble y hermosísima en todo extremo. . . . Fuera estamos de nuestra patria, tú perseguido de tu hermano, y yo de mi corta suerte. Nuestro camino a Roma cuanto más le procuramos, más se dificulta y alarga. Mi intención no se muda, pero tiembla, y no querría que entre temores y peligros me saltase la muerte, y así pienso acabar la vida en religión, y querría que tú la acabases en buen estado. [II, 4, 176–77])

The temptation to settle for the temporary conveniences that Policarpo's island represents also assails Periandro indirectly through the character of King Policarpo, who wants to marry Auristela at any cost. What Policarpo and Sinforosa offer the travel-weary couple is wealth and power. But their wealth and power belong to "the people"; they are not theirs in fact. Were Periandro and Auristela to succumb to the temptations that Policarpo's island represents, they not only would be subject to but would perhaps even provoke popular upheaval. Policarpo says, "I care nothing for what will be said [about marriage to Auristela]; and if it appears as madness, and they take away my kingship, let me reign only in the heart of my Auristela" (No se me dará nada del qué dirán, y cuando por ésta, si pareciere locura, me quitaren el reino, reine yo en los brazos de Auristela [II, 5, 179-80]. The very possibility of such a separation between personal and social desires reveals that Policarpo's proposal is a temptation to be overcome. If Auristela and Periandro were to give up and remain on the island they would condemn themselves to the disharmony between consciousness and unconsciousness that they are trying to resolve through their pilgrimage.

Policarpo and Sinforosa are a clear expression of Auristela and Periandro's impatience with their assumed roles as brother and sister and a sign of what abandoning themselves to each other at this point would cost them. To yield now, with the unconscious powers still potentially in charge, would be to relinquish their claims to the true loyal marriage that is their goal.

Disorder Among the Secondary Characters

The danger into which the hero and heroine fall in Book II is reiterated in the actions of the secondary characters. Clodio, who represents intelligence cut off from its nourishment in love and compassion, plays a major role in Book II where the attractions of a rationally ordered society are highlighted. Clodio works by slander, using fact and literalism to highlight evil and advance himself. Correctly interpreting Auristela's extreme concern for her "brother" as the sign of a lover in disguise, Clodio tries to arouse Arnaldo's suspicions about her. However misguided, Arnaldo proves firm in his love and does not respond as Clodio hoped. Clodio then turns his attentions to Rutilio, who is struggling to overcome the temptation that women represent for him. Clodio suggests that he and Rutilio court Auristela and Sinforosa's sister Policarpa. Though Rutilio ultimately thinks better of the plan, Clodio goes through with his part, giving a letter to Auristela in which he proposes marriage.

The action of Clodio and Rutilio recalls the treasonous behavior of the two sailors in Arnaldo's ship in Book I, except that there the traitors were far removed from the main characters and unnamed, while in Book II they are familiar and close at hand. The results are remarkably similar in both cases, however. The sailors in Book I bring down the whole ship and die. In Book II, Clodio dies, indirectly bringing down with him the whole social order over which King Policarpo reigns.

The concupiscence and treachery of the sailors in Book I was very quickly followed by a female parallel when Rosamunda tried to seduce Antonio. In Book II Clodio's lascivious desires find their equivalent in the witch Cenotia's attempt to snare Antonio. Antonio, who stands for the chastity and inviolability of the true brother-sister pair, loses no time in rejecting Cenotia. Exhibiting the impulsive behavior that was his father's downfall, Antonio takes bow and arrow in hand to kill his temptress. His arrow kills Clodio instead, spearing the arch slanderer in the tongue, just as the lustful savage Bradamiro was killed in Book I.

Clodio's death establishes once again the link between slander and lust. Clodio appeared in Book I chained to the lascivious Rosamunda. He dies in Book II as the lustful barbarian of Book I died. The intertwining of lust and slander continues to be emphasized throughout Book II. Though Antonio has unwittingly killed Clodio in his effort to resist the witch, he has not truly cut out the slandering tongue. Antonio's violent reaction to evil succeeded rather in catching him deeper within it. Cenotia casts a mortal spell on the young man and later goes to King Policarpo and fills him with the same suspicion that Clodio tried to arouse in Arnaldo. As a result of the king's unchecked lust for Auristela and Cenotia's slander, the entire company of pilgrims become the prisoners of Policarpo's desires.

Periandro's Narration

Periandro remains relatively inactive in the first half of Book II. He is well represented in two figures, Arnaldo and Antonio, who stand for the two parts of his separated being. Arnaldo, the prince and suitor of Auristela, represents the Persiles who must remain hidden. Antonio, the fiercely chaste pilgrim brother, represents Periandro's public face. Separately, both are vulnerable, as Clodio's insinuations and Cenotia's advances have shown. Though both resist the temptations of slander and desire offered them, they do not succeed in escaping the troubles such temptations stir up.

Periandro's overt adversary is King Policarpo. True to the behavior that has characterized him all along, Periandro does not seek through violence to free himself from the danger of a powerful rival. Instead he resorts to storytelling, managing, through the brilliance of his imagination, to spellbind his listeners, inspire the pilgrims to faith in their journey, and ultimately liberate his entire group from the malevolent passions that have weighed so heavily upon them. Periandro's story, which occupies most of the second half of Book II, alternates with narrative references to King Policarpo, whose festering desire for Auristela finally breaks into the open, destroying him and Sinforosa while allowing the pilgrims to escape.

Periandro's narration has fascinated many recent critics, largely because of the commentary that his listeners provide, commentary that reveals much about Cervantes' awareness of neo-Aristotelian literary theory.[25] Although Periandro's story is in fact rich in critical theory, it is also highly important in developing the complex time structure of the book and in exploring the relationship between imagination and reality that is so much a part of the literary and metaphysical undergirding of Cervantes' final work.

Periandro's narration marks the first time that the hero in a long novel by Cervantes has told his own story. This study has emphasized the importance, in early works of Cervantes, of the interpolated tales as voices from the unconscious that serve to compensate for an imbalance in consciousness on the part of the main character. Cervantes' work shows a progressive integration of the primary and secondary narratives, which, while indicating the development of literary skill, also signals an expansion in his conception of the hero. This analysis of the *Persiles* has emphasized the degree to which Cervantes' last heroes have opened themselves to the unconscious and the resultant higher level of harmony with the other that they have achieved. The "other" referred to might be the rival, the loved one, or the author; discord at any one point promises discord at all the others.[26]

In earlier long works the secondary narrators—from Timbrio, to Cardenio, to the Captive—experienced release from the conflicts that bound them, or even further successes, after telling their stories. The storytelling process seemed to mark a turning point between a past of struggle and failure and a future in which the old conflicts would be put to rest. The story functions in exactly the same way in the *Persiles*, not only for the secondary characters, but for the main characters as well.

Periandro's tale is different from those his companions or

characters in the earlier works have told, however, because admiration for him, not pity or concern, provokes its telling. Responding to Sinforosa's request, he agrees to tell about his life on the condition that he be "permitted to begin his story where he pleases and not from the beginning" (si se le permitiese comenzar el cuento de su historia no del mismo principio [II, 9, 207]). Distinguishing clearly between life and story, he starts out by saying, " If you desire, sirs, to know the preamble and beginning of my story, I want it to be thus" (El principio y preámbulo de mi historia, ya que queréis, señores, que os la cuente, quiero que sea éste" [II, 10, 207]). The "I want" asserts Periandro's control over his material, and recalls the similar freedom the narrator at the beginning of *Don Quixote* gives himself.[27]

The circumstances under which Periandro agrees to speak further emphasize his control. Faced with the growing disorder that Antonio's killing of Clodio, Cenotia's schemes, and the king's misplaced desires have caused, Periandro tells a story in which he appears—both as narrator and as character—to be in charge. Despite the many interruptions and the frequent expressions of tedium and incredulity that his tale evokes, he is never thrown off course. He always resumes his tale just where he left off, and he remains unperturbed by his listeners' carping.

The principal theme of Periandro's tale is his capacity to prevail over adversity. When his beloved Auristela, along with several other women, is stolen by corsairs early in his story, Periandro says that he inspired the despairing husbands and kinsmen to action by telling them: "Ill fortune was never reversed through idleness or sloth. . . . We ourselves create our fortune, and there is no soul incapable of raising itself to its given place" (La baja fortuna jamás se enmendó con la ociosidad ni con la pereza; nosotros mismos nos fabricamos nuestra ventura, y no hay alma que no sea capaz de levantarse a su asiento [II, 12, 224]).

If mastery over ill fortune is one principal theme of Periandro's narrative, another is the achievement of love within marriage. The first episode in Periandro's story tells how Auristela intervened to prevent four young people from marrying according to their parents' wishes rather than their own. The events inaugurating the adventures of Periandro and Auristela capture, therefore, the essence of their task: to combine love and marriage and to achieve that goal by facing and overcoming all obstacles that rise up to prevent it.

Periandro's narration not only announces the theme of his own journey but also addresses the problems and fates of his listeners. The next two segments of his tale describe the aged King Leopoldio's failed love for a much-younger woman and the brave Sulpicia's fierce defense of her honor. These two episodes relate to the lives of King Policarpo and Transila and foretell their fates.

While Policarpo grows visibly more preoccupied with his desires, Periandro goes on to tell of a beautiful island on which he landed, filled with emerald greens and crystalline waters and flowers and fruits like rubies and topaz. "All of the fruits we know of," he says, "were there in their fullness, without the differences in their seasons impeding them: everything there was spring, everything was summer, all fullness without burden, and all delightful autumn" (Todas las frutas de quien tenemos noticia estaban allí en su sazón, sin que las diferencias del año las estorbasen: todo allí era primavera, todo verano, todo estío sin pesadumbre, y todo otoño agradable [II, 15, 241]). On the island of which Periandro speaks a procession is said to have passed by, featuring carts representing the temptations of Sensuality and the rewards of Continence and Modesty. Among the beautiful damsels in the procession, Periandro says he saw Auristela and was told that she must remain untouched until she reaches Rome. Only after Periandro narrates his experience on the island does he admit that it was a dream.

The interjection of a dream vision prompts a discussion about the difference between reality and imagination, and all seem to agree that the two differ very little from one another. The dream, however, also introduces once again a vision of the atemporal and reminds the listeners that despite the appearance of misery the promise of fulfillment persists. The dream offers a vision of the garden of Paradise, recalls the bounteous island of Ricla and Antonio, and anticipates the beautiful island to which the pilgrims will soon escape.

Between each segment of Periandro's episodic narrative, the principal narrator interjects both incredulous and admiring reactions from Periandro's listeners and describes Policarpo's growing confusion. The frequent interruptions give vent to possible reader objections but also puncture what could be the self-enclosed world of Periandro's tale. Periandro's mastery, the interruptions show, is mastery only over himself. He has no control over the others, nor does he wish to have. Events occur as they will, and Periandro's only task is to hold fast to his own story—the story of his endless determination and his faith in the promise of his journey.[28]

The constant interruption of Periandro's narrative also makes it a microcosm of the work that surrounds it. Like the *Persiles* as a whole, Periandro's narration marks the characters' temporal and spatial advance through a series of discrete episodes, some more fantastic than others, which contain within them the secrets of the journey's beginning and end. As in the work as a whole, Periandro offers stories within stories, while dealing in essence with his separation from Auristela and their effort to reunite. With its emphasis on shipwrecks, storms at sea, and frozen islands, Periandro's tale amplifies on the major episodes of Books I and II, while adding information about the period prior to the beginning of the book.

Periandro's story ends where the principal narrator's began, forming a perfect whole with it. Just as Periandro and Auristela are reunited, at the beginning of the work, on an island that later burns, Periandro narrates his story following their reunion on another island that later burns, again forcing their escape. Nothing in the pattern has changed, from the beginning of Book I to the end of Book II, yet nothing remains the same for the protagonists. Through his narration Periandro reveals his oneness with his author and his concomitant devotion to his pilgrimage.

Periandro's tale is more than a statement of perseverance amid the storms of Policarpo's passions. It can also be read allegorically as his own struggle for mastery, since it does not stop when Policarpo sets fire to the island. The tale continues after the pilgrims escape and echoes the actual events the pilgrims are experiencing, for the fire interrupts Periandro's narration at a point of extreme danger in his story and resumes, the company now safe, with the tale of his and his men's release from danger.

Periandro recounts the final episode in his long tale once he and his company reach a beautiful and fruitful island inhabited by two hermits—Renato and Eusebia—who have lived in isolation, chastity, and devotion together for ten years. Both the hermit couple and the last episode in Periandro's story highlight the heroic struggle for mastery over the passions that is truly Periandro's tale—both as narrator and as character.

Periandro's last story concerns his famous taming of Cratilo's horse, a deed so wild and daring that his skeptical listeners cannot restrain their expressions of disbelief.[29] He tells how he forced his mount to plunge headlong over a cliff, saying that only God's intervention prevented him and the horse from being destroyed. Periandro promptly remounted and again forced the wild beast to the edge of the cliff, urging it to make another leap to the ice below. The horse was so desperate to avoid risking its life again that it finally let Periandro control him. Seen in conjunction with Periandro's dream, which revealed the temptation sensuality still holds for him, and the many examples in Books I and II of characters who have not mastered their passions, the horse perfectly symbolizes Periandro's instincts that must also be brought under the control of his will.[30]

Renato's story links the horse-taming episode with Periandro's real problem: to restrain his passion for Auristela. Falsely accused of improprieties with Eusebia and unable to defend himself in a duel with his accuser, Renato left home to spend his remaining days as a hermit. Eusebia, feeling sorry for him, went to stay with him. Their ten years of chastity are rewarded just as the pilgrims prepare to leave the island: a ship arrives bearing the news that Renato's accuser admitted his slander on his deathbed. Renato and Eusebia agree to return home and marry. The struggle to control passion is reflected not only in Policarpo, Renato and Eusebia, and Periandro's taming of the horse but in Rutilio, the Italian dance master, who decides to stay on the hermit's island in Renato and Eusebia's place to overcome his own still-untamed passions.

Book II ends as the pilgrims separate into two bands: those, like Mauricio, Transila, and Ladislao, who want to return to the northern countries of their origin, and those who intend to travel south to the Mediterranean countries on their way toward Rome. Rosamunda and Clodio are dead, the barbarians and the islanders under King Policarpo have been consumed by flames. The only real threat that remains—Arnaldo—responds to his father's call to war and reluctantly takes leave of his beloved Auristela. The main characters' freedom from so many dangers is reflected in the third and fourth books in the solid ground on which they are now able to walk.

BOOK III

Social and Natural Symbols of Rebirth

The pilgrimage takes a distinct turn in Book III. Finding themselves on the mainland for the first time, the travellers are no longer at the mercy of the high seas or of the pirates and islanders. Everything in the new environment of southern Europe suggests both an advance along the horizontal axis that leads toward Rome and a rise along the vertical axis that points toward the heroes' spiritual development. In the journey through Portugal, Spain, France, and Italy that occupies Book III, Periandro and Auristela, though natives of northern kingdoms, will no longer feel in alien territory. When they arrive in Lisbon, they are celebrated and admired by the townspeople who come out to greet them, but they are left free to continue their journey. Although Cervantes flirts briefly in Chapter 2 of Book III with the idea that Auristela does not understand Spanish, he very quickly abandons that obstacle in the interest of promoting the natural understanding that the travellers now enjoy in all the Catholic countries through which they journey.[31]

The pilgrims agree to travel on foot rather than by coach. When it is suggested, later in Book III, that they take a boat from Barcelona, they refuse, saying that they have seen enough of oceans. As the foot has been taken as the symbol of the soul, since it keeps the body upright, the insistence on walking underscores the higher level of psychic development the pilgrims have now achieved.[32] Less directly assaulted by threats to their own survival, the travellers have the freedom to become self-reflective and to observe the dramas unfolding in the lives of those they encounter along the road.

The new freedom the characters enjoy can also be seen in the composition of the group that travels together. All the divisive elements that made the journeys of Books I and II so difficult have been eliminated in Book III. The pilgrims who land on the shores of Portugal now travel of one accord. Though the group will change somewhat as the book progresses (Antonio and Ricla remain in Spain; two young French women join the pilgrims in France; and another couple, Rupertina and Croriano, will be with them when they reach Rome), none of the new companions seriously threatens the integrity of the central foursome—Auristela and Periandro, Antonio and Constanza—as characters in Books I and II were constantly doing.

The pilgrims' liberation from fear and achievement of harmony and stability is illustrated by a wide spectrum of elements in their new situation. Their journey through southern Europe coincides with spring; the pilgrims reach the border town of Badajoz on the vernal equinox: "The sky held time's course and season suspended in the equal balance of the two equinoxes: neither did the heat tire nor the cold offend one" (Tenía suspenso el cielo el curso y sazón del tiempo en la balanza igual de los dos equinocios: ni el calor fatigaba, ni el frío ofendía [III, 2, 287]).

The fact that Auristela and Periandro reach Rome in Book IV at the onset of summer when the sun is at its zenith reveals that the four books have a correspondence with the seasons and that the heroes are part of a nature allegory that reveals the constancy of change, showing how the figure of birth is imbedded in the image of death. The concept, already present in the opening scene of Book I and belonging to the very core of the Christian message that Auristela and Periandro consciously embrace in Book IV, promotes the harmony between man and nature that the marriage of Antonio and Ricla symbolizes and that Periandro and Auristela seek. The beginning of Book I is not really the beginning, as has already been noted. The end of Book IV is not the end either. When the book ends, Auristela and Periandro have only completed half their journey; they must still return to their places of origin in the Thule and Frislandia.

Harmony and the Feminine

The achievement of harmony with the natural order that is the pilgrims' goal finds frequent expression through the secondary characters in Book III. The first interpolated story in Book III, a tale carefully woven into the experience of the main characters, like those of *Don Quixote* Part II, brings the theme clearly into focus. The story centers on the young woman Feliciana de la Voz and deals with the familiar conflict between love and the dictates of the social order, the very conflict that has spurred

Periandro and Auristela's journey. The pilgrims are deep in the woods at night when a stranger rides up and leaves with them a gold chain and a newborn child. Child, chain, and gold are all symbols of the goals the pilgrims, and through them, Feliciana, seek: the child represents the union of the unconscious and consciousness; the chain, matrimony; and gold, the elusive treasure that is the fruit of the spirit. Though temporarily displaced, they suggest that those to whom they belong will ultimately be restored to their highest good.[33]

The process of piecing together the disassembled fragments of the story resembles the trials the characters themselves must undergo to recover their own shattered harmony. Feliciana narrates part of her story: she was in love with one man, Rosanio, and promised, by her father and brothers, to another. Her love for the wealthy and noble young Rosanio resulted in the birth of their child on the very night when she was to marry the man of her father's choice. Though the story is simple, its unfolding is not. Filled with masked characters, mistaken identities, and interrupted discourses, the story engulfs participants and listeners as well in its seeming confusion.

Nearly dead with exhaustion and fright, Feliciana escapes, without her child, from her enraged father. Taking refuge in the woods, she is cared for by shepherds who hide her in a tree, cover her with sheepskins, and feed her a rustic soup made of goat's milk. Meanwhile, a sister of one of the shepherds nurses the baby, who arrived before Feliciana and whom she will not recognize when he is later brought to her.

When she regains her strength, Feliciana decides to join the pilgrims. The first stop is the monastery at Guadalupe, where Feliciana begins to sing a hymn, as if inspired by angels, to the black Virgin who is there.[34]

> Kneeling, her hands pressed against her breasts, the beautiful Feliciana de la Voz raining tender tears, with a composed face, and without moving her lips or making any other gesture or movement that would indicate that she was a living creature, released her voice to the winds and raised her heart to heaven and sang some verses which she knew by heart.

> (Puesta de hinojos y las manos puestas y junto al pecho, la hermosa Feliciana de la Voz, lloviendo tiernas lágrimas, con sosegado semblante, sin mover los labios ni hacer otra demostración ni

movimiento que diese señal de ser viva criatura, soltó la voz a los vientos, y levantó el corazón al cielo, y cantó unos versos que ella sabía de memoria. [III, 5, 306])

Her song seems to have a miraculous effect, drawing all the conflictive forces in her life together from their disparate places: her father and brother, planning vengeance, enter and are countered by two friends of Rosanio's. Rosanio also appears and makes his defense. Through expressions of mutual love, all are reconciled.

The song Feliciana sings honors the Virgin, and with her, the qualities associated with the feminine. She sings, in the second stanza, "The high and strong foundations / were raised upon deep humility; / and, the more were they mindful of humility, / the more they raised the regal edifice" (Los altos y fortísimos cimientos, / sobre humildad profunda se fundaron; / y mientras más a la humildad atentos, / más la fábrica regia levantaron [III, 5, 309]). The edifice that represents the Virgin is built, according to Feliciana's song, on the foundations of humility, faith, patience, love, and prudence. Her light, though dim, shines brighter than the sun: "More than the sun, the star today gives out her light" (Antes que el sol, la estrella hoy da su lumbre) is the first line of the seventh stanza, which later continues, "Today humility was seen placed upon the summit. / Today the chain of ancient iron / began to break" (Hoy la humildad se vio puesta en la cumbre; / hoy comenzó a romperse la cadena / del hierro antiguo [III, 5, 310]). In the eighth stanza, Feliciana sings to the Virgin: "You were the agreeable medium / through whom the mortal discord of God and man / was reduced to peaceful harmony" (Pues vos fuisteis el medio conveniente, / que redujo a pacífica concordia / de Dios y el hombre la mortal discordia [III, 5, 310-11]). Though Feliciana's song is interrupted by the shouts and accusations of her pursuers, the words she has committed to memory have their effect nonetheless. She who is "the arm of God that held back / from Abraham the harsh knife" (el brazo de Dios, que detuvistes / de Abrahán la cuchilla rigorosa [III, 5, 311]) once again detains the avengers' sword.

As the first episode in the vernal phase of the pilgrims' journey, Feliciana's story is rich in significance. If the iron chain of the old way has been broken, it has been replaced by the necklace of gold. Love and rebirth have triumphed here over a social world no longer associated with barbarians and heretics but with Spaniards and Christians. Feliciana, nearly destroyed in the society of her father and brothers, is restored to life by the combined forces of nature and the feminine.

The story of escape from forced marriage is reiterated at the end of Book III in the comic tale of Isabela Castrucha and Andrea Marulo. There once again feminine powers, now expressed through the exercise of trickery, overcome the forces of authority. The story and the book end with the coincidence, in church, of the baptism of a child, the marriage of a couple, and the death of the man who had tried to prevent their marriage. No clearer method could have been created to express the overall design of Book III, which opens and closes with episodes that celebrate union: the death of the old accompanied by the birth of the new.

Compassion and Forgiveness

The power of the feminine, as articulated in Feliciana's song, continues to be demonstrated in successive interpolated tales in Book III. In Chapter 6 the pilgrims meet Ortel Banedre, who tells them of the unbelievable forgiveness of the Portuguese woman Doña Guiomar de Sosa. Doña Guiomar gives refuge in her house to Ortel, who is being pursued by the police for having killed a man. Though she later discovers that the victim was her own son, she does not retreat from her attitude of compassion, and even gives her son's murderer money before sending him on his way.

In Chapter 7 Periandro takes the opportunity to lecture at length on the power of clemency, advising the same Ortel Banedre who was so mercifully treated earlier not to yield to his own thirst for vengeance. Ortel's wife abandoned him for another man. He tells his listeners: "I am determined to cleanse with their blood the stains on my honor, and, by taking their lives, to remove from my shoulders the heavy weight of their misdeeds." (Voy con voluntad determinada de sacar con su sangre las manchas de mi honra, y con quitarles las vidas, quitar de sobre mis hombros la pesada carga de su delito [III, 7, 324]). In Periandro's declamation against vengeance that runs for a page and a half, he notes that "vengeance punishes but does not remove guilt," and urges Ortel to "come to your senses, and, giving a place to mercy, run no longer after justice" (las venganzas castigan, pero no quitan las culpas: . . . volved en vos, y dando lugar a la misericordia, no corráis tras la justicia [III, 7, 325]).

Constanza will also have an opportunity to demonstrate the literally transforming effects of compassion and forgiveness. Her father reaches his home in Quintanar de la Orden to find that his former enemy has died. Having established that Antonio's offence against him did not require vengeance, the two families have long since become good friends. On the day of the pilgrims' arrival, the nephew and heir of Antonio's former enemy is brought to the house mortally wounded. Also a pilgrim, he was caught in a skirmish between rebelling soldiers and townspeople. On his deathbed he forgives his killer and marries Constanza, leaving her his entire fortune. Two chapters later, on the road to Valencia, some soldiers approach the pilgrims seeking food for one of their number—a young boy being sent to the galleys for his part in the uprising that took Constanza's husband's life. She overcomes her own desire for vengeance and her repugnance for the boy and personally gives him food.

Constanza's act of compassion is startingly repaid in Chapter 12, when a beautiful and well-dressed young woman disembarks from a ship at the port of Barcelona. The woman recognizes the pilgrims, though they do not know her, and invites them to her house. She tells them that she is Ambrosia Agustina, the "boy soldier" whom Constanza had helped. She had dressed as a man to follow her newly wedded husband to war. Constanza's act of compassion has the effect of transforming an offender into a benefactor. The story suggests that compassion can lift the veil of beastliness, and Constanza is rewarded with the hospitality of the elegant and wealthy young woman who had hidden beneath the figure of a dirty, impoverished soldier.

The theme of compassion and forgiveness continues in several other episodes scattered across the pages of Book III. In Chapter 13, having just crossed the border into France, the pilgrims come across a gambler betting his freedom for a small sum of money. If he loses, he goes to the galleys for six months. If he wins, he takes the pittance the gaming officials have loaned him in order to play. The gambler has just lost when the pilgrims appear. They watch the wife plead for her husband's release for her sake and for that of their five children who face starvation in his absence. Constanza and the other pilgrims are so moved that Constanza pays off the king's ministers in charge of the gambling establishment and gives the man more than double the amount he would have earned had he won.

In the next-to-last interpolated tale in Book III, the theme of vengeance transcended is once again highlighted. The story is presented in mock-heroic fashion by an old man dressed in mourning, manservant to a woman also in mourning called Ruperta. The old man tells the pilgrims that Ruperta has carried the skull of her husband in a box for over a year, vowing revenge on his murderer. Handling the affair like a barker at a sideshow, the old servant pulls back the curtains on the scene of the young woman's grim scheme. Having been told that the murderer's son, Croriano, has arrived at the inn, Ruperta decides to avenge her husband's death through him. She waits until the young man is sleeping, and then, like Psyche in Apuleius' "Amor and Psyche," she approaches her victim's bed with a lantern in one hand, a dagger in the other. Such is his beauty, however, that her anger dissolves. When she drops the lantern on him, he awakens and explains that his father is already dead but that they should marry to atone for his wrong.

The narration switches frequently from the voice of the old manservant to that of the principal narrator, concluding: "That night, soft peace won out over harsh war; the battlefield turned into a wedding bed; peace was born out of ire; life from death; and from unhappiness, contentment" (Triunfó aquella noche la blanda paz desta dura guerra, volvióse el campo de la batalla en tálamo de desposorio; nació la paz de la ira; de la muerte, la vida, y del disgusto, el contento [III, 17, 391]). Though heavily overlaid with literary associations, and presented so as to resemble a puppet show more than an actual event, the story carries the concept of vengeance to its extreme. Such grotesque details as Ruperta's having her dead husband's head sawed off and treated with chemicals to reduce it to a skull serve to ridicule the literature of revenge that obviously inspired Ruperta's actions, as did the salting of Durandarte's heart in Don Quixote's dream. Though she merely shifts from one literary situation to another when she gives up playing Judith of Holofernes in favor of Psyche, she moves nonetheless in the direction of love and reconciliation that is the basic trajectory of all the successful characters in the *Persiles*.

Love and reconciliation, as the Ruperta story shows, are powerful because they triumph over a previously conflictive situation that threatens its participants with destruction. Like the basic conflict that motivates the work—the rivalry between Persiles and Magsimino—the Ruperta story is destructive so long as it is based on the triangle. The miraculous appearance of a fourth, in this case the murderer's son Croriano, restores to harmony the imbalance that the triangle promotes. Part of the explanation for the stability that Auristela and Periandro exhibit is that they are always in the company of others who square their relationship, especially of Antonio and Constanza, who represent the ideal image of themselves in their pilgrim's disguise.

Images of Disorder

The lovers who would challenge Auristela and Periandro's serenity—Arnaldo, King Policarpo, Sinforosa—have all disappeared by Book III. Their absence signals an overcoming of the furious desire for possession that the barbarians and the treacherous sailors symbolized in Book I and of the jealousy and fear that characterized the trials of Book II. Though not personally threatened in Book III, however, the heroes still experience struggles. In Chapter 4 they are falsely accused of murder. The handling of their case by the police and at court gives ample evidence of the violence and greed that still reign in their midst. In Valencia in Chapter 11 they escape a raid and the burning of the city by Berber pirates. In Chapter 14 Periandro is nearly killed fighting with a madman who threatens to hurl his two children out of a tower to their death, and in the same chapter Antonio also nearly loses his life helping to rescue a lady in distress.

Behind the crises to which Periandro and Antonio respond in Chapter 14 lie stories of unrequited love. Domicio, the madman in the tower, married for convenience rather than love. His jilted loved one, Lorenza, engages the services of a witch who succeeds in making him crazy by sending him a poisoned shirt. Feliz Flora, a beautiful French woman, is desired by the coarse Rubertino, whose advances she has spurned. In a fury, he gathers together a posse of men with the intention of abducting her.

The important point here is that Periandro and his alter ego Antonio act on behalf of ladies who are strangers, are willing to sacrifice themselves disinterestedly, and are successful. In their response they distinguish themselves from all the former heroes in Cervantes' long fiction. In *La Galatea,* when Elicio faced a challenge similar to Antonio's, Artandro and his men tied him up and easily stole Rosaura away. In *Don Quixote,* the mad gentleman from La Mancha often went to the defense of ladies who neither needed nor wanted his help and then refused to protect the innkeeper when his daughter earnestly pleaded that he do so. In his last work Cervantes created a hero who, having tamed his own passionate impulses and reined in his instinct for possession, is capable of truly offering help to others.

As a result of Periandro's and Antonio's interventions in the catastrophes that confronted them, they become even more open to the feminine. Antonio, who has until now protected himself from the desire the feminine might arouse in him by violently rejecting it, is now accessible to expressions of tenderness. The shift in the valuation of the feminine is shown in the fact that not only his sister Constanza but also Feliz Flora begins to show concern for him. For the first time, Antonio finds himself involved with a woman who is neither sister nor seductress. For Periandro, the softening of the oppositions suggests that, in place of his forced repression, a true tenderness and mutual respect is growing between him and Auristela that will lead them closer not only to their geographical goal but to their spiritual one as well.

Book III is filled with all sorts of characters and situations. There are wayward characters such as the baggage boy Bartolomé, who likes the pilgrims but is susceptible to temptation and runs away from time to time with Luisa, who is a similarly weak character. There are corrupt highborn characters, like the Duke of Nemurs, who has dispatched servants to bring him beautiful women from among whom he plans to select a wife. There are peasants, such as Tozuelo and Cobeña, who reenact in pastoral setting the conflicts of love and marriage that are more violently resolved among the noble. There are rogues, such as the false captives who have decided to make a profit by passing themselves off as escapees from captivity in Algiers. There are also playwrights, wandering pilgrims out more for the fun of it than for their spiritual growth, witches, Berbers, traitors, Moriscos, and even a wise old man, Soldino. The spectrum of characters Cervantes offers in Book III runs the gamut and includes nearly all the facets of contemporary life that have made his work so famous.

So much narrative material so displaced from its mythological underpinnings makes reading the allegories in Book III more difficult.[35] The best that can be said is that Periandro and Auristela have achieved balance and, therefore, no longer figure as much as characters as they do as observers and disinterested participants. The themes of compassion and forgiveness come into prominence, while the problems caused by rivalry, jealousy, and possessiveness drop into the background where they remain as a distant but ever-present reminder of the danger that could rise up to menace the main characters should they forget the lessons they have learned.

Art and Self-Reflexivity

Book III shows that the *Persiles* depends on the very passions that Periandro and Auristela have by and large learned to control. If they figure as observers now, it is because their story no longer claims the reader's attention. The main characters' distance from the conflicts of others, however, permits Cervantes to entertain the question of art and life more directly. The first thing Periandro does on arriving in Lisbon is have a painting made of the pilgrims' adventures—a painting they intend to use to illustrate the narration of their story to any who might be interested in hearing it. And in Chapter 2 Auristela is approached by a poet-playwright who is full of ideas about having Auristela enact on stage the drama of her adventures, which he will cast into poetic form.

The transforming of adventures into art in the opening chapters of Book III suggests that the protagonists not only have overcome the adversities that so threatened to overwhelm them in the first two books but are now capable of seeing themselves in double perspective: both as characters in an ongoing drama and as narrators and spectators. Periandro began to play just such a role in the second half of Book II, when his narration served both to unveil his past and to help him move out of his present danger.

In Chapter 10, halfway through Book III, and again at the end, in Chapters 20 and 21, the theme of representation, implicit in the structure of Book III, is taken up directly. In Chapter 10 the topic is introduced through the False Captives, two students who have decided to make money giving talks about their "captivity" in Algiers, using as their prop a painting other captives sold them. They make some factual mistakes in their presentation and are unmasked by one of the aldermen, who had truly been held captive in Algiers. The resolution comes when another alderman suggests that the students go home with him and get their history straight before taking to the road again with their stories.

The first alderman, who had been angry with the students' ruse, asks the pilgrims: "And you, sir pilgrims, are you also carrying a story that you would have us believe is true even though lies themselves have made it?" (¿Vosotros, señores peregrinos, traéis algún lienzo que enseñarnos? ¿Traéis otra historia que hacernos creer por verdadera, aunque la haya compuesto la misma mentira? [III, 10, 350]). Though they left their painting with Antonio and Ricla in Quintanar de la Orden, the question is a pertinent one. Once the deeds have been done and committed to canvas or the written word, they no longer belong to the one who performed them. They are common property, to be used and abused by whoever so desires. Transformed into art, what is represented is to be questioned no longer for its truth but for its internal consistency. As artists of their lives, Periandro and Auristela are not required to represent themselves as they are. They are only asked to project the image they have chosen of themselves so that it will not contradict itself or betray the truths the image has been designed to protect.

The episode of Isabela Castrucha, mentioned earlier, makes the point even clearer. In order to prevail over her uncle, Isabela feigns possession by the Devil and proclaims that only Andrea Marulo—the young man whom she wants to marry— can release her from his clutches. To carry out her plan, Isabela has to make many arrangements, including writing to Andrea to inform him of his role. The madness she feigns is executed in full consciousness. Were she truly mad, she could not achieve her ends; and were she incapable of pretending to be mad, she could not either. Her success, like that of Basilio and Ginés de Pasamonte in *Don Quixote* Part II and like that of Auristela and Periandro, derives from her ability simultaneously to observe and to participate in a role consciously selected.

The distance Isabela is able to establish between herself and her image allies her not only with the main characters but with the principal narrator, who ends Book III with an observation that reveals his own distance from what might otherwise seem to be the upsetting vicissitudes of life: "And, two days later, a child . . . came into the church to be baptized; Isabela and Andrea, to be married and to bury the body of her uncle, so that one can see how strange are the events of this life: some people are baptized, some are married, some are buried, all at the same time" (De allí a dos días entraron por la puerta de una iglesia un niño, . . . a bautizar, Isabela y Andrea a casarse, y a enterrar el cuerpo de su tío, porque se vean cuán estraños son los sucesos desta vida; unos a un mismo punto se bautizan, otros se casan y otros se entierran [III, 21, 411]).[36] Pulled away from close identification with any one story line, the narrator shows the simultaneity of birth, death, and rebirth—not only how the one situation leads into the next, but also how, at any given moment, all three coincide.

The separation from given roles, the ability to truly be "makers of ones' own destiny" as Periandro had said in Book II, is a major theme in Book III. It is expressed formally in the wide range of secondary stories offered and explicitly in many particular episodes. Ambrosia Agustina, for example, dresses in a man's clothes to find her husband. The peasant Tozuelo, secretly in love with Cobeña, the alderman's daughter, dresses in a woman's clothes, hoping to pass himself off as her while she hides so as not to be noticed as pregnant.[37] Isabela Castrucha not only designs the ploy through which she and Andrea will be married but takes on the role of suitor, being the one to spot her lover in church, fall in love with him, and write him love letters. The reversal of sex roles that Periandro and Auristela were able to affect symbolically at the beginning of Book I is carried out by many of the characters in Book III, each of them demonstrating a skill and maneuverability in the phenomenal world that wins them the marriage with a loved one that they desire.

The artist's and the trickster's visions point toward a high level of consciousness because they require for success a vantage point that transcends the present moment and the limitations of a single perspective. Ginés and Basilio were able to control their surroundings because they could anticipate the expectations of others and manipulate their responses by appearing to conform to a pattern whose outlines they could clearly discern. When Periandro tells of mastering Cratilo's horse in Book II, he is also speaking metaphorically of achieving control over the forces that would otherwise move him. To take charge of the "wild horse" is to be master of one's fate, and it signals an artistry akin to that fleetingly demonstrated by some of the lesser characters in *Don Quixote* Part II.

Mastery, however, as a careful reading of the *Persiles* shows, is acquired in stages. The stages can be clearly delineated by looking at the role of the saving figures who appear in the work. The first such figure rescues Periandro and Auristela early in Book I. He is Antonio, the son, who leads the hero and heroine out of the flames of the Barbarous Island. The second, Mauricio, figured later in Book I as an astrologer who was able to predict the wreck of Arnaldo's ship. In Book III, the guide is Soldino, a hermit who warns the pilgrims of an impending fire and leads them to the shelter of his cave.[38] Soldino is the oldest of the three and represents the highest stage of development.

Antonio's power comes from his physical strength and is appropriate to the needs of the pilgrims in the first phase of their journey. Mauricio is older than Antonio and represents the development of the intellect. His clairvoyance is one dependent on charts and mathematical calculations. Soldino has passed through the phases of physical and intellectual development, having been a soldier and later a man of letters. He appears toward the end of Book III as an authentic wise old man. The hermitage and the cave to which he leads the pilgrims combines the Eden-like bounty of Antonio and Ricla's island paradise in Book I with the dream island of Periandro's narration in Book II. It is, however, neither a gift of nature nor the product of an idle wish, but rather a dwelling place constructed by dint of effort combined with desire. He tells the pilgrims: "I built that hermitage, and with my own hands and ceaseless labor I dug the cave, and made this valley mine, whose water and fruits abundantly supply my needs. Here, running from war, I found peace; the hunger which I suffered, if it can be so said, in the world above found satisfaction here" (Yo levanté aquella ermita, y con mis brazos y con mi continuo trabajo cavé la cueva, y hice mío este valle, cuyas aguas y cuyos frutos con prodigalidad me sustentan. Aquí, huyendo de la guerra, hallé la paz; la hambre que en ese mundo de allá arriba, si así se puede decir, tenía, halló aquí a la hartura [III, 18, 395]).

For Soldino, only in higher degree than for the artist or the trickster, the phenomenal world is but an aspect of reality. For him all times are one, and he can as clearly see events of the past and future as those of the present. Soldino not only completes the orderly process of growth the first three books trace but also gives insight into the structure of the *Persiles* by his presence in the work. The atemporal vision that marks the highest level of spiritual development also informs the construction of the work and explains the presence of myth, symbol, and allegory that were so foreign to the earlier stages of Cervantes' fiction. The complex time structure of the *Persiles,* the constant juxtaposition of images of birth and death, and the gradual distancing of the characters from the traumatic events around them all testify to a unified vision whose clearest novelistic expression in the work is Soldino.

BOOK IV

Recapitulation and Assimilation

The first three books of the *Persiles* trace the main characters' gradual dissociation from the vicissitudes of the phenomenal world and their corresponding growth as physical, intellectual, and spiritual beings. By Book III, Auristela and Periandro have become spectators and disinterested participants in the struggles of others for the most part. The success of their horizontal journey is clear: Book III ends with the pilgrims a few days from Rome.

Book IV, with respect to the geographical aims of the work and the conscious goal of the protagonists, would seem to be superfluous. Indeed, Periandro loses no time pointing out to Auristela in Chapter 1 of Book IV that they have done everything they had intended to and have no reason to remain apart any longer. Auristela resists Periandro's importunings, however, telling him that they are still far from home and that their fates are still too uncertain for them to marry. More remains to be done, and Book IV will focus directly on the hidden obstacles that impede the union of the protagonists for the first time. The dual goals of the characters who set out from the north for Rome come into sharp relief in Book IV: Periandro inclines more to the physical, Auristela more to the spiritual impulses that occasioned their departure from home. The separation between matter and spirit, between consciousness and the unconscious, must be bridged before the royal marriage to which Auristela and Periandro aspire can be achieved.

Book IV, then, constitutes another level of struggle for the
protagonists, one concerned now not so much with their survival and linear progress as with their need to assimilate their
experiences. The horizontal journey having ended, everything
in Book IV contributes to the process of gathering together the
many loose strands of Periandro and Auristela's respective
histories and integrating them into their consciousness. The
process actually began in Book II, when Periandro recounted
his adventures during the time between his initial separation
from Auristela and their reunion on the Barbarous Island. The
effort to bring experience under the control of consciousness
continues in Book III, when Periandro orders a painter to represent the history of the pilgrims' journey on canvas. Later in
Book III, while at the house of Antonio's family in Quintanar de
la Orden, Auristela briefly recounts the story of her separation
from Periandro.

The Sensuous

In Book IV the recapitulation continues on two levels. On
the external plane, characters such as Arnaldo in Chapter 8 and
Rutilio in Chapter 13 rejoin the principal characters in Rome
and tell them of the fortunes of the many secondary characters
who appeared throughout the narration. On the internal plane,
both Periandro and Auristela are forced to break through the
guise as pilgrims that held them at the level of brother and sister to recover their pasts as Persiles and Sigismunda.

The crisis that prompts Periandro's and Auristela's rediscov-
ery of their origins points back to the interpolated tales told
early in Book I. Rutilio's story there emphasized the destructive
power of lust and showed how quickly the attractive young girl,
when seen only as the object of sensual desire, could degenerate
into the image of a witch and a she-wolf. By running off to
Rome with his pupil, Rutilio experienced not the fulfillment of
his desires but a progressive limitation of his freedom as he
found himself first in jail, then alone in the dark and cold of
Norway, and finally cast ashore on a barbarous island where,
reduced to the level of a beast, he had to remain dressed in
animal skins pretending to be a deaf-mute.

Book IV leaves no doubt that Rutilio's story was intended for
Periandro's edification. Already in Chapter 1 of Book IV, Periandro betrays his impatience with the brother-sister role he and

Auristela have imposed upon themselves. Their remaining experiences further expose his continued attraction to the sensuous. In Chapter 2, he and Auristela find Arnaldo and the Duke of Nemurs—the two highborn men whose desire for Auristela had troubled Periandro in the previous books—near death as a result of their struggle for possession of Auristela's portrait.

The first half of Book IV is full of expressions of the mad desire Auristela's beauty awakens. Arnaldo and the Duke of Nemurs, along with Periandro and even some Roman officials, struggle many times to possess her portrait. Everywhere the pilgrims go, crowds mob their carriage for a glimpse of Auristela. At one point Periandro has Auristela cover her face so that the crowds will not overturn the carriage in their desire to see her.

Periandro's susceptibility to desire is revealed not only through his alter egos but through his own experience with the seductress Hipólita. Hipólita is the cosmopolitan woman par excellence, and she tries to engage Periandro's interest, both through her wiles and through her luxurious house and dazzling collection of paintings. Like Antonio with Rosamunda and Cenotia, Periandro betrays his attraction to Hipólita by the excessive ferocity of his resistance. His response, again like that of Antonio in Book II, prompts her anger and exposes him to the malefic powers of a witch.

Book IV brings together all the major themes that have been developing in the previous three books. Hipólita represents the culmination of the theme of the witch that began in Book I with Rutilio, continued in Book II with Cenotia, and returned in Book III with the story of Domicio and the poisoned shirt. In Book IV the witch is no longer identified with other characters but with Periandro and Auristela. She arises when sensuous desire is separated from a true wedding with the spirit, and her influence affects not just the lover but the loved one as well.

The Spiritual

Hipólita engages the skills of the witch Julia, who casts what appears to be a mortal spell on Auristela. Like Isabela of *La española inglesa,* Auristela quickly deteriorates until she comes to resemble death itself. The characters who represent the more superficial aspects of Periandro's attraction to Auristela, the Duke of Nemurs and Arnaldo, lose interest in her and give up their claims to her. Periandro, though he does not abandon her, becomes so sick out of concern for her that Hipólita is forced to tell Julia to call off her spell.

The encounter with Hipólita begins exactly midway through Book IV and is literally central to the book and to the conflicts that inhibit Auristela and Periandro's union. If Hipólita awakens a lingering weakness in Periandro that will finally test his love for Auristela, she also brings back to the surface of Auristela's consciousness the jealousy that nearly overwhelmed her in Book II. Auristela also has her past to relive and overcome in Book IV, and in Chapter 8 while Periandro is visiting the rich and beautiful Hipólita, she remains at home, swamped by fears she is unable to express.

The witch's spell that nearly kills Auristela is, from a psychological point of view, a metaphor for the torments of jealousy that Hipólita's presence inspires. The narrator says of Auristela: "when the tongue is restrained by decorum and modesty, so as to repress all complaints, the heart torments itself within the bonds of silence, till soul and body are almost ready to part" (cuando la honestidad ata la lengua de modo que no puede quejarse, da tormento al alma con las ligaduras del silencio, de modo que a cada paso anda buscando salidas para dejar la vida del cuerpo [IV, 8, 450]). In Book II, faced with Sinforosa's challenge, Auristela also fell ill. In Book IV it is plausible to suppose that the witch Julia is a projection of Auristela's discordant state.

Auristela's conscious response to her dilemma also recalls her earlier bout with jealousy. In Book II, she told Periandro that he should stay on Policarpo's island while she dedicated herself to the religious life. Here, once again, she suggests that they separate, explaining that her instruction in the faith has prompted in her the desire to become a nun. In words similar to those she used in Book II she tells Periandro: "And now I would fain, if possible, go to Heaven without delay, alarms, or anxieties" (Querría ahora, si fuese posible, irme al cielo, sin rodeos, sin sobresaltos y sin cuidados), later adding, "for in order to attain so great a gift as Heaven, one must leave all that one loves best on earth, even one's parents and one's husband or wife. I leave you for no other: He for whom I leave you is God" (que, para alcanzar tan gran bien como es el cielo, todo cuanto hay en la tierra se ha de dejar, hasta los padres y los esposos. Yo no te quiero dejar por otro; por quien te dejo es por Dios [IV, 10, 459]).

Periandro's total despair upon hearing Auristela's words recalls once again the interpolated tales at the beginning of Book I: if Rutilio's story highlighted the weakness that hampered Periandro's progress toward union, Manuel's story brought Auristela's problem to light. The balance the two characters seek requires a harmony between spirit and matter. Rutilio revealed the dangers that an overvaluation of matter can bring; Manuel showed the equally devastating effects of an overvaluation of the spiritual. In reacting to the witch, Auristela swings too far toward the spiritual realm, promoting herself as angelic instead of earthly.

Unification and Marriage

The reactions, Periandro's as well as Auristela's, have a healing effect, even as they push the protagonists to the brink of despair. Periandro leaves Rome when Auristela declares her desire to become a nun. He wanders about in the woods outside the city and then lies down to sleep. He awakens a little later to hear voices conversing in his mother tongue.[39] They belong to none other than his old servant Seráfido, who is telling Rutilio the story of his early life. The story continues until dawn, when Periandro leaves his hiding place to return to Rome and find Auristela.

The conversation between Seráfido and Rutilio links, symbolically, Periandro's true, hidden self with the wandering, repentant image of himself that Rutilio represents. Having all the earmarks of a dream, the magical voice from Periandro's past that rises up through the night in the woods outside Rome has the effect of bringing that which had been dark and hidden back into consciousness. Rutilio's sudden appearance in Rome further suggests a coupling of past and present, night and day, the conscious and the unconscious. Rutilio's name suggests a circle, and his journey, which began when he ran away to Rome, has traced Periandro's in reverse, since he has travelled through the north countries and back to Rome. His wanderings, by intersecting with those of Periandro at the beginning just off the Barbarous Island and again at the end just outside Rome, remind the reader that Periandro's journey is also intended to trace a circle and that what appears to be its end is in fact its midpoint. Once again, then, Cervantes shows how beginning and end join in the middle, so that one has the sense not of a linear journey but of an ever-turning circle around which one travels in search, finally, of oneself.

While Periandro is outside Rome becoming reacquainted with his true origin and destiny, Auristela is in Rome inadvertently revealing to Antonio and Constanza the secrets of her own history. Her declarations of love for Periandro prompt her finally to say "I will tell you who have been sent by Heaven to be indeed a brother and a sister to me that Periandro is not my brother" (quiero que sepais vosotros, pues el cielo os hizo verdaderos hermanos, que no lo es mío Periandro [IV, 11, 462]).

When Periandro and Auristela meet again, both have become openly reacquainted with the Persiles and Sigismunda they had all but left behind on their long, arduous journey from home. Their reidentification of themselves prepares the way for their union with each other, and finally, for the first time in all the long fiction of Cervantes, the quaternity that lay buried in even the earliest work comes out of hiding and asserts its restorative power over the conflicts of the protagonists.

The whole journey of the *Persiles,* with respect to the struggle for union that occupies its main characters, involves uniting the highest and lowest aspects of the self. Periandro and Auristela have to befriend the rival and then discover that the rival is a part of the self before they can truly accept one another. Once Periandro has reembraced Persiles, and Auristela has brought Sigismunda into the light of day—steps each character takes separately but simultaneously--the rest of their story falls quickly and almost effortlessly into place. They meet in front of the church of St. Paul. Like the gathering at the shrine of Guadalupe at the beginning of Book III, the one at St. Paul's at the end of Book IV unites all the forces of union and dissolution that accompanied the pilgrims on their journey. Many friends are there, but two enemies also appear: Hipólita's lover Pirro, who tries to kill Periandro, and Periandro's older brother Magsimino, from whom he thought he had the most to fear. Magsimino, however, is on the brink of death, having caught the summer fever in Rome. Symbolically, then, fire also consumes the last of the obstacles to Periandro's success.[40] As he closes his brother and rival's eyes in death with his left hand, he takes Auristela's in marriage with his right. On the last page of the work, Auristela and Periandro shed their disguises, end their separation, and become not only husband and wife but king and queen, having inherited their respective kingdoms, lands formerly torn by wars but now, like their rulers, joined together in peace.

So much more could be said, for the work is rich in symbols and full of parallels and resonances that this excursion has only briefly touched upon. Enough has been said, however, to make clear that the *Persiles* belongs solidly to Cervantes' opus and that it represents, with respect to the literary, psychological, theological, thematic, and characterological threads his work had been spinning, the culmination of a lifetime of writing.

Conclusion

In this study I have attempted to trace the development of consciousness in the central character as he evolved through Cervantes' long works of fiction and the structural and thematic consequences of that development. I have especially stressed the relation of interpolated matter to its accompanying text, the interaction between character and narrator, the success of the major characters in achieving their stated goals, the role of the secondary characters with respect to one another, and the projection and ultimate autonomy of the female characters. These separate strands of the analysis, as I hope to have shown, are interdependent, and a change in any one of the elements studied from text to text signals a shift in all the others.

The four long works show an overall movement toward greater and greater unity: unity of plot and episode, of character and narrator intentions, of character and environment, of individual and collective aspirations, of lover and loved one. Disunity in any one of these aspects is reflected in the disunity in all the others. Through the constant presence of the quaternity, one is able to see the hero move, in the successive works, from a place of isolation and ineffectuality to a place of centrality and efficacy. In isolation he either failed to perceive the opposites and conjunctions by which he was defined or saw them as alien to himself. In *La Galatea,* Elicio explored what was closest to him —the male world of friends and rivals. The loved one remained but a hazy image in that first work, poorly differentiated and inaccessible. *Don Quixote* Part I carried the development a step further by widening the range of male characters and deepening the hero's exploration of conflict and rivalry. The woman, meanwhile, emerged from her abstract perfection to offer a negative image to balance the overly positive one of the pastoral and chivalric traditions. *Don Quixote* Part II showed the hero probing the unknown, while his principal alter ego, Sancho, freed himself to undergo a process of transformation parallel to Don Quixote's, breaking down at the same time the relation of master to servant that prevailed in Part I. In the *Persiles* the hero was totally immersed in the alien, masterful in his dealings with his same-sex rivals, and attuned to the point of symbolic identity with the loved one. The process showed movement from periphery to center, allowing for both increasing differentiation among the characters and increasing unity. In the final configuration of the the quaternity, therefore, the four became aspects of the one.

The grounding for the structure of the works analyzed here rests not in literary theory and conscious thought alone but in truths emerging from the natural world. The production of twos and fours that I have found throughout the texts follows a natural order that, in the earlier works, conflicts with the one taken from a strictly literary canon. When Cervantes actively eschewed received literary patterns after *La Galatea,* he exposed the dissonance between the imitation of literary form and the imitation of nature. But in its highest evolution, the observation of natural patterns led to an understanding not just of matter but also of spirit. The discovery of the laws of the universe promoted not just an awareness of social failure but also the perfectibility of the observer who learns to apply those rules to himself.

My emphasis on the universality of the patterns apprehended and their relation to mythical, esoteric, and cosmological systems has tended to shift the focus of this study away from the personal and the historical. I have worked on the symbolic level in the textual analysis and have suggested that the material uncovered was largely independent of the instrument through which it emerged. The historical Cervantes may be evident in recounts of shipwrecks and long dusty travels along the highways of southern Spain, but the insights about the nature of our relations to one another and to the world we inhabit belong to us all. My purpose here has not been to squeeze that truth back into the container from which it issued nor to limit its value to the history of a particular man who lived in Spain four hundred years ago. Instead, my aim has been to call attention to those truths as I have perceived them, begging forgiveness for the limitations of my own that have obscured them as I pass them on and asking that they be valued for whatever they have to offer.

Notes

Notes to Introduction—Chapter 1

[1] Umberto Eco, *A Theory of Semiotics* (Bloomington and London: Indiana University Press, 1976), 7.

[2] Edward Said, *Beginnings: Intention and Method* (New York: Basic Books, 1975), 86.

[3] Cesáreo Bandera, *Mimesis conflictiva* (Madrid: Gredos, 1975), 122.

[4] J. Hillis Miller, "Steven's Rock and Criticism as Cure, II," *The Georgia Review* 30 (1976), 337.

[5] See his *Cervantes' Christian Romance* (Princeton: Princeton University Press, 1971), especially the introduction, 1–12.

[6] See Javier Herrero's "Sierra Morena as Labyrinth: From Wildness to Christian Knighthood," *Forum for Modern Language Studies* 17 (1981), 55–67.

[7] Juergen Hahn also discusses this in his "El Capitán Cautivo: The Soldier's Truth and Literary Precept in *Don Quixote*, Part I," *JHP* 3 (1979), 269–303.

[8] The comment, which will be further discussed in Chapter 4 of this study, appears in Chapter 8 of Part II of *Don Quixote*: "It is for us to slay pride by slaying giants; to slay envy by our generosity and nobility; anger by calmness of mind, and serenity of disposition; gluttony, and drowsiness by eating little and watching late into the night; indulgence in lust by preserving our loyalty to those whom we have made ladies of our hearts; and sloth by travelling through all parts of the world in quest of opportunities of becoming famous knights as well as Christians."

[9] In the *Coloquio de los perros*, where the problem of fiction and reality is so thoroughly probed, a witch prophesies that the talking dogs will be restored to their human shape when the elevated proud are knocked down and the battered humble ones are raised up: "Volverán en su forma verdadera / Cuando vieren con presta diligencia / Derribar los soberbios levantados, / Y alzar a los humildes abatidos, / Con poderosa mano para hacello" (*Novelas ejemplares*, ed. Rodríguez Marín, vol. 2 [Madrid: Clásicos Castellanos, 1965], 293).

[10] Several of Cervantes' female characters—Teolinda in *La Galatea*, Leandra in *Don Quixote* Part I, Teodosia in *Las dos doncellas*, and even Auristela in the *Persiles*—show themselves susceptible to the jealousy and despair that are the hallmarks of metaphysical desire. The point here is not to establish an absolute differentiation between male and female characters, for that would be to insist upon the split that in fact Cervantes was seeking, through his works, to heal. The limitations that allow one to seek in another the perfection one feels is lacking in one-self belong to *all* the unredeemed, male and female. The process of redemption requires that the artificial barriers that divide the self from the other fall. That process can best be seen, in Cervantes' works, through the male characters, since they are generally the ones on whom our attention is focused.

[11] Jung, as will be discussed, emphasizes in his work on the struc-ture of the psyche that there are several identifiable layers of the unconscious and that the level of the anima for a man, as that of the animus for a woman, reaches beyond the merely personal unconscious. Unless harmony is established with this level of the psyche, imbalances will be experienced in consciousness. For further discussion, see "The Syzygy: Anima and Animus," in *Aion*, vol. 9, pt. 2, of *Collected Works* (Princeton: Princeton University Press, 1968), 11–22 (hereafter cited as *CW*); and "The Relations Between the Ego and the Unconscious," in *Two Essays on Analytical Psychology*, vol. 7 of *CW*, 127–227.

[12] See my *Novel to Romance: A Study of Cervantes's "Novelas ejemplares"* (Baltimore: Johns Hopkins University Press, 1974).

Notes to "La Galatea"—Chapter 2

[1] For a discussion of neo-Platonism in the pastoral romances, see J. B. Avalle-Arce's *La novela pastoril española* (Madrid: Ediciones Istmo, 1974), 35–68; A. Solé-Leris' *The Spanish Pastoral Novel* (Boston: Twayne Publishers, 1980), 27–30; and D. H. Darst's "Renaissance Platonism and the Spanish Pastoral Novel," *Hispania* 52 (1969), 384–92.

[2] The term *naive* comes from Northrop Frye's discussion in *The Critical Path: An Essay on the Social Context of Literary Criticism* (Bloom-ington and London: Indiana University Press, 1973) of Schiller's dis-tinction between "naive" and "sentimental" reading. Naive reading is linear, participating, precritical, whereas sentimental reading attends to the organizing patterns of convention, genre, and archetype in order to perceive structure. Frye uses the distinction to point out that modern fiction tends to "abolish the teleological plot" (p. 30) in search of unity or intensity, through which the ideal world may be glimpsed (pp. 29–33). I find the distinction useful in approaching a work such as *La Galatea*, whose lack of resolution also forces the reader into a vertical perception of the text's structure.

[3] See especially Francisco López-Estrada's *La "Galatea" de Cervantes*

(La Laguna de Tenerife: Universidad de la Laguna, 1948), 22 and 32–35; and Avalle-Arce's *La novela pastoril,* 247. Just as I was sending this manuscript to press I ran across Mary Gaylord Randel's "The Language of Limits and the Limits of Language: The Crisis of Poetry in *La Galatea,*" *MLN* 97 (1982), 254–71. She writes eloquently not so much of the text's ambiguity as of its awareness of itself as cast out from the center toward which it is oriented. "In the genre which supposedly allows its characters to concern themselves with being rather than contingency, wholeness shines precisely by its absence. The text's internal distances —between philosopher and philosopher, poet and poet, between debate and verse and narrative and event—confirm the inevitable exteriority of all discourse to the vision of truth or of self that it pursues" (p. 265).

[4] In René Girard's *Deceit, Desire, and the Novel: Self and Other in Literary Structure,* trans. Yvonne Freccero (Baltimore: Johns Hopkins University Press, 1965), Girard shows the mechanism by which the lover, attracted less by the loved one than by the desire for her expressed by another, is caught in a spiral of failure that leads to despair. The triangular situation he describes is well suited to capture the dynamics of courtly love as it is experienced in pastoral literature. Bandera, who has applied Girard's model to Cervantes and Calderón, has shown in *Mimesis conflictiva* (Madrid: Gredos, 1975) that endless repetition, and the inability to conclude, characteristic as much of *La Galatea* as of *Don Quixote* Part I, are literary signals of the presence of metaphysical desire within the work. See especially his discussion of Sancho's tale, pp. 112–21.

[5] The words come during the priest's dismantling of Don Quixote's library, in Chapter 6 of Part I.

[6] The division of the world into "good" and "bad" is essential not only to the pastoral enterprise but to the chivalric as well. Bandera has shown in *Mimesis* how much Cervantes, in *Don Quixote,* is entangled unconsciously with the figure of the mad knight whom he thought he had invented to ridicule. In *La Galatea* Cervantes does not launch a fullblown attack on characters who have absorbed the pastoral ideology, but he does show a disinclination to limit his perspective to theirs. If William Empson is correct, in *Some Versions of Pastoral* (New York: New Directions, 1968), in proposing that the pastoral tradition's nostalgia for the countryside emerges out of a consciousness imbedded in the complexities of urban life, it is understandable that Cervantes, with his vast experience outside the courts and centers of power, would accept with difficulty the pastoral mystique. Renato Poggioli, in *The Oaten Flute* (Cambridge: Harvard University Press, 1975), also emphasizes the split implicit in the pastoral between the author's worldly existence and the peaceful poetic world he imagines, "for pastoral poetry appears whenever the hustle and bustle of metropolitan life

grows hard to bear and man tries to evade its pressures at least in thought" (p. 4). He later notes: "If the artist or the poet dons so often a pastoral disguise, it is only because he wishes to emphasize his personality in private rather than in public terms. The emphasis is but a symbolic protest and acts as a romantic and nostalgic denial of those cultural or material circumstances that condition his social status and make him at the same time a public figure or a civil servant" (p. 23). The pastoral is clearly not a genre entirely suited to a relatively poor soldier just returned to Spain after five years of captivity in Algiers.

[7] Poggioli says, "The courtly pastoral is but a costumed garden party, where even the great personages of the world play for a while, if only in emblematic fashion, the conventional role of shepherds and shepherdesses" (*The Oaten Flute*, 23–24). Cervantes, in his prologue to *La Galatea*, acknowledges that most of his characters are in fact courtiers in disguise: "I will not be too worried if someone criticizes me for having mixed philosophy with the love complaints of shepherds, who rarely talk in fact about anything but things to do with the countryside, and that with great plainness. But noting—as in the work I sometimes do— that many of the shepherds are only shepherds in disguise, the objection is answered" (Así no temeré mucho que alguno condemne haber mezclado razones de filosofía entre algunas amorosas de pastores, que pocas veces se levantan a más que a tratar cosas del campo, y esto con su acostumbrada llaneza. Mas advirtiendo—como en el discurso de la obra alguna vez se hace—que muchos de los disfrazados pastores della lo eran sólo en el hábito, queda llana esta objectión [prologue, 8]) Erastro's presence, in such a literary atmosphere, is all the more arresting.

[8] See my "Structural and Thematic Discontinuity in Montemayor's *Diana,*" *MLN* 86 (1971), 182–98. See also Joaquín Casalduero's discussion of the homosexual tradition in ancient bucolic literature that surfaces—as ornament, he says—in *La Diana*, in his article "*La Galatea,*" in *Suma Cervantina* (London: Tamesis, 1973), especially pp. 29–30. The point is not so much that love is primarily homosexual in *La Diana*—it is not—but that the sexual polarities do not function as the basis of attraction in the work. Bandera, in *Mimesis*, has provided a theoretical explanation for the blurring of sex differentiation, pointing out that eros is an expression of metaphysical desire and that it has no sex: "The 'eroticism' of which we are speaking is truly a metaphysical 'eroticism'. In fact, we are dealing with an 'eroticism' that, instead of basing itself on sexual differences, tends to abolish them. . . . Its object has no sex, is not a 'he' nor a 'she', but rather an *other*, shaped and defined by literature, around whom the irresistible attraction of being appears to shimmer" (p. 29).

[9] Casalduero, in "*La Galatea,*" displaying his sensitivity to the fine details of a work, mentions, but does not comment on the significance of, the separation between shepherds and shepherdesses that distin-

guishes *La Galatea* as a pastoral novel (see pp. 37–45). Renato Poggioli elaborates much more on Cervantes' deviation from the pastoral manner of representing the sexes. Pointing out that the pastoral is essentially a man's world, in which woman figures as an object valued only for her youth and beauty, he registers surprise at Marcela's role in *Don Quixote* Part I: "In this case the divergence [from the stock pastoral situation], almost without precedent in the whole of pastoral literature, is seen in the fact that the willing or unwilling leader, the person taking the initiative, or at least setting an example, is a woman and not a man. Now we know that in the pastoral story we are about to hear there will be not simply two leading characters of different sex but an antagonist and a protagonist, which is extravagant enough; and we also know that by an even more extraordinary exception the latter will be a feminine one" (*The Oaten Flute*, 169). The comment could well be made about *La Galatea*, however, a work Poggioli mentions in passing without ever discussing, for it is in *La Galatea* that Marcela's predecessor Gelasia appears. The point is that the stronger role accorded the woman in Cervantes' work, even in his earliest writings, distinguishes him from his contemporaries. Louis Combet's *Cervantès ou les incertitudes du désir* (Lyons: Presses Universitaires de Lyon, 1981) explores this phenomenon at great length. Though I do not share his conclusions (see my review article on his book in *MLN* 97 [1982], 422–27), his observations are valid to a point and must be taken into account.

[10] Avalle-Arce (*La novela pastoril*) beautifully expresses the presence of the polarities in *La Galatea*: "What is the meaning of this enormous pendular movement which intentionally embraces such distinct aspects of literary reality, or even physical reality on occasion? The most likely thing is that we are dealing with a rigorous pairing of opposites: poetic, myth and real circumstances, court and countryside, with alternate primacy, feminism and antifeminism, paganism and Christianity. The method by which this is carried through—note that I am not speaking of a dialectic method, but rather of that compatible with artistic creation —that method is evidence of a vision of the poeticizable cosmos as something susceptible of synthesis" (p. 246). But he also adds: "The harmony of the poeticizable cosmos is not achieved, and the most that one gets is a lining up of opposites" (p. 247).

[11] See previous note.

[12] The pattern, which will be traced throughout the novels of Cervantes, finds its abstract formulation in C. G. Jung's writings on the levels of the psyche. See for example "The Syzygy: Anima and Animus," in *Aion*, vol. 9, pt. 2, of *CW*, 11–22; "The Relations Between the Ego and the Unconscious," in *Two Essays on Analytical Psychology*, vol. 7 of *CW*, 127–227; and *The Archetypes and the Collective Unconscious*, vol. 9, pt. 1, of *CW*. The process of reaching beyond the limitations of the ego begins, as Jung describes it, by recognizing the shadow as a projection

of unwanted qualities outside of the self. He says: "I should like to emphasize that the integration of the shadow, or the realization of the personal unconscious, marks the first stage in the analytic process, and that without it a recognition of anima and animus is impossible. The shadow can be realized only through a relation to a partner, and anima and animus only through a relation to the opposite sex, because only in such a relation do their projections become operative" ("The Syzygy," 22).

[13] Evaluation of the symbolic meaning of the number four can be found in any standard dictionary of symbols. See, for example, J. C. Cooper, *An Illustrated Encyclopaedia of Traditional Symbols* (London: Thames and Hudson, 1978), 115–16; J. E. Cirlot, *A Dictionary of Symbols*, trans. Jack Sage (London: Routledge and Kegan Paul, 1962), 201; and Ad de Vries, *Dictionary of Symbols and Imagery* (Amsterdam and London: North-Holland Publishing Company, 1974), 201, 344–45. Jung has amplified greatly on the subject of the quaternity, especially in "The Structure and Dynamics of the Self," in *Aion*, vol. 9, pt. 2, of *CW*, 222–65; and in "The Psychology of the Transference," in *The Practice of Psychotherapy*, vol. 16 of *CW*, 219ff.

[14] Among the commentators of *La Galatea* whom I have read, Jennifer Lowe is alone in making explicit reference to the link between the implied jealousy of Elicio and Erastro and the interpolated tales that are presented in the novel, in her excellent effort to demonstrate the structural unity of *La Galatea*. See her "The *cuestión de amor* and the Structure of Cervantes' *Galatea*," *BHS* 43 (1966), 98–109.

[15] Howard Patch, in *The Other World According to Descriptions in Medieval Literature* (Cambridge: Harvard University Press, 1950), mentions lakes, enclosed gardens, and caves in their role as passages to places that served as analogues of the other world in medieval romance. For my purposes here, the "other world" belongs to the realm of the unconscious since it is inaccessible to intellectual understanding. Responses to the other world–unconscious can be evoked, moreover, only through appeal to the imagination and to the senses. At the heart of the neo-Aristotelian rejection of medieval romance was romance's appeal to the imagination, considered the realm of the common people and inferior to the intellect. The intense sixteenth-century debate about the values and dangers of literature revolved around a dispute over the merits of the various faculties of the soul. Alban Forcione shows, in his brilliant analysis of the debate between Don Quixote and the Canon in *Cervantes, Aristotle, and the "Persiles"* (Princeton: Princeton University Press, 1970), that Cervantes, through Don Quixote, was capable of making a strong defense of literature's appeal to the senses and the imagination. The Lisandro episode reveals that Elicio's "descent" into the "other world" is essential to his well-being, for it allows him to correct a severe imbalance in consciousness that, unattended, would inevitably lead to violence.

[16] See, for example, Alan Deyermond, "El hombre salvaje en la novela sentimental," *Filología* 10 (1964), 97–111; Paul Ilie, "Grotesque Elements in the Pastoral Novel," in *Homenaje a William L. Fichter* (Madrid: Editorial Castalia, 1971), 319–28; Oleh Mazur, "Various Folkloric Impacts upon the *Salvaje* in the Spanish *Comedia*," *HR* 36 (1968), 207–35; the collections of essays, especially Edward Dudley's "The Wild Man Goes Baroque," in *The Wild Man Within*, ed. Edward Dudley and Maximillian Novak (Pittsburgh: University of Pittsburgh Press, 1972); Barbara Mujicia, "Violence in the Pastoral Novel from Sannazaro to Cervantes," *Hispano-Italic Studies* 1 (1976), 39–55; and Harry Sieber, "Society and the Pastoral Vision in the Marcela-Grisóstomo Episode of *Don Quijote*," in *Estudios literarios de hispanistas norteamericanos dedicados a Helmut Hatzfeld con motivo de su 80 aniversario* (Barcelona: Ediciones Hispam, 1974), 185–94.

[17] The process is well discussed in "The Shadow" (in *Aion*, vol. 9, pt. 2, of *CW*, 8–10), where he says, in part: "To become conscious of it [the shadow] involves recognizing the dark aspects of the personality as present and real. This act is the essential condition for any kind of self-knowledge, and it therefore . . . meets with considerable resistance" (p. 8). He goes on to note the *emotional* (as opposed to the intellectual) nature of the shadow's eruption into consciousness, using words that can well be applied to Elicio's relation to Erastro/Lisandro: "Affects occur usually where adaptation is weakest, and at the same time they reveal the reason for its weakness, namely a certain degree of inferiority and the existence of a lower level of personality. On this lower level with its uncontrolled or scarcely controlled emotions one behaves more or less like a primitive . . ." (p. 9). To assimilate the shadow, he adds, requires "insight and good will" (p. 9).

[18] The narrator describes Elicio as preoccupied both with his love and with the shepherds as he goes out alone at night into the woods: "Elicio could not stop thinking about what had moved the shepherds to such a desperate state, and he felt badly that he had not followed the homicidal shepherd to find out from him, if it were possible, what he wanted. With this thought and with the many others that his love caused him . . . he went out from his cabin" (su sosiego [de sus ganados] y el poco que sus cuidados le concedían [no] podían apartar a Elicio de pensar qué causas habían movido a los dos pastores para venir a tan desesperado trance; y ya le pesaba de no haber seguido al pastor homicida, y saber dél, si fuera posible, lo que deseaba. Con este pensamiento, y con los muchos que sus amores le causaban . . . se salió de su cabaña [I, 30]).

[19] Both characters, fleeing from and terrified of love, fall victims of their desire for Gelasia, who reveals the destructive nature of the self-enclosed female character. Lenio goes mad for her, and Galercio attempts suicide because of her. The situation will recur in the Marcela/

Grisóstomo episode in *Don Quixote* Part I. The problem for Cervantes will be, as Marcela's well-known speech in her own defense shows, that desire, though devastating when rejected, cannot be engendered in one who is indifferent. Psychologically speaking, the presence of a Gelasia or a Marcela in Cervantes' early works testifies to a not fully developed relationship to the feminine in his nature and in his work, which is reflected in less exaggerated terms in the fortunes of his main character.

[20] The twin motif is widely remarked upon by commentators of this work, though rarely are the observations on its roots in folklore and mythology integrated into the structure of relationships in *La Galatea* itself. The motif will be analyzed in the body of the text. Here I want to point out that the presence of female twins is something of a departure from tradition, once again heralding the incipient tendency in Cervantes to perceive feminine development as an important aspect of the masculine drive for union. Also rarely commented upon is the significance of the fact that Teolinda and Leonarda are not actually twins but identical sisters, an event far stranger than the already rare phenomenon of twinship. Since Cervantes sacrifices considerable credibility by this evasion of the natural, the situation warrants scrutiny.

[21] Both images, the hunted rabbit and the slaughtered deer, capture symbolically the imbalance in the relationship between the sexes that the pastoral as well as the chivalric sustain. The woman is viewed, in this imagery, as pure and vulnerable, much like the ermine with whom Lotario compares the young woman in his discourse to Anselmo in "The Tale of Foolish Curiosity" in *Don Quixote* Part I. She is, in the final analysis, prey, pursued by the hunter, the dog, or the lion. E. C. Riley has discussed the symbolic relation between the rabbit and the woman in his article "Symbolism in *Don Quixote*, Part II, Chapter 73," *JHP* 3 (1979), 161–74.

[22] René Girard, in *Violence and the Sacred*, trans. Patrick Gregory (Baltimore: Johns Hopkins University Press, 1977), notes the danger that resemblance invokes, since it suggests reciprocity and hence a susceptibility to violence that differentiation serves to check. A similar point is made by C. K. Ogden in his book *Opposition: A Linguistic and Psychological Analysis* (Bloomington and London: Indiana University Press, 1967): "Opposition is not to be defined as the maximun degree of difference, but as a very special kind of repetition, namely of two similar things that are mutually destructive in virtue of their very similarity" (p. 41). The appearance of identity, then, masks the presence of opposing forces. This in itself seems to suggest that the Teolinda/Leonarda/Artidoro/Galercio pairings are doomed to failure.

[23] It is true that the Silerio/Timbrio story is told from the point of view of the weaker character, since the primary narrator of the tale is Silerio. What is significant is that Silerio has appropriated the values of the stronger character, through whose ego he must necessarily perceive

himself as of lesser value. The embryo of a transformation process can be found, however, in Silerio's search for a spiritual orientation. His actions contrast sharply with those of the traditional despairing lover, a prime example of which is Cardenio in *Don Quixote* Part I. In the *Persiles*, the "weaker" character is no longer concerned at all with the value system that relegates him to the position of *segundón*. Louis Combet (*Cervantès ou les incertitudes du désir*), who believes that all of Cervantes' male heroes correspond to the role of the "rival" or secondary male figure, has entirely neglected the possibility of another orientation that would turn wordly values upside down.

24 The problem is well analyzed in Denis de Rougemont's *Love in the Western World*, trans. Montgomery Belgion, rev. and aug. ed. (New York: Pantheon, 1956), as well as in C. S. Lewis' *The Allegory of Love: A Study in Medieval Tradition* (Oxford: Clarendon Press, 1936).

25 See his *Mimesis*, especially pp. 19–33.

26 Some critics, encouraged by Cervantes' already cited comment in the preface to *La Galatea* that most of his shepherds are courtiers in disguise, have sought for historical counterparts for the most prominent characters in the work. Lauso has frequently been seen as a stand-in for Cervantes himself, as López-Estrada points out in *La "Galatea,"* 161–62, and the loved whom Lauso has ceased to desire is seen as the mysterious Ana Franca with whom Cervantes is said to have had a brief liaison.

27 Interestingly, it is precisely these three who have attracted the most attention from those critics concerned with uncovering historical characters in *La Galatea*. Avalle-Arce, in *La novela pastoril*, suggests that Tirsi is probably Francisco de Figueroa but discounts F. Egea Abelenda's suggestion ("Sobre la *Galatea* de Cervantes," *Revista de Archivos, Bibliotecas y Museos* 42 [1921] 548–54) that Damon was Pedro Lainez, saying, "This identification does not explain the close friendship between Damon and Tirsi." What *can* be observed is that the apparently automatic doubling—Tirsi *must* appear with his inseparable friend Damon—corresponds to the deep structure of the work as has been shown throughout this analysis of *La Galatea*. Perhaps Tirsi does represent a historical figure. But when transformed into fiction, that figure is doubled and appears as two friends. For more on the hidden identities of the characters in *La Galatea*, see Geoffrey Stagg, "A Matter of Masks," in *Hispanic Studies in Honour of Joseph Manson*, ed. D. M. Atkinson and A. H. Clark (Oxford: Clarendon Press, 1972), 255–67.

28 The brevity of this analysis has not allowed all of the many characters who dart in and out of this most complex and confusing pastoral novel to be mentioned. But no loved one in the work is available to a would-be lover uncontested. Even the pale, scarcely developed Blanca has a suitor to complicate her relation to Silerio. The suitor is Darinto, who, on hearing that Silerio has been found, leaves the company of

Blanca, Nísida, and Timbrio in despair, knowing that Blanca prefers Silerio to him (Book IV).

[29] I do not use the term *conversion* here lightly, nor do I make the leap from character to authorial consciousness unaware of the chasm that we have been taught to see between them. I very much share René Girard's belief, however, that the resolved novel—the one that ends in the hero's death or marriage—signals the attainment of higher consciousness on the part of the author. Girard expresses the notion of such a conversion in the last chapter of his *Deceit, Desire, and the Novel*.

Notes to "Don Quixote" Part I—Chapter 3

[1] Félix Martínez-Bonati, in his "Cervantes y las regiones de la imaginación," *Dispositio* 2 (1977), 28–53, reveals a similar unity of vision beneath the disorder of the surface narrative in *Don Quixote* Part I.

[2] *Mimesis conflictiva* (Madrid: Gredos, 1975), see particularly Chapter 1, "Cervantes frente a don Quijote," pp. 39–56.

[3] The discrepancy between formal subdivisions and the natural flow of the narrative has been ably analyzed by Raymond Willis in his *The Phantom Chapters of the "Quijote"* (New York: Hispanic Institute in the United States, 1953).

[4] It is interesting to note the conflict and yet the complementarity of the stated positions of author and character as the book begins. Cervantes' prologue and the literary discussions throughout Part I call into question not only all the literary norms employed in his day but the very practices and assumptions of lettered men. Don Quixote, on the other hand, has absolute faith in the written word his author is questioning. What the two have in common, however, is the sense of being outside of and of feeling aggressive toward the established order—literary for Cervantes, social for Don Quixote. For a good discussion of the social implications of Don Quixote's madness, see Charles Aubrun's "Pour quelle raison déraisonna Don Quichotte," in *Homenaje a Casalduero* (Madrid: Gredos, 1972), 37–44.

[5] "I find myself incapable of supplying them [the many things lacking] because of my inadequacy and scanty learning, and because I am too spiritless and lazy by nature to go about looking for authors to say for me what I can say myself without them" (I, Prologue, 27) (Yo me hallo incapaz de remediarlas, por mi insuficiencia y pocas letras, y porque naturalmente soy poltrón y perezoso de andarme buscando autores que digan lo que yo me sé decir sin ellos [I, Prologue, 57]).

[6] It is curious how few critics have pointed out that the words so strongly written against the chivalric novels were spoken by the friend who emerged as Cervantes' interlocutor in the prologue. Most people who choose to contend that *Don Quixote* was written as a burlesque of the books of chivalry (e.g., Anthony Close, *Cervantes and the Romantic Approach to "Don Quixote"* [Cambridge: Cambridge University Press,

1978]; P. E. Russell, *"Don Quixote* as a Funny Book," *MLR* 64 [1969], 312–26; and Martín de Riquer, *Aproximación al "Quijote"* [Barcelona: Editorial Teide, 1967], 59–75), attribute the friend's words to Cervantes himself. Bruce Wardropper (in *"Don Quixote*: Story or History?," *Modern Philology* 63 [1965], 1–11) does point out, though without elaborating, that the speaker is a friend. Though the main weight of current opinion tends to discredit the attack on chivalric novels as the single motivating factor for the work (see, for example, Forcione, *Cervantes, Aristotle, and the "Persiles"* [Princeton: Princeton University Press, 1970], 124–30 and E. C. Riley, *Cervantes's Theory of the Novel* [Oxford: Clarendon Press, 1962]), most agree that the motive, be it to destroy or to outdo the chivalric novels, was a factor. See Salvador de Madariaga's "Cervantes y los Libros de Caballerías," in *Guía del lector del "Quijote,"* 2d ed. (Buenos Aires: Editorial Sudamericana, 1943): "We have seen that the attitude of Cervantes, as a critic, toward the books of chivalry, though complex, was, all told, adverse. But Cervantes was also, and above all, a creator, and a creator almost always in unconscious rebellion against Cervantes as critic. We ought not to be surprised, then, if in the attitude of the author of *Don Quixote* with respect to the books of chivalry we notice elements in surprising contradiction to the expressed end for which *Don Quixote* was written" (pp. 40–41). See also Otis Green, "El 'Ingenioso' Hidalgo," *HR* 25 (1957), 193. Robert Flores, in "The Role of Cide Hamete in *Don Quixote*," *BHS* 59 (1982), 3–14, offers an interesting further interpretation of the 1605 Prologue: "In Chapter 6 of Part I Cervantes (not to be confused with any of his characters, who should not be trusted as spokesmen for their creator) criticizes specific romances of chivalry, not the genre as a whole, and his statement in the Prologue to the effect that the sole purpose of the novel was to discredit the ill-founded edifice of the books of chivalry is, in all probability, a direct and immediate spin-off from the discussion between Don Quixote, the priest, and the Canon concerning literature in general and books of chivalry in particular (Chapters 47–50; Part I has fifty-two chapters). Hence, Cervantes' remarks are probably after-thoughts rather than statements of purpose, and they should be taken with a pinch of salt . . ." (p. 13, n. 12).

[7] A book devoted entirely to the difficulties of perceiving a single ideology behind the novel is Manuel Durán's *La ambigüedad en el "Quijote"* (Xalapa, Mexico: Universidad Veracruzana, 1961), which will here represent the perspectivist tendency that has dominated *Quijote* criticism in recent years. For critical evaluations of the perspectivist position, see Arthur Efron, *Don Quixote and the Dulcineated World* (Austin and London: University of Texas Press, 1971) and Anthony Close, *Cervantes and the Romantic Approach*. Despair over the difficulty in coming fully to grips with the novel, however, continues to be expressed in the most recent commentaries. See, for example, Helena Percas de Ponseti's introduc-

tion to her two-volume *Cervantes y su concepto del arte* (Madrid: Gredos, 1975): "Reading the book itself, along with all the criticism, opens us to a world of perspectives unsuspected for their breadth and contradictions. Instead of leading us closer to the author, the reading makes even less graspable the nature of his artistic creation, especially in *Don Quixote*. . . . Every episode has evoked controversy about the essential meaning it encloses, since the critics begin with irreconcilable basic premises" (p. 12). She cites in support of this lament a similar passage by Angel del Río in his "El equívoco del *Quijote*," *HR* 27 (1959), 201–2.

[8] The best short analysis of this immense amalgam of verbal expression remains Leo Spitzer's "Linguistic Perspectivism in the *Don Quijote*," in *Linguistics and Literary History: Essays in Stylistics* (Princeton University Press, 1948). Others who have worked the same vein in recent Cervantes criticism are Mia Gerhardt, *"Don Quijote": La Vie et les livres* (Amsterdam: North Holland Publishing Company, 1955); and Marthe Robert, *L'Ancien et le nouveau (De "Don Quichotte" à Franz Kafka)* (Paris: Grasset, 1963). This approach rightly makes of *Don Quixote* a favorite case for theorists concerned with the role of language in the world of experience and hence *Don Quixote*'s appearance in Michel Foucault's *The Order of Things*, translated from *Les Mots et les choses* (New York: Random House, 1970).

[9] Leo Spitzer, in "Linguistic Perspectivism," articulates well the presence of Cervantes' affirmative spirit: "And yet, beyond this perspectivism, we may sense the presence of something which is not subject to fluctuation: the immovable, immutable principle of the divine . . . " (p. 41).

[10] *Mimesis.* See, for example, pp. 40–60.

[11] Leaving aside for a moment the fact that Don Quixote is in any case a fictional entity, the difficulty of representing "reality" is an enormous one, one that Laurence Sterne addressed in his effort to catch up to the present moment in *Tristram Shandy*.

[12] J. J. Allen presents one analysis of Cervantes' dissociation from Don Quixote in his study of the patterns of success and failure in *Don Quixote: Hero or Fool? A Study in Narrative Technique* (Gainesville: University of Florida Press, 1969).

[13] Cesáreo Bandera makes Cervantes' mixed fascination with and resistance to fiction the cornerstone of his analysis of *Don Quixote* in *Mimesis*.

[14] Arthur Efron, in *Don Quixote and the Dulcineated World*, brings Don Quixote's cruelty toward the body—his own as well as Sancho's—under close scrutiny.

[15] *Beginnings: Intention and Method* (New York: Basic Books, 1975), 137–47.

[16] Edward C. Dudley, in his article "The Wild Man Goes Baroque" (In *The Wild Man Within*, ed. Edward C. Dudley and Maximillian Novak [Pittsburgh: University of Pittsburgh Press, 1972], 115–39), specifically

calls the retreat into the Sierras the turning point of Part I and links the mountains in Chapter 23 of Part I with the cave in Chapter 23 of Part II to signal a shift from an extroverted to an introverted orientation on Don Quixote's part.

[17] See Avalle-Arce's discussion of the Sierras in his portion of the article "*Don Quijote*," in *Suma Cervantina* (London: Tamesis, 1973), especially pp. 51–55, and also in his *Don Quijote como forma de vida* (Madrid: Fundación Juan March, 1976), where he links the question of gratuitousness with that of free will in the chapter entitled "La vida como obra de arte," pp. 144–72. The chapter is an elaboration of an article, "Don Quijote o la vida como obra de arte," previously published in *Cuadernos hispanoamericanos* 242 (1970), 247–80. In quite another context Helena Percas de Ponseti (*Cervantes y su concepto del arte*, 135–37) also discusses the question of gratuitousness, relating it to the theological debate on grace that belonged to the theoretical climate of the times in which Cervantes wrote. She writes about not only the absurdity of Don Quixote's penance but his willingness to love his lady without expecting return. The center as well as the apex of Part I (since Don Quixote is on a mountain and *Don Quixote* is halfway finished) shows the hero turning to the unconscious side of his search for the first time. The actions he performs seem gratuitous, because, like everything from the unconscious, they cannot be justified along rational lines.

[18] Avalle-Arce, in his portion of the article on *Don Quixote* in *Suma Cervantina*, sees important correspondences between the Sierra Morena episode of Part I and the cave of Montesinos episode in Part II. It is worth noting, beyond the similarities Avalle-Arce established between the two, that at both crucial moments Don Quixote has to deal with Dulcinea's dark side, as reflected in Aldonza Lorenzo in Part I and in the coarse peasant girl in Part II.

[19] In choosing to adopt a schema for the interpolated tales of Part I of *Don Quixote*, I am aware of the wide variety of ways in which critics have explained, ordered, and even numbered them. Most critics today agree that the stories have a significance integral to the novel as a whole, though there is considerable disagreement over what that significance is. René Girard (*Deceit, Desire, and the Novel: Self and Other in Literary Structure*, trans. Yvonne Freccero [Baltimore: Johns Hopkins University Press, 1965]) offers an excellent defense for the underlying coherence of "The Tale of Foolish Curiosity" within the novel in which it is lodged, as does Bruce Wardropper in "The Pertinence of *El curioso impertinente*," *Publications of the Modern Language Association* 72 (1957), 587–600; Harry Levin, in "The Example of Cervantes," in *Contexts of Criticism* (Cambridge: Harvard University Press, 1957), 76–96; and Frank Pierce in his introduction to *Two Cervantes Short Novels: "El curioso impertinente" and "El celoso extremeño"* (Oxford: Pergamon, 1970).

For a summary of approaches to the question of the interpolated tales in *Don Quixote* Part I see Edward Dudley's "Don Quixote as Magus: The Rhetoric of Interpolation," *BHS* 49 (1972), 355–68, especially pp. 355–57.

More dissention among recent critics is evident when the question becomes one of ordering. Marthe Robert (in *L'Ancien et le nouveau*) disavows any significant internal ordering pattern (*"Don Quixote* could be read in any order . . . because it does not develop through situations emerging one out of another. . ." [p. 125]), but Raymond Immerwahr ("Structural Symmetry in the Episodic Narratives of *Don Quijote,* Part One," *Comparative Literature* 10 [1958], 121–35) takes pains to show how perfectly placed and balanced the episodes are. A middle view is taken by Félix Martínez-Bonati in "La unidad del *Quixote" (Dispositio* 2 [1977], 118–39): "The sequence of adventures, . . . looked at as a whole, acquires a meaning, since the character of the adventures changes slowly, according to the changes in personality of the characters, and this gives a certain order to the succession of parts. But this order is not causal, it does not have a strong logic, nor can it be discerned in each one of the adventures" (p. 121). The problem of the ordering and significance of the interpolated tales remains an unresolved one, to which I add my interpretation, not as The Definitive Solution but as a part of my overall analysis of the development of the consciousness of harmony as it is expressed in the sequence of Cervantes' fiction. That Cervantes himself was interested in the ordering of the interpolated tales might be indicated by evidence brought by Robert Flores ("Cervantes at Work: The Writing of *Don Quixote,* Part I," *JHP* 3 [1979], 135–60) and Geoffrey Stagg ("Revision in *Don Quijote,* Part I," *Hispanic Studies in Honour of I. Gonzáles Llubera* [Oxford, 1959], 347–66) that Cervantes shifted the Marcela/Grisóstomo tale from a place late in the novel to its present position in Chapters 11–14. Helena Percas de Ponseti also discusses the question of ordering in her *Cervantes y su concepto del arte,* 127. What the Flores studies (see also his "The Loss and Recovery of Sancho's Ass in *Don Quixote,* Part I," *MLR* 75 [1980], 301–10) reveal clearly is that Cervantes spent a great deal of time adding to, revising, and reshuffling the material that eventually became *Don Quixote* Part I, all of which suggests that *some* ordering principle was involved in the selection process. See also Harold G. Jones' "Grisóstomo and Don Quixote: Death and Imitation," *Revista canadiense de estudios hispánicos* 4 (1979), 85–92.

As for numbering, the list of interpolated tales varies from five (my count) to six (Casalduero) to seven (Immerwahr and Dudley), to nine (in the Porrúa edition of *Don Quixote* [Mexico, 1966]).

[20] The link between romantic love and death is very clearly made in Denis de Rougemont's *Love in the Western World,* trans. Montgomery Belgion, rev. and aug. ed. (New York: Pantheon, 1956), 18–23 and 50–53. He also asserts the equality of the sexes that is the precondition of

true marriage: "Once she is man's equal, woman cannot be man's goal. Yet at the same time she is spared the bestial abasement that sooner or later must be the price of divinizing a creature" (pp. 312–13).

²¹ A discussion of the juxtaposition of the Marcela, Rocinante, and Maritornes episodes can be found in Casalduero's *Sentido y forma del "Quijote,"* 3d ed. (Madrid: Insula, 1970), 89–94.

²² Javier Herrero ("Arcadia's Inferno: Cervantes' Attack on Pastoral," *BHS* 55 [1978], 289–99), in discussing the similitudes between Leandra and Marcela, has also pointed out that neither has a mother. He uses the observation to explain their respective hardheartedness, saying that they "have no experience of the limitations of human love" (p. 298). Another possible explanation is that such young women have had to bear directly the projections of eros from the men in their households, men who were forced by the situation to repress their instincts of desire. The young women grew up, in other words, surrounded by the dynamics of what we have come to call "Platonic" love. Their role has always been to extinguish the fires of eros that are inevitably, if unconsciously, ignited by their presence.

²³ Cervantes develops the situation described here to a far greater degree in his *El casamiento engañoso.* For more on that work, see my *Cervantes' "El casamiento engañoso" and "El coloquio de los perros": A Critical Study* (London: Tamesis, 1976).

²⁴ Edward Dudley, in "Don Quijote as Magus," using a somewhat different construct, has also underscored the lifesaving importance of characters being able to escape the limitations of their own stories. See especially page 362 of his article. His point that "Don Quijote does not fit within his own novel" (p. 367) relates well to my more general idea that Don Quixote has confused an aspect of himself with his whole being, thus distorting truth and endangering his very life. Cesáreo Bandera, in his discussion of the interrupted tale, makes a similar point, showing that interruptions break the hermeticism of fiction: "To interrupt the narration is nothing other than to introduce into it another perspective distinct from that of the narrator, to open the facts to the possibility of a different interpretation, and, as a consequence, to make clear the purely formal nature of the narrator's subjectivity" (*Mimesis,* p. 86).

²⁵ Bandera, *Mimesis,* see especially pp. 141–52.

²⁶ Cesáreo Bandera sees something similar when he makes the observation: "There is no essential difference between the passionate, romantic and 'true' love of Cardenio for Luscinda, and the 'lascivious' obsession of don Fernando for such a beautiful lady. There is no essential difference, because in both cases we find ourselves precisely before a desire that derealizes, de-essencializes its own object" (*Mimesis,* 106–7).

²⁷ Edward Dudley, in "Boccaccio and Cervantes: *Novella* as Novella," *Hispano-Italic Studies* 2 (1979), 23–40, proposes that Camila might have

entirely lost herself within the various roles she is called upon to play, being "the actress in everything she does" (p. 37), but concludes that the essence of the interpolated *novela* is that the human heart, in this case Camila's, is in any event unknowable through the faculty of the intellect. The point is an important one for my argument here, for it suggests once again that the human heart can be apprehended through another faculty, perhaps, but not through the intellect. When the latter is overvalued, when the feminine remains unconscious, it necessarily leads to the imbalances that end in destruction, as "The Tale of Foolish Curiosity" so well reveals.

[28] The lord might here be called "reason," or the "order of things." Time after time, in the main story as in the interpolated ones, we see those characters associated with fantasy and passion directing the proceedings: Don Quixote, considered mad, generates all the activity, challenging along the way everyone associated with the established order. Grisóstomo also leaves home in order to live out an erotic impulse. Cardenio leaves home to be taken over by the irresponsible and lustful younger brother of the Duke's household, and, as we have just seen, it is Anselmo's passion that dethrones Lotario's reason. Only in the next tale, where paternal authority in all its representations is respected, however, does the encounter with the feminine lead to union. All of this testifies, it seems to me, not to Cervantes' anarchic or conservative tendencies, but to his fidelity to a quest motif that demands above all the development of a strong ego, or conscious position, as a prelude to the descent that leads ultimately to fulfillment with the other of the opposite sex.

[29] Avalle-Arce (*La novela pastoril española* [Madrid: Ediciones Istmo, 1974], 71ff.), Dudley ("Don Quixote as Magus," 363), and Bandera (*Mimesis,* 136) comment on the inn as the locus in which love difficulties are magically resolved. Though the resolution, as Bandera points out, is an ironic one, forced and therefore incomplete, I do not think it is entirely false. The inn serves rather as a theater, providing the observers with insight, inasmuch as they constitute the audience, but leaving them still caught in their own limitations, inasmuch as they remain entities of fiction.

[30] Juergen Hahn, in "El Capitán Cautivo: The Soldier's Truth and Literary Precept in *Don Quijote,* Part I," *JHP* 3 (1979), 269–303, also singles out the Captive's tale for special notice, saying that it reveals the religious truth that undergirds the novel and provides the background against which the vanity and presumptuousness of the other characters, from Anselmo to Cardenio to Don Quixote, can be seen. The Captive's tale stands out as distinct from the others. Avalle-Arce has discussed the differences between it and "The Tale of Foolish Curiosity" from the point of view of the historical and the poetic in *Deslindes cervantinos* (Madrid: Edhigar, 1961). What I hope to show is

how the religious aspect of the story is reflected in the transformational process undergone by the hero, a process that will be expanded to occupy the entire work in the *Persiles*.

[31] See note 13, Chapter 2, for reference to number symbolism. In the elaborate exchange between father and sons that prefaces the Captive's tale, what stands out are the numbers one, three, four, and seven, all of which have significance in the symbolic structure of the story.

[32] In Part II, when Don Quixote finally meets his "lady" in the cave of Montesinos, he too proves incapable of responding adequately to her need. Being himself incomplete, he cannot serve to complete another.

[33] Although Jaime Oliver Asín, in "La hija de Agi Morato en la obra de Cervantes" (*Boletín de la Real Academia Española* 27 [1947/48], 245–333), has taken pains to identify Zoraida with a real Moorish girl, Francisco Márquez Villanueva, in *Personajes y temas del "Quijote"* (Madrid: Taurus, 1975) has shown that her story corresponds well with two folk motifs written up in Stith Thompson's *Motif-Index of Folk-Literature* (Berkeley: University of California Press, 1977): (R162) "Rescue by Captor's daughter (wife, mother)" and (T 91.6.4.1) "Sultan's daughter in love with captured knight," see p. 102, n. 28. Luis Murillo, in "El Ur-Quijote: nueva hipótesis," *Cervantes* 1 (1982), 43–50, also confirms the idea that Zoraida is a legendary figure, pointing out that her name means "star" (as does Auristela's in the *Persiles*).

[34] Since to the conscious mind the union of opposites is impossible, it is natural that one would revert to the miraculous when trying to describe the story of the Captive and Zoraida, as Luis Murillo does when he says: "The polarity between them underlines the miraculousness of the case. The verisimilitude of their motives and actions is the operation of the miraculous in the moral sphere of the human" ("El Ur-Quijote," 49).

[35] Luis Murillo notes that when the Captive arrives at the inn with Zoraida, the couple resembles Joseph and Mary ("El Ur-Quijote," 46). The Christian theological position that identifies Jesus with God makes Mary's relationship to the two not unlike that of Isis, Horus, and Osiris. Joseph Campbell discusses a number of deities who are at once the consorts and the sons of the Great Goddess of the Universe in his *The Masks of God: Primitive Mythology* and *The Masks of God: Oriental Mythology* (New York: Viking Press, 1959 and 1962). Although the dogma of the trinity has served to suppress the feminine aspect of the godhead, the cults of Mary and stories such as this one recall the importance of the feminine in the process of creation and transformation. See also Erich Neumann, *Art and the Creative Unconscious: Four Essays*, trans. Ralph Manheim (Princeton: Princeton University Press, 1974), 13, and Jung "The Components of the Coniunctio," in *Mysterium Coniunctionis*, vol. 14 of *CW*, 17–37.

[36] Helena Percas de Ponseti suggests, in fact, that Don Quixote was

not present for the Captive's tale: "As for Don Quixote, we do not know if he is or is not present during the Captive's narration. Before the narration they are preparing his bed. Is he going to sleep through this *novela* also?" (*Cervantes y su concepto del arte,* 161) In a footnote on the same page, she adds: "It appears that Don Quixote is present only a little after the telling of his life story that the Captive offers" (p. 161, n. 32).

[37] Jung, who devoted many years to the study of alchemical texts, discusses the deformation and psychic suffering that the adept undergoes in the context of Job and the Passion of Christ in "Rex and Regina," in *Mysterium Coniunctionis,* vol. 14 of *CW,* 349–55, and also in "The Visions of Zosimos," in *Alchemical Studies,* vol. 13 of *CW,* 67–73, among many other places.

[38] In its fullest expression, the marriage evolves out of the brother-sister pair, as Jung points out in "Religious Ideas in Alchemy," in *Psychology and Alchemy,* vol. 12 of *CW,* 412–17. In later works, for example, *La española inglesa* and the *Persiles,* the couple will figuratively represent a brother-sister pair. Here, where the relation to the feminine is still in its beginning stages in Cervantes' work, the female character's distance from the consciousness of the hero is symbolized by her being foreign.

Notes to "Don Quixote" Part II—Chapter 4

[1] I have already pointed out in Chapter 3 that one of the oppositions that remains to be resolved in *Don Quixote* is that established between author and character. The antagonism is far from one-sided, and Cide Hamete finds his own opportunities to rail against the limitations of his relationship to Don Quixote as he perceives them. In one of his most famous comments, Cide Hamete complains that "to have his mind, his hand and his pen always confined to a single subject and to so scanty a list of characters was an unbearable hardship.... To avoid this inconvenience in the first part he had resorted to short tales ..." (II, 44, 745–46) (el ir siempre atenido el entendimiento, la mano y la pluma a escribir de un solo sujeto y hablar por las bocas de pocas personas era un trabajo incomportable ... y ... por huir deste inconveniente había usado en la primera parte del artificio de algunas novelas [II, 44, 368]). One of the signs that *Don Quixote* Part II is a work in which some levels of resolution among terms in opposition is achieved comes in Chapter 74, when Cide Hamete, through his pen, finally recognizes his union with his protagonist-antagonist: "For me alone Don Quixote was born and I for him. His was the power of action, mine of writing. Only we two are at one ..." (II, 74, 940) (Para mí sola nació don Quijote, y yo para él; él supo obrar y yo escribir; solos los dos somos para en uno [II, 74, 608]).

A different point of view, stressing the total irreconcilability of Don Quixote and Cide Hamete has recently been propounded by J. J. Allen in *Don Quixote: Hero or Fool? Part II* (Gainesville: University of Florida Press, 1979), 3–15, and expanded upon by Howard Mancing in "Cide

Hamete Benegeli vs. Miguel de Cervantes: The Metafictional Dialectic of *Don Quijote,*" *Cervantes* 1 (1982), 63–81. Robert Flores, however, in "The Role of Cide Hamete in *Don Quixote*'" (*BHS* 59 [1982], 3–14), shows that Cide Hamete emerges in Part II offering the central point of view and that he proves himself to be both reliable and honored by Cervantes, who nonetheless remains clearly distinct from his narrator.

[2] Félix Martínez-Bonati, in "La unidad del *Quijote,*" *Dispositio* 2 (1977), 118–39, refers to Don Quixote as acting out of two archetypes, the "miles gloriosus" and the "wise old man" (p. 126). If one considers the two parts of the novel as distinct entities, the one emerging from and reflecting the other while contrasting sharply with it, one can see how the two archetypes identified by Martínez-Bonati shift with respect to one another. In Part II the wise old man comes into prominence, leaving the "miles gloriosus" little room for action.

[3] Cesáreo Bandera has carried this point one step further, suggesting in *Mimesis conflictiva* (Madrid: Gredos, 1975) that Cervantes himself, being fascinated and repelled by Don Quixote, fell into the fiction from which he believed himself free. If Bandera's understanding of the dynamics of Cervantes' relation to his character is correct, the secondary characters would be the images of Cervantes himself. In Part II, when Cervantes has recognized his entanglement and withdrawn himself partially, the characters who ridicule Don Quixote clearly reveal the same limitations he does. Don Quixote, on the other hand, like Cervantes, has moved away from the full identification with his role that seemed to characterize him in Part I. J. J. Allen has analyzed, from an entirely different angle, the resultant shift in reader perception, showing how we tend to sympathize more with Don Quixote in Part II than in Part I in *Don Quixote: Hero or Fool? A Study in Narrative Technique* (Gainesville: University of Florida Press, 1969). The point is that the entire network of relationships—between Don Quixote and his role, between Don Quixote and the characters around him, between Don Quixote and Cide Hamete, between Cervantes and Don Quixote, and between Don Quixote and the reader—has undergone a major change, one surely motivated by a change in the way Cervantes himself perceived his role as author.

[4] The association becomes nearly overt in Chapter 17 of Part I, when Cide Hamete points out that he is related to the Moorish muleteer who caused Don Quixote and Sancho so much distress at Juan Palomeque's inn. Don Quixote is convinced that the considerable upset is the work of a Moorish enchanter. Having nearly reached the end of his rope, the gullible Sancho wails, while he and his master are still in the midst of their troubles, "Will this perhaps be the Moorish enchanter come to give us another hiding, in case there's anywhere he forgot to hit us last time?" (I, 17, 126) (Note that this translation is not quite accurate. Sancho's actual words were "Señor, ¿si será, a dicha, el moro

encantado, que nos vuelve a castigar, si se dejó algo en el tintero?" [I, 17, 206]. Thus he clearly establishes the link between the Moor at the inn and the Moor who is writing Don Quixote's history.

[5] Examples of Cide Hamete's manipulation of the reader can be found in the episodes of the Knight of the Mirrors, Camacho's wedding, Master Peter, the pinching of Don Quixote and Doña Rodríguez, the Talking Head, and the Knight of the White Moon. In each case, Cide Hamete waits until we have participated with Don Quixote in the confusion to which he has been subjected before explaining the machinations by which the illusion was created. This control over the reader was very little in evidence in Part I. It reflects, however, the narrative technique of withholding information from the reader practiced by Heliodorus, whom Cervantes openly admits to having imitated in the *Persiles*.

[6] It is curious that animals and bad omens are associated with both the onset and the conclusion of Don Quixote's search for Dulcinea. In Chapter 73 Don Quixote finds in a hunted rabbit that Sancho catches a sign that he will never find Dulcinea. (E. C. Riley discusses the finding of the rabbit in "Symbolism in *Don Quixote,* Part II, Chapter 73," *JHP* 3 [1979], 161–74). Animals associated with feminine images were also present in *La Galatea*. It is no accident that in Part II of *Don Quixote*, where the interest in the feminine rises to prominence in Don Quixote's self-creation, there is also an increased effort to confuse the boundaries between the human and the animal. See, for example, the highlighting of the friendship between Rocinante and Sancho's donkey, the war over the mayors who could bray like donkeys, and the presence of bulls, pigs, monkeys, and cats. Though each incident, taken separately, has a different symbolic meaning, taken together, they bear witness to a rise of the beast in the novelistic world of Don Quixote.

[7] Every aspect of the third sally—from the conversations with the women, to the omens, to the animal sounds, to the night, to the search for Dulcinea—points toward a responsiveness to the symbols of the unconscious that entirely reverses the thrust of Don Quixote's journey in Part I.

[8] The distortion of time and space, clearly experienced in the cave of Montesinos, where one and one-half hours for Sancho is three days and nights for Don Quixote, seems to be involved in this opening nighttime journey of Don Quixote and Sancho. In Chapter 1 of Part I we are told that Don Quixote chose for his lady a good-looking farm girl from a village nearby. When Don Quixote sets out in Chapter 8 to find her in Toboso, he urges Sancho on, hoping to arrive in Toboso by daybreak. At the end of Chapter 8, however, the narrator indicates that knight and squire spent two full days and nights travelling the short distance to the neighboring village: "In this and other such conversations they spent that night and the following day. . . . Finally, on the

next day, at nightfall, they made out the great city of El Toboso . . . " (II, 8, 520) (En estas y otras semejantes pláticas se les pasó aquella noche y el día siguiente, sin acontecerles cosa que de contar fuese. . . . En fin, otro día, al anochecer, descubrieron la gran ciudad del Toboso [II, 8, 81]). In the semihallucinatory world to which we are introduced in Part II, Toboso has grown in size and distance, exaggerating the difficulty of its access that is part of Don Quixote's delusion. But here we, along with Sancho, are so caught up in the distortions that we are likely not to notice them at all.

⁹ Of the "inferior function," i.e., that aspect of the self generally neglected by the conscious personality, Jung says, "the inferior function is practically identical with the dark side of the human personality. . . . A man who is possessed by his shadow is always standing in his own light and falling into his own traps" (*The Archetypes and the Collective Unconscious*, vol. 9, pt. 1, of *CW*, 123).

¹⁰ Though working on the plane of rhetoric and text, Ramón Saldívar's interesting article "Don Quijote's Metaphors and the Grammar of Proper Languages," *MLN* 95 (1980), 252–78, makes a similar point regarding the inherently contradictory nature of the elements that constitute the text: "Whenever the text is described in terms of the truthful expression of any one of these polarities, it is always possible to point to the presence of the opposite term inextricably tied to it, deconstructing its supposed truth value" (p. 274). The text, like the world, is a composite of contradictory and mutually self-negating signs. What that tells us, it seems to me, is that our concern as critics should be to reflect upon a character's (and ultimately an author's and a critic's) misplaced valoration of some signs over others, some entities over others, and to see how such misinterpretation distorts not only the objects of a character's environment, but the character himself or herself.

¹¹ Not all commentators take Don Quixote's words here as signs of a wiser, saner Don Quixote. J. J. Allen (*Don Quixote: Hero or Fool? Part II*) does not read the statement ironically, but Anthony Close ("Don Quixote's Sophistry and Wisdom," *BHS* 55 [1978], 103–14) finds in it yet another example, albeit mixed in with wisdom, of Don Quixote's chivalric rhetoric.

¹² As has already been discussed, Don Quixote's search for the ideal is by its very nature death-oriented, since it rejects all that is here and now. Denis de Rougemont has shown this clearly in the context of courtly love, and Arthur Efron, using a Reichian model, has also demonstrated the degree to which Don Quixote reflects a whole culture devoted to a rejection of the body. See Efron's *Don Quixote and the Dulcineated World* (Austin and London: University of Texas Press, 1971) and his recent "The Problem of Don Quixote's Rage," *Denver Quarterly* 16 (1981), 29–46.

13 Arthur Efron, in "Don Quixote's Rage," notes the degree to which the Moor was imaged as the enemy in the chivalric hero's fantasy (see his discussion of Machuca, pp. 38–39). To come to the point where Don Quixote is prepared to validate Cide Hamete's version of himself above all others is truly to have achieved, at least in some degree, a union of opposites, as already discussed in note 1 of this chapter.

14 The identity that underlies and guarantees all eruptions of violence has been thoroughly documented in René Girard's *Violence and the Sacred*, trans. Patrick Gregory (Baltimore: Johns Hopkins University Press, 1965). When Sansón Carrasco stops playacting and becomes emotionally involved in unseating Don Quixote, he becomes the very knight he thought he was ridiculing.

15 Both the Knight of the Green Coat's attire and his concern over the safety of his mare in Rocinante's presence have attracted critical attention. Francisco Márquez Villanueva, in "El Caballero del Verde Gabán y su reino de paradoja," in *Personajes y temas del "Quijote"* (Madrid: Taurus, 1975), 219–29, has associated the green of Don Diego's coat with madness. See also his article "La locura emblemática en la segunda parte del *Quijote*," in *Cervantes and the Renaissance* (Easton, Pa.: Juan de la Cuesta—Hispanic Monographs, 1980), 87–112. Vernon A. Chamberlin, in "Symbolic Green: A Time-Honored Characterizing Device in Spanish Literature," *Hispania* 51 (1968), 29–37, sees green as a symbol of lust. Though Chamberlin notes, "Cervantes did not choose to develop the characterization of his 'Caballero del Verde Gabán' . . . along those amorous lines" (p. 30), John G. Weiger, in *The Individuated Self: Cervantes and the Emergence of the Individual* (Athens: Ohio University Press, 1979), cites Chamberlin and wholeheartedly adopts the view that green in this episode signifies sensuality. Helena Percas de Ponseti makes a strong case for relating green in Cervantes to deception: "Cervantes separates himself from the traditional symbolism of green from ancient times. Instead of being for him the symbol of love with its variants of sensuality, concupiscence, eroticism or hope, green is the symbol of all kinds of deceptions and falsehoods on the human plane" (*Cervantes y su concepto del arte*, 2 vols. [Madrid: Gredos, 1975], 386).

Interpretations regarding the green in Don Diego's costume are usually affected by one's overall assessment of his role in the work, since the range of possible meanings of the color is wide. Many of the interpretations can be assimilated if one sees in Don Diego a figure, like the others in Part II analyzed so far, displaying to Don Quixote an image of himself. Dressed in green, Don Diego suggests not only madness but the vegetation of the natural world, which is subject, like all its elements, both to growth and to decay. The interpretation provides a place not only for Weiger's emphasis on the erotic in the episode but for Ponseti's concern with deception and illusion. Green does suggest growth, but it is the illusory growth of the natural world that is automatically coupled with its opposite, decline. Both eroticism and decline are aspects of Alonso Quijano's life, but he has recreated himself as the fictional entity Don Quixote in order to deny them. It is no wonder that Don Quixote must perforce shy away from the image of himself that the Knight in Green offers him.

[16] The role of the Knight of the Green Coat in *Don Quixote* has been the subject of considerable controversy, ranging from a rejection of all that Don Diego represents in Américo Castro's "La estructura del *Quijote*," in *Hacia Cervantes* (Madrid: Taurus, 1967), 308–17, and Helena Percas de Ponseti's *Cervantes y su concepto del arte*, 332–82, to a more favorable evaluation of the Knight in Green's presence by Unamuno, in *Vida de don Quijote y Sancho*, 3d ed. (Madrid: Espasa-Calpe, 1938), and Marcel Bataillon, in *Erasmo y España*, trans. A. Alatorre, 2 vols. (Mexico City: Fondo de Cultura Económica, 1950), 2: 417. A summary of opinions on the figure of the Knight of the Green Coat can be found in Alberto Sánchez's "El Caballero del Verde Gabán," *Anales Cervantinos* 9 (1961/62), 169–201. See also Randolf D. Pope's "El 'Caballero del Verde Gabán' y su encuentro con Don Quijote," *HR* 47 (1979), 207–18.

[17] Randolf Pope, in "El 'Caballero del Verde Gabán,'" attributes Don Quixote's hostile reaction to Don Diego to the envy a poor country gentleman would feel in the presence of Don Diego's wealth and well-being. Judging from the size of their respective libraries, however, it is not at all clear that Alonso Quijano was significantly poorer than Don Diego. Indeed, it is their very similarity that evokes Don Quixote's resistance to the gentleman in green.

[18] The idea that Don Quixote fails to interpret the dream, insisting on its pleasant associations only, is well documented in Gethin Hughe's article "The Cave of Montesinos: Don Quixote's Interpretation and Dulcinea's Disenchantment," *BHS* 54 (1977), 107–13.

[19] Peter Dunn's excellent article "La cueva de Montesinos por fuera y por dentro: estructura épica, fisonomía," *MLN* 88 (1973), 190–202, discusses the parallels with the classic descent motif not only in the cave episode but in the epic structure of Part II itself and shows how Cervantes' cave parodies the classic journey to the underworld by offering Don Quixote no enlightenment whatsoever. Helena Percas de Ponseti, on the other hand, draws parallels with mystic expression and symbolism in her study of this episode, concluding that Don Quixote glimpsed there the infernal illusion in which he was trapped but from which he was unwilling to detach himself (*Cervantes y su concepto del arte*, 420–29). A good discussion of the episode can also be found in Agustín Redondo's "El proceso iniciático en el episodio de la cueva de Montesinos del *Quijote*," *Iberoromania* 13 (1979), 47–61.

[20] John G. Weiger (in *The Individuated Self*, 62–65) has chosen to emphasize the sexual implications of this episode, attaching a lascivious quality

to the humanist cousin that I find unpersuasive and insisting on the much more certain feminine qualities suggested in the cave imagery. The fact that the address to Dulcinea precedes the descent does, however, clearly link this episode to the opening and closing moments of Don Quixote's third journey from home. In all cases the search for the feminine motivates Don Quixote, which is why he is not tilting at windmills but lowering himself into caves in the 1615 novel.

[21] Peter Dunn, in "La cueva de Montesinos," makes a similar point when he suggests that *everything* in Part II reflects the inner split of the hero: "The most salient characteristic of Part II is the reciprocity between Don Quixote and the surrounding world, which reflects, in its turn, the internal split within the hero" (p. 20). This idea, that the cave experience mirrors that of the aboveground world, is exactly my point throughout this study of Part II.

[22] Don Quixote's inadequacy, which I see in all its metaphysical implications, is often interpreted in a sexual manner. See Manuel Durán, *La ambigüedad en el "Quijote"* (Xalapa, Mexico: Universidad Veracruzana, 1961), 216, who refers to the Freudian interpretation of impotence without wholeheartedly adopting it, and John G. Weiger, *The Individuated Self*, 61, who does.

[23] For a general discussion of the trickster figure, see Paul Radin, ed., *The Trickster: A Study in American Indian Mythology* (New York: Schocken Books, 1972) and Karl Kerenyi's essay therein, "The Trickster in Relation to Greek Mythology," 173–91. Jung also provided a commentary to Radin's book, which is reprinted in *The Archetypes and the Collective Unconscious*, 255–72. What all the discussions have in common is the revelation of the redeeming nature hidden in the trickster's amorality. Jung says of the trickster: "He is a forerunner of the saviour, and, like him, God, man, and animal at once. He is both subhuman and superhuman, a bestial and divine being . . . " (p. 263). For a discussion of the trickster as Proteus, and as an essential element in the works of Cervantes, see Alban Forcione's *Cervantes, Aristotle, and the "Persiles"* (Princeton: Princeton University Press, 1970), 305–37.

[24] See especially the *entremeses* "La cueva de Salamanca" and "El retablo de las maravillas" and the *comedia Pedro de Urdemalas*.

[25] See Edith Kern's recent study *The Absolute Comic* (New York: Columbia University Press, 1980), especially her analysis of *El celoso extremeño*, pp. 61–63.

[26] Northrop Frye makes use of these two opposing terms in *The Secular Scripture* ([Cambridge: Harvard University Press, 1976], 65–93), attributing to romance the proclivity for fraud and to the novel the tendency to rely on force.

[27] The moon seems primarily a symbol of the feminine in patriarchal cultures, according to Erich Neumann in *The Great Mother: An Analysis of the Archetype*, trans. Ralph Manheim (Princeton: Princeton

University Press, 1963). As reflector, it represents the secondary, passive role of woman, a role that is also played by mirrors. The moon of course has other associations—with changeability, with the night, and with roundness—that have also traditionally linked it with the feminine. The mirror, for its part, also has different sets of associations, the most prevalent of which is self-awareness. The juxtaposition of the two—mirrors in the shape of moons—would suggest self-awareness as something to be discovered through the feminine.

[28] See above, note 23.

[29] Similarities between Master Peter's puppet play and the episode in the cave are also pointed out by Helena Percas de Ponseti, *Cervantes y su concepto del arte*, 584–92, as well as by Alban Forcione, in his *Cervantes, Aristotle, and the "Persiles,"* 147. The relation of this episode to the structure of the entire novel is masterfully presented in George Haley's "The Narrator in *Don Quijote*," *MLN* 81 (1966), 145–65.

[30] See my *Distance and Control in "Don Quijote": A Study in Narrative Technique* (Chapel Hill: University of North Carolina Studies in Romance Languages and Literatures, 1975), Chapter 3, for a long discussion of this point.

[31] Although, like most symbols, that of the monkey is polyvalent, the dominant association is with trickery, mischief, and the baser instincts. In the context in which he appears here, along with the other animals, such an interpretation seems warranted. See J. C. Cooper, *An Illustrated Encyclopaedia of Traditional Symbols* (London: Thames and Hudson, 1978), 106.

[32] Arthur Efron, in "Don Quixote's Rage," suggests that Don Quixote intervenes when he does to prevent the happy return to France of the escaping couple Gaiferos and Melisendra. The text makes it quite clear, however, that Don Quixote becomes disturbed at the sight of the hordes of Moorish puppets pursuing them. The last thing the interpreter of the show says is: "See what a numerous and resplendent cavalcade rides out of the city in pursuit of the pair of Christian lovers! . . . I am afraid they will catch them and bring them back tied to their own horse's tail" (II, 26, 641) (Miren cuánta y cuán lúcida caballería sale de la ciudad en seguimiento de los dos católicos amantes; . . . Témome que los han de alcanzar, y los han de volver atados a la cola de su mismo caballo [II, 26, 238]). That Don Quixote knows and even approves of the later reunion of the married couple is clear later when he tells Master Peter, ". . . if all goes well, she is now with her husband in France, taking her pleasure for all she is worth" (II, 26, 644) (si viene a mano, ahora [está] holgándose en Francia con su esposo a pierna tendida [II, 26, 242]). Don Quixote's motives here do not seem to be based on rejection of the body.

[33] See J. J. Allen's discussion of Melisendra's slip in "Melisendra's Mishap in Maese Pedro's Puppet Show," *MLN* 88 (1973), 330–35.

[34] In a lecture given at the 1981 MLA Convention in New York, Arthur Efron also pointed out the importance in Part II of *Don Quixote* of women engaging in activities normally carried out by men. His lecture was entitled "Bearded Waiting Women, Lethal Lovely Female Piratemen: Sexual Boundary Shifts in *Don Quixote*, Part II."

[35] Arthur Efron, who emphasizes Sancho's importance in the novel as a presence not entirely overcome by the idealisms of literary and social acculturation, of course attends carefully to this episode. See his *Don Quixote and the Dulcineated World*, 92–93.

[36] For further discussion of the symbolic importance of the rabbit in Chapter 73, see E. C. Riley's article "Symbolism in *Don Quixote*, Part II, Chapter 73."

[37] See Cesáreo Bandera's discussion in *Mimesis.*

Notes to the "*Persiles*"—Chapter 5

[1] Alban Forcione, in *Cervantes' Christian Romance* (Princeton: Princeton University Press, 1971), discusses the allegory in the *Persiles* with relation to Renaissance aesthetics, showing that a modern allegorical reading is not only possible but acceptable, despite the reigning neo-Aristotelian view that saw allegory as a more limited form and associated it with the false and inverisimilar. (See especially pp. 51–63.) My reading, like Forcione's, does not call for a one-to-one correspondence between every element in the text and another, superimposed allegorical structure. Rather, it proposes that beyond the level of the plot one can perceive a larger, more generalized pattern that the characters trace in their journey toward Rome.

[2] Antonio Vilanova, in "El peregrino andante en el *Persiles* de Cervantes," *Boletín de la Real Academia de Buenas Letras de Barcelona* 22 (1949), 97–159, provides a full background, from biblical, classical, and Renaissance sources, on the theme of the pilgrim in Spanish letters, and most particularly, on its application to Cervantes' *Persiles*. Vilanova makes it clear that the pilgrim represented one's stay on earth: "[Persiles and Sigismunda's pilgrimage] is at the same time an enormous pilgrimage, a pious pilgrimage to Rome, and an image of human life as a difficult pilgrimage over the earth" (p. 145). See also Avalle-Arce's discussion in "*Los trabajos de Persiles y Sigismunda,*" in *Suma Cervantina,* (London: Tamesis, 1973), 209–11.

[3] See Chapter 4, note 23 for references to the connection between the trickster and the savior figure. Alban Forcione, in *Cervantes, Aristotle, and the "Persiles"* (Princeton: Princeton University Press, 1970) offers a good discussion of the relation between the artist and the rogue in Cervantes' work but does not extend his observations to include the perfection that Periandro represents in his fullest expression. Periandro is obviously a character who shows the highest evolution of the trickster, and the thievery and lying of that figure are very much a part of his own portrait.

[4] Cf. Mack Singleton, "El misterio del *Persiles,*" *Realidad* 2 (1947), 236–53, who, along with so many other nineteenth- and twentieth-century commentators, had difficulty reconciling the "idealism" of *La Galatea* and the *Persiles* with the rich realism of *Don Quixote.* Singleton believed that the *Persiles* was a product of Cervantes' earliest period and that he submitted it for publication at the end of his life because his reputation by that time was well established and anything bearing his name could be published. Other well-known critics who have resisted accepting all or parts of the *Persiles* as a late work are William Entwistle (*Cervantes* [Oxford: Clarendon Press, 1940], 176) and Rafael Osuna ("Las fechas del *Persiles,*" *Thesaurus: Boletín del instituto caro y cuervo* 25 [1970], 383–433), who says: "No one can explain how Cervantes could have written this novel after having written the *Quijote,* the *Coloquio,* and *Rinconete*" (pp. 402–3).

[5] For a fuller discussion of the commingling of the narrator's voice and that of his main character see my "Periandro: Exemplary Character, Exemplary Narrator," *Hispanófila* 69 (1980), 9–16.

[6] Avalle-Arce notes, in the introduction to his edition of the *Persiles* (Madrid: Clásicos Castalia, 1969), that the narrator is much more in evidence in Books III and IV than in Books I and II. I think the difference might be overstated here, but in general it is worth noting the degree to which the narrator intervenes to comment on the events taking place, an intervention that has the effect of minimizing, as so much else also does in the work, the distinctions between "fiction" and "reality" so important in earlier works by Cervantes. For a full discussion of the changing role of the narrator in the four books of the *Persiles,* see Forcione, *Cervantes, Aristotle, and the "Persiles,"* Chapter 8.

[7] The in medias res technique was highly recommended by literary theorists of Cervantes' day, including Jacques Amyot, the French translator of Heliodorus' *Aetheopica,* Julius Caesar Scaliger, Torquato Tasso, and, of course, Alonso López Pinciano. A good discussion of that technique and others important to neo-Aristotelian theorists can be found in Alban Forcione's *Cervantes' Christian Romance,* his *Cervantes, Aristotle, and the "Persiles,"* and in E. C. Riley's *Cervantes's Theory of the Novel* (Oxford: Clarendon Press, 1962).

[8] Here it is useful to cite Cesáreo Bandera's observation (*Mimesis conflictiva* [Madrid: Gredos, 1975], 132) that in the *Persiles* "the journey to the mind of God is nothing other than the journey to the mind of the other" (El *itinerarium mentis ad Deum* no es otro que el *itinerarium mentis ad proximum*).

[9] See C. G. Jung, "The Psychology of the Transference," in *The Practice of Psychotherapy,* vol. 16 of *CW,* 218, for a discussion of the importance of the brother-sister stage of the development of the royal couple, who, in alchemical texts of the sixteenth and seventeenth centuries, stood for the completion of the opus—the transformation of base material

into gold. Jung is careful to stress, throughout his extensive writing on the alchemists, that their works represent projections of the human psyche and that they belong to a symbology of transformation that cuts across time and culture. I have no idea whether Cervantes was exposed to the writings of alchemists. He mentions them jokingly in *El coloquio de los perros,* and their work was widely published in the sixteenth and seventeenth centuries. Whether he knew them directly or not, the transformation his characters undergo in their advance from lover–loved one to a couple joined in marriage is astoundingly similar to that which Jung has discovered in the alchemists' writings.

[10] Cervantes' boasting was always tinged with self-doubt as well. It is in the prologue to the *Novelas ejemplares* that he refers to the Heliodoran imprint on the *Persiles,* calling it "a book which dares to compete with Heliodorus, if for its temerity it does not come out with its hands on its head." Later, in the dedication to Part II of *Don Quixote,* he says that his forthcoming *Persiles* will be "either the worst or the best that has been written in our language." Judging from the work's early reception—it went through six editions in the year of its publication and subsequently enjoyed translation into many languages—it would seem that Cervantes' last work was indeed considered a masterpiece in its time.

For a most thorough examination of Cervantes' literary debt to Heliodorus and to the neo-Aristotelian literary school that brought his work to prominence in the late sixteenth century, see Alban Forcione's *Cervantes, Aristotle, and the "Persiles,"* 49–87, and his subsequent *Cervantes' Christian Romance,* especially pp. 3–28. Other major works on this aspect of the *Persiles* are E. C. Riley's *Cervantes's Theory of the Novel;* Sanford Shepard's *El Pinciano y las teorías literarias del Siglo de Oro* (Madrid: Gredos, 1962); Albinio Martín Gabriel, "Heliodoro y la novela española: Apuntes para una tesis," *Cuadernos de literatura* 8 (1950), 215–34; Rudolph Schevill, "Studies in Cervantes. Persiles y Sigismunda: The Question of Heliodorus," *Modern Philology* 4 (1907), 677–704; W. C. Atkinson, "The Enigma of the *Persiles,"* *Bulletin of Spanish Studies* 24 (1947), 242–53; and Stanislav Zimic, "*El Persiles* como crítica de la novela bizantina," *Acta neophilologica* 3 (1970), 49–64.

[11] The vertical axis established at the beginning links the work clearly with romance, as described by Northrop Frye in the *Anatomy of Criticism: Four Essays* (Princeton: Princeton University Press, 1957; reprint, 1971), 186–205, and later in *The Secular Scripture* (Cambridge: Harvard University Press, 1976).

[12] Dorotea in *Don Quixote* Part I, Teodosia in *Las dos doncellas,* Ana Fénix in *Don Quixote* Part II, and Ambrosia Agustina in Book III of the *Persiles* all dress as men to pursue their lovers, but only in Cervantes' last works—in *Don Quixote* Part II and in the *Persiles*—do men reciprocally dress as women. In the case of Ana Fénix's lover Don Gregorio,

the change has a novelistic explanation, since as a captive among the Turks he runs more danger of encountering lascivious desire as a young man than as a woman in a harem. But in the case of the brother and sister on Sancho's island, there is no apparent reason, apart from the pure reciprocity that signals the final crossing of the male-female barrier, for the young girl's brother to dress in her clothes. In Chapter 35 of Part II the Duke's servant dresses as Dulcinea and later, in Chapters 36–42, as the Countess Trifaldí. As for men who dress in costumes appropriate to a lower class in order to approach their ladies, one can find examples in Cervantes' works in Tomás de Avendaño in *La ilustre fregona* and Juan de Cárcamo in *La Gitanilla*. The need to lower oneself in order to come into contact with the feminine reveals the collective context in which Cervantes was writing.

[13] My understanding of the role of the weaker member of the rivalry in Cervantes' last works contrasts sharply with that of Louis Combet (*Cervantès ou les incertitudes du désir* [Lyons: Presses Universitaires de Lyon, 1981]), who sees the figure throughout Cervantes' work as a sign of an inherent masochism. Periandro fits into Combet's description as the image of the lover who automatically desires that which his superior desires, following the pattern of triangular desire described by Girard. The fact that Periandro succeeds where earlier "inferior" rivals—Cardenio is the prime example—failed is not really taken into account by Combet. Our analyses do coincide to some extent, however, for I relate the behavior patterns that lead to Periandro's success to strategies associated with the feminine, strategies the dominant male figure would never be required to employ.

[14] The situation is well represented, of course, in many of the late *novelas* in the *Novelas ejemplares,* as I have tried to show in *Novel to Romance: A Study of Cervantes's "Novelas ejemplares"* (Baltimore: Johns Hopkins University Press, 1974).

[15] Forcione, in *Cervantes' Christian Romance,* discusses the series of near deaths and symbolic rebirths that are a basic part of the overall imagery of the work.

[16] An interesting article by Eduardo González ("Del *Persiles* y la isla bárbara: Fábulas y reconocimientos," *MLN* 94 [1979], 222–57) describes in detail this portion of the *Persiles* and points out the essential difference between the men, who arrive on the island by a regular and predictable pattern of catastrophe, and the women, who must be sought after and bargained for. Though the study does not attempt to explore the implication of this difference for masculine and feminine psychology, the observation makes clear the masculine consciousness from which the law of succession has been fabricated and thus reveals the distinction, on the horizontal, narrative plane, that must be transcended in the course of Periandro's journey.

[17] Northrop Frye discusses the symbolism of fire, which he asso-

ciates with the apocalyptic, in *Anatomy of Criticism,* 146. In the *Persiles* fire destroys those characters caught in uncontrolled desire at the same time that it liberates the pilgrims.

[18] Other discussions of the interpolated tales of Book I can be found in Forcione's *Cervantes' Christian Romance,* 109–16; Avalle-Arce's *Deslindes cervantinos* (Madrid: Edhigar, 1961), 81–96; and Casalduero's *Sentido y forma de "Los trabajos de Persiles y Sigismunda"* (Buenos Aires: Editorial Sudamericana, 1947), 21–40. For a longer discussion of Manuel's story and its relation to the plan of the *Persiles* see my "Tres imágenes claves de lo feminino en el *Persiles,*" *Revista canadiense de estudios hispánicos* 3 (1979), 219–36.

[19] The custom, described in El Inca Garcilaso de la Vega's *Comentarios reales* (1609) and earlier in Francisco Thámara's *El libro de las costumbres de todas las gentes* (1556), allows the bridegroom's kinfolk first rights in the bed of his wife-to-be. The reference to such a custom provides the basis for much of the speculation regarding the dating of this portion of the *Persiles.* For a summary, see Rafael Osuna's "Las fechas del *Persiles,*" 395–97.

[20] It must be noted that Transila also served as translator for the barbarians on the Barbarous Island. Her skill with language inverts both Rutilio's muteness and the role that she was expected to play as captive woman, making her a negotiator rather than an item of exchange. Eduardo González ("Del *Persiles* y la isla bárbara") makes this point for a different purpose. Here I want only to indicate that all those who managed to escape captivity did so by first anticipating their liberation internally by taking an opposite-sex role. Transila's skill with language and with sword signals the forthright activity of the feminine that precedes masculine development. That she is found on the island of Golandia suggests again that she has activated the male principle from its enslavement to collective values and that giving in to the search through the unconscious, represented by the voyage at sea, yields union.

[21] Many instances of fear of the sea and of its dangerous, capricious nature appear in Cervantes' work. The opening pages of *El celoso extremeño* offer an explicit link between inner turmoil and storms at sea. The Captive in *Don Quixote* Part I also experiences the sea's danger. Elicio and Timbrio both use the image of storms at sea in *La Galatea* to represent metaphorically their experience with romantic love. The sea also disturbs Recaredo in *La española inglesa* and Ricardo in *El amante liberal.* See Avalle-Arce's study of the sea and its relation to shipwreck and captivity in Cervantes' work in "La captura de Cervantes," *Boletín de la Real Academia Española* 48 (1968), 237–80.

[22] In a very nicely written paper, J. J. Allen convincingly elucidates the role of providence in the less clearly theological *Don Quixote,* as well as in the *Novelas ejemplares* ("The Providential World of Cervantes'

Fiction," *Thought* 55 [1980], 184–95). Javier Herrero, in a discussion of the Sierra Morena episode of Part I also stresses the importance of divine grace in the resolution of conflict in Cervantes' work ("Sierra Morena as Labyrinth: From Wildness to Christian Knighthood," *Forum for Modern Language Studies* 17 [1981], 55–67). In the *Persiles*, the insistence on salvation through God's grace cannot be mistaken.

The survival of the major characters is described as a miracle and given the overtones of the story of Jonas and, by traditional Christian extension, of the death and resurrection of Christ. The hull of the overturned ship is likened to a whale, and the pulling out of the victims to a birth. Forcione also discusses these associations in *Cervantes' Christian Romance*, 68–70.

[23] The possibility of female alter egos becoming rivals is hinted at in *La Galatea* in the Teolinda/Leonarda relationship and gets full expression in *Las dos doncellas*. The exploration of male friendship and rivalry, on the other hand, is clearly present in *La Galatea* in the secondary stories told to the men. The development of an independent female consciousness is latent in Cervantes' earliest work but does not appear as an explicit force until very late. For a woman to have a rival, she must not only be loved, but love. Early Cervantine women, especially the heroines, rarely knew they were in love.

[24] It is the unconscious resistance common to many of Cervantes' heroines, from Galatea to the Isabela of *La española inglesa*, that causes Louis Combet to see such characters, Auristela included, as cruel. That women as well as men have resistances—unconscious forces that inhibit union—to overcome is clear in all of Cervantes' fiction. A case similar to Auristela's at this point can be found in *El amante liberal*, where Leonisa is required to act as a mediator between her lustful mistress Halima and her would-be lover Ricardo. In both works the women's efforts to represent the desires of another give them a chance to express in legitimate fashion a love that might otherwise be so suppressed as not even to be acknowledged.

[25] *Persiles'* narration has been the focus of several astute readings by recent critics interested in Cervantes' engagement with literary theory. The best of these close readings is Forcione's in his *Cervantes, Aristotle, and the "Persiles,"* where he devotes an entire chapter to it (187–211). Another good study can be found in Stanislav Zimic's *"El Persiles como crítica."* I have taken up the relation between Periandro's storytelling and his character in "Periandro: Exemplary Character, Exemplary Narrator."

[26] Cervantes flirts briefly with the idea of taking an ironic stance toward the primary narrator just at the beginning of Book II, when he offers a commentary on the work: "It seems that the author of this history knew more about being a lover than about being a historian, because he spends almost all of the opening pages of the second book

on a definition of jealousy. . . . But in this translation, for that is what it is, it is taken out as excessive . . ." (Parece que el autor desta historia sabía más de enamorado que de historiador, porque casi este primer capítulo de la entrada del segundo libro le gasta todo en una difinición de celos . . . pero en esta tradución, que lo es, se quita por prolija [II, 1, 159]). The effort to create a distance between himself as narrator and himself as translator is abandoned, however, almost as soon as it has been adopted. For further discussion, see Forcione's *Cervantes, Aristotle, and the "Persiles,"* 260–84, and Avalle-Arce, in notes 51 and 143 of his edition of the *Persiles*.

[27] I refer, of course, to the famous introductory sentence in *Don Quixote* Part I, "In a certain village in La Mancha, which I do not wish to name," that so interested Américo Castro for its indication of the power of the will to shape a life. But what must be stressed here is that avoiding origin is part of Periandro's *conscious* strategy. When the origin is being suppressed or avoided for the unconscious disturbances it has produced, as was the case with Don Quixote and other novelistic heroes, the main character has no such freedom but is instead burdened and finally overcome by whatever he is trying to oppose. Much closer to Periandro's situation is Ginés de Pasamonte, though the latter goes too far in the other direction and has lost all touch with his plan in life, which is why he can only deal with it retroactively, as his famous comment on his autobiography suggests: "How can it [my autobiography] be finished if my life isn't? What is written begins with my birth and goes down to the point when I was sent to the galleys this last time" (*DQ* I, 22, 177) (¿Cómo puede estar acabado si aun no está acabada mi vida? Lo que está escrito es desde mi nacimiento hasta el punto que esta última vez me han echado en galeras [*DQ* I, 22, 268]).

[28] Periandro's reaction to interruption can be interestingly compared with that of Sancho in his narration of Part I of *Don Quixote*. Like the whole of *Don Quixote* Part II, Periandro's narration has a direction of its own that cannot be impeded. The interruptions, in addition to giving vent to feelings of incredulity the reader might be experiencing, function like the episodes that slow down Periandro and Sigismunda's journey toward Rome. Most critics (e.g., Forcione, *Cervantes, Aristotle, and the "Persiles,"* and Stanislav Zimic, "El *Persiles* como crítica") have stressed the theoretical implications of Mauricio's frequent interruptions of Periandro's narration. Equally important to note, however, is Persiles' imperturbability. Unlike Sancho's or Cardenio's, his tale does not depend upon the listener's rapt attention. Periandro's serenity despite the interruptions testifies to his freedom, both as character and as narrator, as I have explained in my "Periandro: Exemplary Character, Exemplary Narrator."

[29] There are many examples of Cervantes' effort to preserve a semblance of verisimilitude within the context of the marvelous. When a

woman falls unharmed from a tower in Book III, he explains that her billowing skirts had a braking effect; when later in Book III a fire in Valencia does not burn the pilgrims who have hidden in a tower, he tells us that the metal doors prevented the flames from reaching the Christians. In more fantastic cases involving the transformation of witches into she-wolves and the success of astrological prediction, Cervantes covers for himself by having the characters themselves engage in discussions about the possibilities and probabilities of such happenings.

[30] Casaldureo reads the *Persiles* (*Sentido y forma de "Los trabajos de Persiles"*) as an example of the Christian Baroque. Although my approach is quite different, many of our particular readings of the events in the work are similar. Like him, I see the horse in this episode as a sign of passion, a symbology, in fact, very common in the Spanish Baroque.

[31] The narrator says: "Auristela replied that she had not understood a single word of all he had been saying, for she was ignorant of the Castilian language, as he might plainly see, and even if she did know it, her plans were other" (Auristela le respondió que no había entendido palabra de cuantas le había dicho, porque bien se veía que ignoraba la lengua castellana, y que puesto que la supiera, sus pensamientos eran otros [III, 2, 286]). The problem, of course, arises much earlier. Antonio and his family also speak Spanish, yet they were able to communicate perfectly with Periandro and Auristela in Book I.

[32] We should remember that Zoraida in "The Captive's Tale" also insisted on going by foot up the mountain that rose from the sea coast when she and the others from Algiers landed in Spain.

[33] The resemblances between this episode and the exemplary tale *La señora Cornelia* are strong and serve to reinforce the late dating for the latter that I proposed in my *Novel to Romance*. Here, however, the powerful presence of the feminine gives a slightly different emphasis to the tale whose central problem is nonetheless so similar.

[34] Dr. Fred Gustafson has studied the significance of the figure of the black Virgin in his doctoral thesis *The Black Madonna of Einsiedeln: A Psychological Perspective* (Zurich: The Jung Institute, 1975). Gustafson notes her importance in combining images of the dark and light side of the feminine and her association with strength and humility, as Cervantes uses her in this episode.

[35] Avalle-Arce has sharply distinguished between the mythical world of the first two books of the *Persiles* and the more historical, verisimilar orientation of Books III and IV in "*Los trabajos de Persiles y Sigismunda, historia setentronial,*" in *Suma Cervantina* (London: Tamesis, 1973) 199–212. Both halves of the work, however, clearly participate in an overall trajectory leading from bondage to freedom that Avalle himself affirms, and both halves are therefore open to the kind of allegorical reading

that Forcione, among others, proposes in his *Cervantes' Christian Romance.*

[36] In this constellation of birth, marriage, and death it is also tempting to see a displacement of the Oedipal conflict, in which the dead uncle represents the father, who is symbolically replaced by the child. This resolution, involving the son's acceding to the father's place, is reiterated in the Feliciana de la Voz episode that initiated Book III and is central to Periandro's fortunes as well. What is interesting to note, however, is that the father figure is in all cases overcome not by violence but by art or deceit and that the instrument of the art or deceit is a woman. This fits in well with the opposition Frye establishes in *The Secular Scripture* between "froda" and "forza," 65–93.

[37] Here again the phenomenon of men wearing women's clothing seems to underscore the process the men's assimilation of the feminine that is expressed at so many levels in Cervantes' late works.

[38] Alban Forcione in *Cervantes' Christian Romance* makes a major point of the recurrence of cave images to represent the moment of rebirth.

[39] Walter Ong, in *Interfaces of the Word* (Ithaca and London: Cornell University Press, 1977), sharply distinguishes between the "mother tongue," which "not only comes primarily from our mother but belongs to some degree intrinsically to our mother's feminine world" (p. 23), and the learned language of scholarly discourse, which until this century was generally Latin and was the nearly exclusive preserve of males. Significantly, Periandro, when about to take the step that will allow him to integrate the feminine and his origins, hears his story told just outside Rome in the language of his mother.

[40] See note 17 of this chapter.

Bibliography

Abenlenda, F. Egea. "Sobre la *Galatea* de Cervantes." *Revista de Archivos, Bibliotecas y Museos* 42 (1921), 548–54.

Allen, John J. *Don Quixote: Hero or Fool? A Study in Narrative Technique.* Gainesville: University of Florida Press, 1969.

———. *Don Quixote: Hero or Fool? Part II.* Gainesville: University of Florida Press, 1979.

———. "Melisendra's Mishap in Maese Pedro's Puppet Show." *Modern Language Notes* 88 (1973), 330–35.

———. "The Providential World of Cervantes' Fiction." *Thought* 55 (1980), 184–95.

Asín, Jaime Oliver. "La hija de Agi Morato en la obra de Cervantes." *Boletín de la Real Academia Española* 27 (1947/48), 245–333.

Atkinson, William C. "The Enigma of the *Persiles*." *Bulletin of Spanish Studies* 24 (1947), 242–53.

Aubrun, Charles. "Pour quelle raison déraisonna Don Quichotte." In *Homenaje a Casalduero.* Madrid: Gredos, 1972.

Avalle-Arce, Juan Bautista. "La captura de Cervantes." *Boletín de la Real Academia Española* 48 (1968), 237–80.

———. *Deslindes cervantinos.* Madrid: Edhigar, 1961.

———. *Don Quixote como forma de vida.* Madrid: Fundación Juan March, 1976. Pp. 144–72.

———. "Don Quijote o la vida como obra de arte." *Cuadernos hispano-americanos* 242 (1970), 247–80.

———. "Introducción." *Los trabajos de Persiles y Sigismunda,* by Miguel de Cervantes Saavedra. Madrid: Clásicos Castalia, 1969.

———. *La novela pastoril española.* Madrid: Ediciones Istmo, 1974.

———. "Los trabajos de Persiles y Sigismunda, historia setentrional." In *Suma Cervantina.* London: Tamesis, 1973. Pp. 199–212.

Avalle-Arce, Juan Bautista, and Edward C. Riley. "*Don Quixote.*" In *Suma Cervantina.* London: Tamesis, 1973. Pp. 47–59.

Bandera, Cesáreo. *Mimesis conflictiva.* Madrid: Gredos, 1975.

Bataillon, Marcel. *Erasmo y España*. Translated by A. Alatorre. 2 vols. Mexico City: Fondo de Cultura Económica, 1950.

Campbell, Joseph. *The Masks of God: Oriental Mythology*. New York: Viking Press, 1962.

_____. *The Masks of God: Primitive Mythology*. New York: Viking Press, 1959.

Casalduero, Joaquín. "*La Galatea*." In *Suma Cervantina*, edited by J. B. Avalle-Arce and E. C. Riley. London: Tamesis, 1973. Pp. 27–46.

_____. *Sentido y forma de "Los trabajos de Persiles y Sigismunda."* Buenos Aires: Editorial Sudamericana, 1947.

_____. *Sentido y forma del "Quijote."* 3d edition. Madrid: Insula, 1970.

Castro, Américo. "La estructura del *Quijote*." In *Hacia Cervantes*. Madrid: Taurus, 1967. Pp. 308–17.

Chamberlin, Vernon A. "Symbolic Green: A Time-Honored Characterizing Device in Spanish Literature." *Hispania* 51 (1968), 29–37.

Cirlot, Juan Eduardo. *A Dictionary of Symbols*. Translated from the Spanish by Jack Sage. London: Routledge and Kegan Paul, 1962.

Close, Anthony. *Cervantes and the Romantic Approach to "Don Quixote."* Cambridge: Cambridge University Press, 1978.

_____. "Don Quixote's Sophistry and Wisdom." *Bulletin of Hispanic Studies* 55 (1978), 103–14.

Combet, Louis. *Cervantès ou les incertitudes du désir*. Lyons: Presses Universitaires de Lyon, 1981.

Cooper, J. C. *An Illustrated Encyclopaedia of Traditional Symbols*. London: Thames and Hudson, 1978.

Darst, David H. "Renaissance Platonism and the Spanish Pastoral Novel." *Hispania* 52 (1969), 384–92.

Deyermond, Alan. "El hombre salvaje en la novela sentimental." *Filología* 10 (1964), 97–111.

Dudley, Edward C. "Boccaccio and Cervantes: *Novella* as Novella." *Hispano-Italic Studies* 2 (1979), 23–40.

_____. "Don Quixote as Magus: The Rhetoric of Interpolation." *Bulletin of Hispanic Studies* 49 (1972), 355–68.

_____. "The Wild Man Goes Baroque." In *The Wild Man Within*, edited by Edward C. Dudley and Maximillian Novak. Pittsburgh: University of Pittsburgh Press, 1972. Pp. 115–39.

Dunn, Peter. "La cueva de Montesinos por fuera y por dentro: estructura épica, fisonomía." *Modern Language Notes* 88 (1973), 190–202.

Durán, Manuel. *La ambigüedad en el "Quijote."* Xalapa, Mexico: Universidad Veracruzana, 1961.

Eco, Umberto. *A Theory of Semiotics*. Bloomington and London: Indiana University Press, 1976.

Efron, Arthur. "Bearded Waiting Women, Lethal Lovely Female Piratemen: Sexual Boundary Shifts in *Don Quijote*, Part II." (Lecture given at the 1981 MLA convention.)

_____. *Don Quixote and the Dulcineated World.* Austin and London: University of Texas Press, 1971.

_____. "The Problem of Don Quixote's Rage." *Denver Quarterly* 16 (1981), 29–46.

El Saffar, Ruth. *Distance and Control in "Don Quixote": A Study in Narrative Technique.* Chapel Hill: University of North Carolina Studies in Romance Languages and Literatures, 1975.

_____. *Cervantes' "El casamiento engañoso" and "El coloquio de los perros": A Critical Study.* London: Tamesis, 1976.

_____. *Novel to Romance: A Study of Cervantes's "Novelas ejemplares."* Baltimore: Johns Hopkins University Press, 1974.

_____. "On *Cervantès ou les incertitudes du désir.*" *Modern Language Notes* 97 (1982), 422–27.

_____. "Periandro: Exemplary Character, Exemplary Narrator." *Hispanófila* 69 (1980), 9–16.

_____. "Structural and Thematic Discontinuity in Montemayor's *Diana.*" *Modern Language Notes* 86 (1971), 182–98.

_____. "Tres imágenes claves de lo feminino en el *Persiles.*" *Revista canadiense de estudios hispánicos* 3 (1979), 219–36.

Empson, William. *Some Versions of Pastoral.* New York: New Directions, 1968.

Entwistle, William. *Cervantes.* Oxford: Clarendon Press, 1940.

Flores, Robert. "Cervantes at Work: The Writing of *Don Quixote,* Part I." *Journal of Hispanic Philology* 3 (1979), 135–60.

_____. "The Loss and Recovery of Sancho's Ass in *Don Quixote,* Part I." *Modern Language Review* 75 (1980), 301–10.

_____. "The Role of Cide Hamete in *Don Quixote.*" *Bulletin of Hispanic Studies* 59 (1982), 3–14.

Forcione, Alban K. *Cervantes, Aristotle, and the "Persiles."* Princeton: Princeton University Press, 1970.

_____. *Cervantes' Christian Romance.* Princeton: Princeton University Press, 1971.

Foucault, Michel. *The Order of Things.* Translated from *Les Mots et les choses.* New York: Random House, 1970.

Frye, Northrup. *Anatomy of Criticism: Four Essays.* Princeton: Princeton University Press, 1957. Reprint, 1971.

_____. *The Critical Path: An Essay on the Social Context of Literary Criticism.* Bloomington and London: Indiana University Press, 1973.

_____. *The Great Code: The Bible and Literature.* New York: Harcourt, Brace, Jovanovich, 1982.

_____. *The Secular Scripture.* Cambridge: Harvard University Press, 1976.

Gerhardt, Mia. *"Don Quijote": La Vie et les livres.* Amsterdam: North Holland Publishing Company, 1955.

Girard, René. *Deceit, Desire, and the Novel: Self and Other in Literary Structure.* Translated by Yvonne Freccero. Baltimore: Johns Hopkins University Press, 1965.

———. *Violence and the Sacred.* Translated by Patrick Gregory. Baltimore: Johns Hopkins University Press, 1977.

González, Eduardo. "Del *Persiles* y la isla bárbara: Fábulas y reconocimientos." *Modern Language Notes* 94 (1979), 222–57.

Green, Otis. "El 'Ingenioso' Hidalgo." *Hispanic Review* 25 (1957), 175–93.

Gustafson, Fred. *The Black Madonna of Einsiedeln: A Psychological Perspective.* Zurich: The Jung Institute, 1975.

Hahn, Juergen. "El Capitán Cautivo: The Soldier's Truth and Literary Precept in *Don Quijote,* Part I." *Journal of Hispanic Philology* 3 (1979), 269–303.

Haley, George. "The Narrator in *Don Quixote:* Master Peter's Puppet Show." *Modern Language Notes* 81 (1966), 145–65.

Herrero, Javier. "Arcadia's Inferno: Cervantes' Attack on Pastoral." *Bulletin of Hispanic Studies* 55 (1978), 289–99.

———. "Sierra Morena as Labyrinth: From Wildness to Christian Knighthood." *Forum for Modern Language Studies* 17 (1981), 55–67.

Hughe, Gethin. "The Cave of Montesinos: Don Quixote's Interpretation and Dulcinea's Disenchantment." *Bulletin of Hispanic Studies* 54 (1977), 107–13.

Ilie, Paul. "Grotesque Elements in the Pastoral Novel." In *Homenaje a William L. Fichter.* Madrid: Editorial Castalia, 1971. Pp. 319–28.

Immerwahr, Raymond. "Structural Symmetry in the Episodic Narratives of *Don Quijote,* Part One." *Comparative Literature* 10 (1958), 121–35.

Jones, Harold G. "Grisóstomo and Don Quixote: Death and Imitation." *Revista canadiense de estudios hispánicos* 4 (1979), 85–92.

Jung, Carl Gustav. *The Archetypes and the Collective Unconscious.* Vol. 9, pt. 1, of *Collected Works.* Princeton: Princeton University Press, 1968.

———. "The Components of the Coniunctio." In *Mysterium Coniunctionis.* Vol. 14 of *Collected Works.*

———. "The Psychology of the Transference." In *The Practice of Psychotherapy.* Vol. 16 of *Collected Works.*

———. "The Relations Between the Ego and the Unconscious." In *Two Essays on Analytical Psychology.* Vol. 7 of *Collected Works.*

———. "Religious Ideas in Alchemy." In *Psychology and Alchemy.* Vol. 12 of *Collected Works.*

———. "Rex and Regina." In *Mysterium Coniunctionis.* Vol. 14 of *Collected Works.*

———. "The Shadow." In *Aion.* Vol. 9, pt. 2, of *Collected Works.*

———. "The Structure and Dynamics of the Self." In *Aion.* Vol. 9, pt. 2, of *Collected Works.*

———. "The Syzygy: Anima and Animus." In *Aion.* Vol. 9, pt. 2, of *Collected Works.*

———. 'The Visions of Zosimos." In *Alchemical Studies.* Vol. 13 of *Collected Works.*

Kerenyi, Karl. "The Trickster in Relation to Greek Mythology." In Paul Radin, *The Trickster: A Study in American Indian Mythology.* New York: Schocken Books, 1972.

Kern, Edith. *The Absolute Comic.* New York: Columbia University Press, 1980. Pp. 61–63.

Levin, Harry. "The Example of Cervantes." In *Contexts of Criticism.* Cambridge: Harvard University Press, 1957. Pp. 76–96.

Lewis, C. S. *The Allegory of Love: A Study in Medieval Tradition.* Oxford: Clarendon Press, 1936.

López-Estrada, Francisco. *La "Galatea" de Cervantes.* La Laguna de Tenerife: Universidad de la Laguna, 1948.

Lowe, Jennifer. "The *cuestión de amor* and the Structure of Cervantes' *Galatea.*" *Bulletin of Hispanic Studies* 43 (1966), 98–109.

Madariaga, Salvador de. "Cervantes y los Libros de Caballerías." In *Guía del lector del "Quijote."* 2d edition. Buenos Aires: Editorial Sudamericana, 1943.

Mancing, Howard. "Cide Hamete Benengeli vs. Miguel de Cervantes: The Metafictional Dialectic of *Don Quijote.*" *Cervantes* 1 (1982), 63–81.

Márquez Villanueva, Francisco. "El Caballero del Verde Gabán y su reino de paradoja." *Personajes y temas del "Quijote."* Madrid: Taurus, 1975.

_____. "La locura emblemática en la segunda parte del *Quijote.*" In *Cervantes and the Renaissance.* Easton, Pennsylvania: Juan de la Cuesta–Hispanic Monographs, 1980. Pp. 87–112.

Marín, Rodríguez, ed. *Novelas ejemplares,* by Miguel de Cervantes. Vol. 2. Madrid: Clásicos Castellanos, 1965.

Martín Gabriel, Albinio. "Heliodoro y la novela española: Apuntes para una tesis." *Cuadernos de literatura* 8 (1950), 215–34.

Martínez-Bonati, Félix. "Cervantes y las regiones de la imaginación." *Dispositio* 2 (1977), 28–53.

_____. "La unidad del *Quijote.*" *Dispositio* 2 (1977), 118–39.

Mazur, Oleh. "Various Folkloric Impacts Upon the *Salvaje* in the Spanish *Comedia.*" *Hispanic Review* 36 (1968), 207–35.

Miller, J. Hillis. "Steven's Rock and Criticism as Cure, II." *The Georgia Review* 30 (1976), 330–48.

Mujica, Barbara. "Violence in the Pastoral Novel from Sannazaro to Cervantes." *Hispano-Italic Studies* 1 (1976), 39–55.

Murillo, Luis. "El *Ur-Quijote:* nueva hipótesis." *Cervantes* 1 (1982), 43–50.

Neumann, Erich. *Art and the Creative Unconscious: Four Essays.* Translated by Ralph Manheim. Princeton: Princeton University Press, 1974.

_____. *The Great Mother: An Analysis of the Archetype.* Translated by Ralph Manheim. Princeton: Princeton University Press, 1963.

Ogden, Charles K. *Opposition: A Linguistic and Psychological Analysis.* Bloomington and London: Indiana University Press, 1967.

Ong, Walter. *Interfaces of the Word.* Ithaca and London: Cornell University Press, 1977.

Osuna, Rafael."Las fechas del *Persiles.*" *Thesaurus: Boletín del instituto caro y cuervo* 25 (1970), 383–433.

Patch, Howard. *The Other World According to Descriptions in Medieval Literature.* Cambridge: Harvard University Press, 1950.

Percas de Ponseti, Helena. *Cervantes y su concepto del arte.* 2 vols. Madrid: Gredos, 1975.

Pierce, Frank. *Two Cervantes Short Novels: "El curioso impertinente" and "El celoso extremeño."* Oxford: Pergamon, 1970.

Poggioli, Renato. *The Oaten Flute.* Cambridge: Harvard University Press, 1975.

Pope, Randolf D. "El 'Caballero del Verde Gabán' y su encuentro con Don Quijote." *Hispanic Review* 47 (1979), 207–18.

Radin, Paul. *The Trickster: A Study in American Indian Mythology.* New York: Schocken Books, 1972.

Randel, Mary Gaylord. "The Language of Limits and the Limits of tanguage: The Crisis of Poetry in *La Galatea.*" *Modern Language Notes* 97 (1982), 254–71.

Redondo, Augustín. "El proceso iniciático en el episodio de la cueva de Montesinos del *Quijote.*" *Iberoromania* 13 (1979), 47–61.

Riley, Edward C. *Cervantes's Theory of the Novel.* Oxford: Clarendon Press, 1962.

_____. "Symbolism in *Don Quixote,* Part II, Chapter 73." *Journal of Hispanic Philology* 3 (1979), 161–74.

Río, Angel del. "El equívoco del *Quijote.*" *Hispanic Review* 27 (1959), 200–221.

Riquer, Martín de. *Aproximación al "Quijote."* Barcelona: Editorial Teide, 1967.

Robert, Marthe. *L'Ancien et le nouveau (De "Don Quichotte" à Franz Kafka).* Paris: Grasset, 1963.

Rougemont, Denis de. *Love in the Western World.* Translated by Montgomery Belgion. Revised and augmented edition. New York: Pantheon, 1956.

Russell, Peter E. "*Don Quixote* as a Funny Book." *Modern Language Review* 64 (1969), 312–26.

Said, Edward. *Beginnings: Intention and Method.* New York: Basic Books, 1975.

Saldívar, Ramón. "Don Quijote's Metaphors and the Grammar of Proper Languages." *Modern Language Notes* 95 (1980), 252–78.

Sánchez, Alberto. "El Caballero del Verde Gabán." *Anales Cervantinos* 9 (1961/62), 169–201.

Schevill, Rudolph. "Studies in Cervantes. *Persiles y Sigismunda:* The Question of Heliodorus." *Modern Philology* 4 (1907), 677–704.

Shepard, Sanford. *El Pinciano y las teorías literarias del Siglo de Oro.* Madrid: Gredos, 1962.

Sieber, Harry. "Society and the Pastoral Vision in the Marcela-Grisóstomo

Episode of *Don Quijote.*" In *Estudios literarios de hispanistas norteamericanos dedicados a Helmut Hatzfeld con motivo de su 80 aniversario.* Barcelona: Ediciones Hispam, 1974. Pp. 185–94.

Singleton, Mack. "El misterio del *Persiles.*" *Realidad* 2 (1947), 237–53.

Solé-Leris, Amadeu. *The Spanish Pastoral Novel.* Boston: Twayne Publishers, 1980.

Spitzer, Leo. "Linguistic Perspectivism in the *Don Quijote.*" In *Linguistics and Literary History: Essays in Stylistics.* Princeton: Princeton University Press, 1948.

Stagg, Geoffrey. "A Matter of Masks." In *Hispanic Studies in Honour of Joseph Manson,* edited by D. M. Atkinson and A. H. Clark. Oxford: Clarendon Press, 1972. Pp. 255–67.

———. "Revision in *Don Quixote,* Part I." *Hispanic Studies in Honour of I. González Llubera.* Oxford, 1959. Pp. 347–66.

Thompson, Stith. *Motif-Index of Folk-Literature.* Berkeley: University of California Press, 1977.

Unamuno, Miguel de. *Vida de Don Quijote y Sancho.* 3d edition. Madrid: Espasa-Calpe, 1938.

Vilanova, Antonio. "El peregrino andante en el *Persiles* de Cervantes." *Boletín de la Real Academia de Buenas Letras de Barcelona* 22 (1949), 97–159.

Vries, Ad de. *Dictionary of Symbols and Imagery.* Amsterdam and London: North-Holland Publishing Company, 1974.

Wardropper, Bruce. "*Don Quijote:* Story or History?" *Modern Philology* 63 (1965), 1–11.

———. "The Pertinence of *El curioso impertinente.*" *Publications of the Modern Language Association* 72 (1957), 578–600.

Weiger, John G. *The Individuated Self: Cervantes and the Emergence of the Individual.* Athens: Ohio University Press, 1979.

Willis, Raymond. *The Phantom Chapters of the "Quijote."* New York: Hispanic Institute in the United States, 1953.

Zimic, Stanislav. "*El Persiles* como crítica de la novela bizantina." *Acta neophilologica* 3 (1970), 49–64.

Index

214

Designer: Lisa A. Mirski
Compositor: Editorial Excelsior Corporation
Text: 10/12 Palatino
Display: Palatino
Printer: McNaughton & Gunn, Inc.
Binder: McNaughton & Gunn, Inc.